# Anthropological Practice

# Anthropological Practice
## Fieldwork and the Ethnographic Method

**Judith Okely**

*London • New York*

English edition
First published in 2012 by
**Berg**
Editorial offices:
50 Bedford Square, London, W1CB 3DP, UK
175 Fifth Avenue, New York, NY 10010, USA

Berg is an imprint of Bloomsbury Publishing Plc.

**Library of Congress Cataloging-in-Publication Data**

Okely, Judith, date.
Anthropological practice : fieldwork and the
ethnographic method / Judith Okely.
pages cm
Includes bibliographical references and index.
ISBN 978-1-84520-602-4 (hardback)
1. Ethnology—Fieldwork.   2. Ethnologists—Interviews.   I. Title.
GN346.O275   2012
301—dc23          2011050410

**British Library Cataloguing-in-Publication Data**

A catalogue record for this book is available from the British Library.

ISBN 978 1 84520 602 4 (Cloth)
978 1 84520 603 1 (Paper)
e-ISBN 978 0 85785 092 8 (Institutional)
978 0 85785 091 1 (Individual)

Typeset by Apex CoVantage, LLC, Madison, WI, USA
Printed in the UK by the MPG Books Group

**www.bergpublishers.com**

Dedicated to
EDMUND LEACH
who first introduced me to
Social Anthropology

# Contents

# Preface and Acknowledgements

This volume has emerged from years of research, lecturing, thinking and writing. I am grateful to the many undergraduates and graduates who encouraged me to pursue the questions raised when considering and conveying what anthropological fieldwork entails. I explain through this text how there have been entire issues missing or hidden in social anthropology's unique research practice in understanding the full range of humanity across place and time around the globe.

There is now a range of edited collections of individual accounts of fieldwork experience. In these the editors indeed elicit a common theme. However, the narratives necessarily take their own paths, often resulting in haphazard comparative themes. Given each contributor's independent chapter, there is less possibility of synthesizing very specific commonalities or contrasts. Here, by contrast, the anthropologists have each been asked similar questions while simultaneously being given freedom to pursue relevant follow-ups, all during taped dialogues with the author. The single interviewer/anthropologist has then selected and explored key extracts and themes. The book is unique in that it is ultimately interpreted by the one author.

When Professor at Edinburgh University, I was awarded an Economic and Social Research Council one-year senior research fellowship, where I had intended to complete a methods book based on course lectures. However, the impromptu inspiration of tape recording a dialogue extending over four hours with Brian Morris encouraged me to transform the entire project. Gradually, the recorded and brilliantly evocative voices of over twenty anthropologists pushed my drafts to the margins. I had the huge task of selecting, then editing relevant quotes from the hours upon hours of transcripts. I had also to watch for repetition and conversational fillers in the unrehearsed oral accounts. The quotations are, after months, indeed years, of learning from them, as succinct as possible, all the while retaining the spontaneity of the spoken words. My selection entailed authorial choices, but the anthropologists should also be allowed to speak for themselves without overbearing justifications and explanations, both before and after each quotation. Poetry likewise cannot be reduced to explanatory prose.

Details of the individuals are outlined further on. They reveal the extraordinary range, both across the different anthropologists' research topics and localities, but also within individual trajectories. Many may have done 'classical' fieldwork. But they have also pursued innovative directions, proving that anthropology can extend to all contexts of human activity. Participant observation is ever malleable.

I thank Hull University for financial assistance in transcribing several interviews in the late 1990s. The vast majority of the transcription costs have been at my expense. I am grateful for the meticulous transcriptions and comments by Sinead Ni Shuineer, Carol at Darlington and finally Niamh Hyland who also copyedited this text before submission. Katherine Earle first encouraged me to apply for a contract when I explained this was not a first-year manual. Hannah Shakespeare, through regular e-mails, and then Anna Wright kept faith, despite delays and distractions.

Some of the ideas and dialogue extracts I have presented in earlier lectures. It was a privilege to try them out in different contexts:

1997    The Distinguished Lecture, Society for the Anthropology of Europe, American Anthropological Association, Washington DC.
1998–2008    Methods lectures for the Roma course at the Central European University, Budapest, then as partner through the International Gender Studies Centre, Oxford, to an EU Marie Curie initiative.
2006    The Third Eric Wolf Lecture, Vienna, sponsored by the International Research Centre for Cultural Studies, Commission of Social Anthropology of the Austrian Academy of Sciences and Department of Social and Cultural Anthropology, Vienna University.
2010    The Obi Igwara Memorial lecture 'Crossing Borders', The Association for the Study of Ethnicity and Nationalism, the London School of Economics, London University.

I tried out fieldwork themes in papers at the following international conferences:

1996    The European Association of Social Anthropologists, Barcelona; 2002 The Ethnological Society Conference, Providence Rhode Island, USA: 2004 The European Association of Social Anthropologists (EASA), Vienna, and 2006 Bristol; 2005 the 37th World Congress of the International Institute of Sociology, Stockholm; and 2008 The Helsinki Collegium for Advanced Studies.

I thank the editorial board of the *Sociological Review* and Keele for permission to republish an amended version of 'Fieldwork Embodied' from Shilling (2007). A small number of examples from the Vienna EASA (Okely 2010b) are reproduced here.

I engaged with broad issues with George Marcus in *Social Anthropology* (Marcus and Okely 2007) and a reply to Amy Pollard in *Anthropology Matters* (Okely 2009b). I tried out aspects at conferences of The Association of Social Anthropologists at Manchester 2003 and Belfast 2010. I outlined aspects of fieldwork when I addressed the President of Finland at the Annual Gypsy Lore Society Conference in Helsinki 2009.

At the following universities I gave an occasional lecture or seminar on research practice: Manchester, Cardiff, Smith College, USA, Essex, Humbold University,

East London, Stockholm, Madrid, Nottingham, Wroklov, Glasgow, Leipzig, Vienna and the University of West Bohemia, Pilsen.

Over the years, I have convened or contributed to methods courses, as staff or visiting professor at the Universities of Edinburgh, Hull and Copenhagen, and more recently in masters courses at Malta, Brunel and Bristol universities. The students from many varied contexts and cultures brought superb intellectual exchanges. Innovative possibilities of anthropological fieldwork, in ever-changing contexts, have been pursued by my postgraduate students. Some of their topics are outlined in chapter 3. Their varied nationalities and cultural histories are inspiring. These included not only individuals from England and Scotland, but also those self-defined as Algerian, Australian, Belgian, Brazilian, Bulgarian, Canadian, Danish, Finnish, Egyptian, Ghanaian, Greek, Indian, Japanese, Maltese, Saudi, Swedish and Turkish. Anthropology does indeed engage students and scholars around the world.

This book concentrates on aspects of the unique field practice of anthropology. It is framed, especially in the opening chapter, by ongoing theoretical discussions of key themes in or indeed missing from the existing literature. Thus there are informed references to standard debates combined with my evaluations. Some readers may prefer to plunge into examples before a theoretical overview, although I argue that a theoretical overview provides a crucial context. Subsequent chapters are combined with the analysis of the original case studies emerging from the extended taped dialogues with over twenty widely published anthropologists of international standing based in Britain, Scandinavia, the Netherlands, Poland, Canada, the United States and Japan. They are of sixteen different nationalities.

While initially asking the same open-ended questions, I allowed the anthropologists free range as the dialogue progressed. I pursued relevant contextual leads. These exchanges moved beyond interview format. Each dialogue addresses the same fieldwork concerns experienced in a wide variety of locations around the globe. Some of the anthropologists had not explored such issues before my intervention, let alone written about them.

These were dialogues between two anthropologists where the questioner could exchange parallel or contrasting experiences. Contrary to some still prejudiced views within social science practice which insist on the interviewer and interviewee being 'uncontaminated' by prior communication, I did not select strangers. The relaxed atmosphere of mutual trust ensured free flowing narrative and intellectual honesty (Okely 2010a).

The anthropologists were predominantly persons who had published extensively; often several monographs of international reputation. They had the confidence to reveal hitherto unrecorded vulnerabilities and mistakes, all of which are crucial for unravelling and systematizing anthropological practice. The investigation focused not on what they *ought* to have done but what they *had* done. Invariably, their practices contradicted the formulaic injunctions in methods 'cook books'. They proved brilliantly articulate. The recent increased sensitivity towards research 'training' had not usually figured in the postgraduate preparation of many of these now established anthropologists. Yet their monographs, and the fieldwork which created them, provide the core to the discipline. The book rescues the embedded, often unarticulated centrality of anthropological practice(s).

Major questions (see the Appendix), include: pre-fieldwork preparation, initial ideas, choice of locality and subject, possible change of focus once in the field, encounters and rapport with key associates, the role of serendipity, learning through the body and the senses, key incidents, learning by mistakes, language, relational implications of the gender, ethnicity, nationality, age and personality of the fieldworker, political dialogue and key associates. Other questions on visual recording, field notes, memory, analysis, and writing up have been reserved for alternative or future publication. Aspects of archives and publication would have rested more on my own research and forthcoming discussions.

In contrast to edited collections of individual anthropologists' fieldwork accounts, the analysis of the material reveals both an extraordinary set of commonalities and pertinent contrasts, all open to systematic theorizing. The consistent findings are indeed of scientific value in the broadest meaning of science.

While working on this book, I co-edited two others. I thank my co-editors for the shared enterprise: Deborah Fahy Bryceson and Jonathan Webber (Okely 2007a), Narmala Halstead and Eric Hirsch (Okely 2008). My sister Elaine designed and pruned my wildlife garden offering welcome outdoor distractions. I have appreciated the support and intellectual community of the International Gender Studies Centre, Oxford. I celebrate the life of Marianne Gullestad who shared the past academic exclusions of those who did fieldwork in 'home space'. I celebrate my former Hull colleague Obi Igwara whose referee described her as 'a force of nature' (Okely 2010a).

I dedicate this book to my original mentor, Edmund Leach, who taught us five graduates in a 'conversion' course at Cambridge 1969–70. We had two hours a week for the entire academic year devoted to the works of Malinowski. By the autumn of 1970, I would be living on a temporary Gypsy camp, taking with me the holistic perspective which Leach had inspired. When hearing that I was engaged in fieldwork among Gypsies, just a short drive from Kings College Cambridge, Leach declared how important such work was. Later, he supported me at a conference (Okely 1983: 8). I had imbibed Malinowski's emphasis on the current significance of a group's self-selected culture rather than a search for 'origins' as explanation. I was not to predict the venom this would arouse among non-anthropologists, especially linguists (Okely 1997: 240; and a 2010 interview on www.Cingeneyiz.org).

I am indebted to Leach for confirming the importance of intensive fieldwork. His publications rescue social anthropology from diffident and destructive proclamations. Research, as lived daily practice, is not the distancing, acclaimed abstract theorizing which reduces Malinowski's experiencing the 'imponderabilia of everyday life' to perverse voyeurism. I was fortunate to have been initiated into social anthropology by one of Malinowski's pupils. This book celebrates some of that legacy.

# Theoretical and Historical Overview

Anthropological fieldwork is the subject in practice. It cannot be reduced to the implementation of techniques. No one can rote learn what to do and how to be when moving among people whose daily lives and total context, unfamiliar or seemingly familiar to the researcher, are to be studied over an extended passage of time.

When anthropology applicants are asked to outline their research proposals and methods, would they dare reveal the following? That they will learn to shin up tree trunks, as Morris (see chapter 6) kept attempting in Tropical forest India; or pound manioc hour upon hour like Christine Hugh-Jones (1979); ride horses on migration in Afghanistan, as Lindisfarne (see chapter 6); take peyote on a sacred journey, as Myerhoff (1974); hunt monkeys for dinner with poison darts, like Stephen Hugh-Jones (1977); dance as did Smith-Bowen (1954) and Powdermaker (1967); learn to gut fish day long in Iceland (Johnson 1984); or walk Greek mountain paths barefoot on a pilgrimage, then write about the smell of incense like Kenna (2005). Should the monitoring committee know that anthropologists also make friends rather than interrogate 'informants'?

Will research proposals suggest the anthropologist will clean lavatories in a hospice (Hockey 1990), weep with the bereaved, play children's games the day long (Hardman 1973), or drink the water of the Ganges, as Parry (see chapter 6), when it contains the remnants of a burning ghat? I did not know that I would have to drive a 1,500-weight van for scrap collection, hand-milk cows and join twelve-hour Normandy banquets. I was to appear as character witness at the central London criminal court for a Traveller charged with kidnap, possessing a firearm and attempted murder. Rewarded as intellectuals, anthropologists use their bodies. Long out of the armchair, they have moved down from the verandah. They are at the mercy of their hosts' acceptance and then set on unpredictable paths. They can hardly mimic bureaucratic research designs and pursue a preordained project, increasingly set by a top-down managerial culture. Grounded theory may have recognized the back and forth of knowledge through process (Glaser and Strauss 1967), but not grounded in the whole being and the researcher's body. Such theory is interview-privileged and rooted in text and word, divorced from hand, heart, movement and the senses. By contrast, as chapter 6 will explore with vivid examples, the anthropologist puts his or her body on the line, at the disposal of the subjects. Knowledge comes through the skin and all the senses (Stoller 1989; Howes 2003; Okely 2006c) There is a relationship with the people(s) through continuing, not one-off, shared experiences. We are forever changed in mysterious, unpredictable ways (Young and Goulet 1994; Coffey 1999; Borneman and Hammoudi 2009).

This book is about the possibilities and creative potential in ethnographic field-work. Although primarily addressed to anthropologists, there are lessons for other social scientists and beyond. Social anthropological fieldwork provides unique insights into long-term cross-cultural encounters. Few anthropology academic textbooks explicitly analyze fieldwork as what is done in practice. Courses have privileged sociological definitions of ethnography with positivist remnants. I explore the contrasts between pre-fieldwork assumptions with what anthropologists actually did. I had initially hoped to find the lived examples in the introductions, or even footnotes of anthropological monographs. These were elusive. I was thus drawn to tape-record informal dialogues, many up to four hours. The anthropologists were willing to divulge hitherto unrecorded accounts as superb narrative.

The book concentrates on aspects of the largely unique field practice of anthropology. Clifford (1988) and others argue that while the method of long-term immersion via participant observation is the hallmark of the discipline, few have explored its intellectual implications. Of the ethnographic method, Sanjek suggests 'anthropologists have done a better job of using than articulating it' (1991: 617). In Okely and Callaway (1992), progress was made in the discussion of the individual encounter and the need to explore further the means by which fieldwork is accomplished.

Autobiographical accounts have served as alternative approaches and subversions, defying any suggestion of universalistic rules of method. Through the personal, they undermine the notion of the neutral data gatherer. I argued for their integration into the mainstream rather than as marginalized narrative for entertainment (Okely 1992). Fortunately, numerous edited collections of personalized fieldwork accounts have emerged (Bell, Caplan and Karim 1993; Young and Goulet 1994; Kulick and Willson 1995; Amit 2000; Dresch, James and Parkin 2000; De Soto and Dudwick 2000; Hume and Mulcock 2004; James and Mills 2005). These necessarily, by their format of individualized articles, remain detached from linked monographs and indeed from each other.

By contrast, this book synthesizes through one author/analyst the commonalities and contrasts in multifaceted individual dialogues. I have therefore inserted extended extracts from the spoken (not written) voices of each anthropologist. Nevertheless, the selection, editing and commentaries are my responsibility alone. Ultimately, texts 'are written from a particular author's point of view' (Hastrup 1992: 125).

These exchanges moved beyond any rigid interviewing formulae which the sociologist Anne Oakley (1981) so convincingly challenged long ago. They were dialogues between anthropologists where they could exchange parallel or contrasting experiences. Burgess rightly suggests that interviews can be conversations, but his example is of an adult researcher with school children, where there is a power imbalance with little or no reciprocity in the process (1984: 101–22). Similarly, while Dwyer attempts to avoid potential imbalance in *Moroccan Dialogues* (1982) to give the perspective of the Faqir, there is little reciprocity, thus restricting the full meaning of dialogue as exchange. At the time, it was considered innovative merely to record individual lives (Crapanzano 1980), as later creatively confirmed by Caplan (1997).

For my dialogues, I chose individuals I knew, ensuring a trusting exchange. The occasional recorded encounter with relative strangers failed. Unease inhibited free dialogue. The majority of my dialogues were recorded in either the anthropologists' or my home space, with notable exceptions. That with Michael Herzfeld was recorded in a Copenhagen airport lobby. Malcolm McLeod, then Curator of the Huntingdon Museum, Glasgow, welcomed me to his office, while Helena Wulff and I sat in a Stockholm café. Her tape recorder malfunctioned, so I hand-wrote the answers. When she did not want personal confidences noted, she said: 'Turn the tape recorder off!' Indeed, many anthropologists trusted me to turn off the real machine at important, sometimes dramatic junctures. Louise de la Gorgendière, in her Edinburgh flat, insisted on ironing throughout the interview. Roy Gigengack and Raquel Alonso López brought their toddler son to my home. He, like Hélène Neveu's crawling baby daughter, found plenty of objects to play with in an academic's paper and book-heaped spaces. The anthropologists had the confidence to reveal hitherto hidden, unrecorded aspects of fieldwork. The extended, vivid quotations eventually pushed earlier chapter drafts to the edges.[1]

In reproducing quotations in this text, some of my own interjections and comparisons have been largely deleted to avoid repetition across interviews or the recycling of published narratives (e.g. Okely 1994b, 1996b: chapter 1, 2005, 2008). With a very limited word length, I have been obliged to reserve some aspects for publication elsewhere. These included: acts of recording through field notes and memory, then analysis and writing up (cf. Okely 1994a).

Although the book is ultimately one author's interpretation, nevertheless the text is dominated by multiple voices. The anthropologists proved to be brilliant narrators.[2] I challenge any high theorists' triumphant put-down that ethnography is 'just descriptive'. They are immune to the detail of human possibility. The minutiae in the anthropologists' testimonies carry profound theoretical implications, if the reader will only surrender to the emergent flow of knowledge.

These anthropologists have lived fieldwork in Afghanistan, in India, whether the tropical forest, Banaras, an iron and steel complex or a stone quarry south of Delhi. Others have lived fieldwork in Iran, tropical forest Malaysia, Indonesia, the Amazon region of Venezuela or Mexico City. Many have researched in Africa, in Ghana, Senegal, Uganda, Malawi, Sudan, Kenya or Nigeria (Okely 2010a). Others have done fieldwork in Europe, both before and after the collapse of communism, in Poland, Bulgaria, Macedonia and Slovakia. There are fieldwork testimonies from Western and Northern Europe, namely Sweden, Germany, Norway, the Basque country, England, Ireland, several Greek islands and New York. The continents are Africa, Asia, South America, North America, and Europe, north, south or central. Fieldwork collectively spans the late 1960s to the present. The anthropologists have done fieldwork both in so-called remote localities (Ardener 1987) and in or near the Western metropolises.

For the younger researchers included here, fieldwork only commenced from 2001 and is continuing. My own fieldwork has been in Europe, namely Ireland, the United Kingdom and France, mainly from the late 1970s and through the 1990s. The work of these ethnographers around the world thus extends across space and time. While anthropologists have experienced the wonders and sometimes dangers of participation in alternative cultures, they have also confronted aspects of their own cultures which were taken for granted or controversial, indeed dangerous.

The anthropologists were of sixteen nationalities, including individuals of Japanese, Indian, Senegalese and Mexican descent. While the majority were of European and North American descent, the anthropologists included Polish, Swedish, Norwegian, Dutch, Basque, French, Maltese, English, Scottish, Franco-Canadian and US citizens. Their religious and ethnic identities also varied.

The narratives refute the critique that anthropologists have done interesting things but produced boring texts (Pratt 1986). The analysis of the material reveals an extraordinary set of both commonalities and some pertinent contrasts; all open to systematic theorizing. The consistent findings are indeed of generalized scientific value in the broader meaning of science (Okely1996a). What emerges, indeed cascades, from the accounts are the tumultuous and unexpected experiences across the multiplicity of cultures. Anthropologists have quietly challenged the straightjacket of Euro-American prescribed scientized methods which are now finally being questioned beyond anthropology (Law 2004). While methods 'training' had been persistently institutionalized through the 1990s in the United Kingdom, little or no interest was shown in earlier textbooks towards those approaches which did *not* fit a positivist, ultimately ethnocentric agenda.

Informally, it has been taken for granted that anthropologists should be open to what confronts them in the field. Indeed these anthropologists responded to the people's *own* interests and the specific context, avoiding pre-formed questions dictated by the anthropologists' academic cultural contexts. Thus anthropologists have in practice experimented for decades with alternatives. Yet these ingenuities and differences have not been formally and creatively expounded to challenge dominant models in social science.

Anthropological methodological silence has not been restricted to the United Kingdom. In 1997, it was claimed that 'most leading departments of anthropology in the United States provide no formal (and very little informal) training in fieldwork methods' (Gupta and Ferguson 1997b: 2). When lecturing at conferences and at Smith College in the United States, exposing the anthropologists' flexible practices, I was surprised by the relieved responses from US postgraduates, for example at the annual conference of the Ethnological Society (Okely 2003c).

There was likewise an absence of detailed discussion of anthropological practice. Postgraduates were puzzled as to why they had not been told what *actually* happens in fieldwork. They were reassured to learn that established anthropologists had encountered experiences similar to their own. They had believed that changing research perspectives and making mistakes were proof of personal failure. Many methods textbooks circulated for anthropologists in North America and on book display, for example at the 2003 American Ethnological Conference, reveal similar positivist, pre-meditated intent. Fortunately, some informative wider-ranging methods books are emerging, for example that by Aull Davies (1999), although without the range of direct examples offered here.[3]

Without knowing in advance the outcome of my dialogues, I discovered many commonalities in the anthropologists' experiences and responses. All the anthropologists found very different concerns and conditions than anticipated, either on first arrival or after the initial period of participant observation. Everyone changed focus to a large or lesser extent. They delved into their own resources. Any prior reading, cross-cultural knowledge and indeed a range of disciplines and earlier life experiences, became a rich resource for comparative comprehension. When the verb 'to conduct' is used in relation to fieldwork, this implies that fieldwork is managed and pre-directed. The more satisfactory verb is 'to experience'. This is consistent with Borneman's concern with what 'anthropology does or can do in and through experience-based fieldwork' (2009: 6). Regrettably, a managerial *modus operandi* has increasingly been imposed on university research (Okely 2006a).

Fieldwork, in the tradition explored in this volume, is embarked upon and completed by the anthropologist, often alone. This is not as part of a multi-disciplined research team, as implicitly critiqued by Shostak (1981). The anthropologist is the embodied participant observer, researcher, scribe, analyst then author. The anthropologist can be a vulnerable figure in the field often, but not always, the outsider with prior affinities. Additionally, some anthropologists I recorded for this study were accompanied by their partners and children, with creative consequences (see chapter 7).

I have aimed to explore the total context whereby the anthropologist acquires knowledge through experience. Autobiographical insertions and accounts can always give illumination (Okely 1992). Too often, however, we have to search the crevices of the text for those throwaway remarks and anecdotes about lived practice. My doctoral supervisor, Godfrey Lienhardt tried to discourage me from including a chapter on fieldwork methods in my thesis. He advised relegating anything of this to an appendix. I refused and this became chapter three of my monograph (Okely 1983). My interest in practice had also been influenced by the obsessive questioning I faced when 'ordinary' non-Gypsy people discovered my seemingly dramatic and 'dangerous' field subject just a few miles' drive from Oxford (Okely 2008).

Many classical monographs have proved thoroughly engaging to anthropological readers and beyond. Subsequent generations have brought innovations to the genre. Regardless of the excitement of the texts, there remain absences and deceptions in the practice. Anthropologists, caught in the nets of scientism, have claimed to be, or pretended to mimic, the detached observer, turned voyeur, when it has been thought that mere co-residence was sufficient. A few it seems (though not among those recorded here) never learned the first elements of the language and, like other social scientists, delegated 'data-gathering' to local interviewers armed with questionnaires. Somehow, it passed as anthropology merely because the fieldworker was in a foreign place. Some pioneers did not engage with their own bodies, except as passive sufferers of disease or as conspicuous strollers. They were living elsewhere, emotionally and bodily detached, while the data gathering proceeded perfunctorily. By contrast, anthropologists in this volume revealed a wide range of potential participation, depending on the appropriateness. The numerous examples are explored in chapter 5.

## Methodological Silence

Preparation for anthropologists, in Britain at least, where the majority of the anthropologists in this book were educated as postgraduates, has too easily relied on a notion of 'instinct', ideally detached interaction but in practice an open-ended approach. The absence of formal methods courses has changed in recent years. But it is important to examine the historical context of recent decades. Johnny Parry, whom I recorded, stated:

> Edmund [Leach] was the most incredibly good supervisor, both as an undergraduate and as a post/fieldworker. But in the period when you're actually preparing and doing the research, this was general in Cambridge in those days—you were just left to get on with it. And: 'Come back and talk to us when you've got the data and we'll see what we can make of it'.

Suzette Heald described a similar approach in the late 1960s:

> I had no fieldwork training. It wasn't done in those days. We had fieldwork seminars where someone recommended a particular HB pencil and someone else told us that notebooks six inches by three were a good idea as they'd fit into your pockets. In the field it was largely as though one was treading in the footsteps of one's ancestors, trying to learn the techniques by remote control through their books, and then finding out that it was all much more complicated. It was a question of establishing relationships. So, as to what works and what doesn't, there can't be a uniform answer since everyone will form a different kind of relationship.

When I studied with Leach, who was running a year-long postgraduate course devoted entirely to the works of Malinowski, the reading list included everything except his diary (Malinowski 1967), but this, as subsequently argued, gave unique insights into fieldwork practice (Okely 1975, 1996b: chapter 2). Leach declared that this diary should never have been published.

Traditionally it has been a stiff-upper-lip model (cf. Asad 1986: 142) or the dated sink-or-swim British attitude (Kenna 1992: 160). Anthropologists risked absorbing such values regardless of whether they had been schooled this way. The British elite 'public' school ethos of maturity through severance from the mother, and emotional detachment, in accord with an ideology exported with British colonialism, fits with the ideal of a cerebral, detached observer. Emotions and creative imagination are treated as disruptive, if not dangerously 'feminine'. Just as neophytes may be sworn to secrecy in the liminal stage, so the returning anthropologist had been encouraged to keep quiet. Self-revelation might be perceived as a loss of face or cracking of the masculine mask of competence (Okely 1992).

A researcher's pose as detached and trained 'data gatherer' is undermined by the leakage of tales of incompetence revealing sensitivity and entanglement. The self-possessed social scientist does not want to appear as buffoon but as the all-confident hero. Sondheim aptly suggested, as a female outsider, that anthropology 'is one of the rare intellectual vocations that do not demand a sacrifice of one's manhood' (1970: 189). Silences preserve the mystique of the researcher in control. By contrast, tales of mistakes, tears and laughter allow the hero(ine) to be someone with feet of clay and fractured ego. It is also clear that mistakes are made, whatever the prior field experience of the anthropologist, precisely because the relevant and detailed contexts cannot be predicted because they are part of the emergent discoveries (cf. Hume and Mulcock 2004). In this book, unique and original dialogues confirm the inescapable relevance of mistakes for vital insights, as Needham (1967) found out when he removed a tick from his flesh and threw it into the fire, to the consternation of his companions, the nomadic Penan of Sarawak.

## The Demand for Methods

In British and North American universities, methods courses are now de rigueur, but initially in response to political scepticism. The social sciences have long been pressured to prove their credibility. Steven Rose (1997: 8) suggests the 'predictive tag' was added:

> precisely to privilege simple sciences like physics and chemistry . . . physics is . . . a 'hard' science, whose principles can be expressed mathematically and so it is supposed to be the model to which all other sciences should aspire. By contrast the social and human sciences are seen as the 'softest' because they are the least capable of precise mathematical expression.

Ironically, science has its own hierarchies of value. Rose argues how even biology has 'physics envy' (Rose 1997: 9). Some anthropologists now have 'biology envy'. Yet some early anthropologists brought some of the practices of biological enquiry to social anthropology, though not socio-biological reductionism.

The background to this volume has a specific history. In the early 1980s sociology was conflated by the political Right with communism and dubbed a 'non-subject'. Thatcher, a trained chemist, despite the fact that her successful 1979 election campaign was organized by Maurice Saatchi, with a first class sociology degree from the London School of Economics, attempted to abolish the UK Social Science Research Council. Her minister, Keith Joseph, selected the chairman of an independent enquiry. Lord Rothschild conducted a fulsome in-depth investigation and unpredictably defended, indeed celebrated, social science disciplines. He declared it would be an act of extreme vandalism if the Council were to be disbanded. In response, the Conservative government decreed that the Council drop the word 'science' and privilege economics; re-naming it the Economic and Social Research Council (Kuczynski 2006).

The new title privileged economics in an era of monetarism, Reaganomics and deregulation. The lucid prose of Keynesian economics had been lost in de-contextualized metric paradigms which set the agenda for all social science strategies.Increasingly phantom quantification, detached from any grounded knowledge, was to lead decades later to the banking crisis; then studied by an anthropologist experienced in ethnographic fieldwork (Tett 2009). It seems no coincidence that Lord Browne who devalued the arts, humanities and social sciences in his 2010 report for higher education, has an undergraduate degree in physics, though no PhD.

In the 1980s the newly named ESRC was indeed vulnerable (Bell 1984) and pressurized to prove its 'utility' in training for 'transferrable skills'. All social science disciplines in the United Kingdom were at first to be subjected to a one-size-fits-all methods training. Fortunately, each discipline successfully argued for its specificity. The pressure, however, for formulaic methods mounted. Anthropology, with its practice-based traditions, had no ready cookbooks. Instead, anthropology students were filtered into other methods courses. Quantitative techniques, more appropriate to surveys, were simplistically downsized for 'qualitative hangers-on'. In the 1990s I watched my Edinburgh postgraduates' creative confidence crushed by course conveners from other disciplines. Anthropology was mocked for its lack of hypotheses and 'advance management'.

Such research priorities could already be inventions. Long before, the sociologists Ditton and Williams (1981) declared that 'the doable is unfundable and the fundable is undoable'. Theoretical sociologists may have abandoned positivism, but their colleagues who privileged survey research continued to teach methods asserting the primacy of 'replicability', the alleged dangers of 'contamination' and the ideal of numerical majorities for generalization. The aims of such 'rigorous' training hint at the rigor mortis of mind and body. Such positivist priorities hold their sway, like physics envy, in public discourse. In 2009 the influential journalist Polly Toynbee (2009) cited, as gospel, a psychologist's assertion:

It is as good a science as physics, says Rutter. A hypothesis is tested, each result raises further questions, and progress is incremental. Proof of accuracy is in replication.

The irony is that social science positivism has only vaguely replicated aspects of science practice. Scientists have also, as in anthropological fieldwork, exploited the role of chance and accident. Likewise, anthropologists in this study embraced serendipity (see chapter 3).

Some readers of earlier drafts of this chapter have questioned my ensuing discussion of the theoretical and historical context of anthropological research, paradoxically wanting me to launch immediately into 'descriptive' examples. There will be plenty in subsequent chapters. However, it is crucial to disentangle the many presumptions and diversions in research proposals, their application and conclusions. While the abstracted theoreticians would dismiss ethnography as 'mere description', anthropologists need to expose the pseudo science or positivism long embedded in social science research. There is always theoretical potential in anthropological research and science in the broadest sense, as knowledge (Okely 1996a).

## The Hypothesis

In the 1980s the sociologist David Silverman (1985) argued that hypothesis testing was usually, although not exclusively, associated with quantitative research. He repeats his reservations about the potential of hypotheses in qualitative research (Silverman 2000: 7–8). Nevertheless, such approaches were largely overlooked in government funding. Steven Rose noted, 'so enthusiastically were Popper's ideas taken up that during the 1970s and 1980s grant applications in Research Councils in Britain tended to be turned down if they failed to state that the purpose of the proposed research was to "test the hypothesis that. . ." ' (1997: 46). This continued well into the 1990s in ESRC application forms including those for doctoral grants. Eventually the request was changed to more open-ended 'research questions'. Nonetheless, Rose (1997) aptly commented that the 'testing mode' was replaced by 'relevance' and 'wealth creation'.

The State has obliged academic grant-giving bodies to prove their 'usefulness', something made more explicit over a decade later in the dying days of the 2010 UK Labour government and to be reaffirmed in the Browne Report by Lord Browne, formerly head of the maligned oil company BP. He advised no funding for the teaching of the Arts, Humanities and Social Sciences. Only 'science' was to be ring-fenced. At the same time the 2011 Coalition government attempted to impose its own political agenda on the seemingly independent Arts and Humanities, causing academic fury ('Academic Fury over Government Order' 2011).

Already, utility for universities had been extended in the mid 1990s to a demand for 'income generation' via links with businessmen as users. Benefits to minorities or the powerless were ignored, or dismissed. In my annual self-assessment for my head of department at Hull University, in answer to proof of 'outreach', I recorded having lectured (without payment) in the local prison and even recruiting two undergraduates after their release. But this initiative was rejected as 'not income generating'. No matter that I later celebrated witnessing the ex-prisoners graduating.

The view of research, as producing short-term monetary utility as well as the predictable, destroys 'blue skies' openness which paradoxically brings *both* the unpredictable and unforeseen utility. Fortunately, many anthropology departments are increasingly open to innovation and creative scrutiny in methods courses. Elsewhere, positivist research practices are being challenged. A major sociologist has unpicked predetermined designs which ignore or deny the creative 'chaos' of the research process (Law 2004). Such debates continue. Felicia Hughes-Freeland, in our dialogue, declared:

> Sometimes all the verbiage is meaningless. It's what the ESRC want with their datasets instead of our versions of events. It's as if you can go and collect 'stuff'. The words are the data, but there's something more. You get big chunks of quotation. I fall into that dodgy area. That criticism of interpretive analysis where your voice merges with that of the people you represent.

Research planning, based largely on quantitative criteria, is misleading not simply inappropriate. The anthropologist can never fully plan. Indeed, as this book demonstrates, she or he should *not* plan with precision. The unplanned incident or 'anecdote' can be the most informative. The anthropologist may indeed have to jettison preconceived notions. Chapter 3 explores the experiences of anthropologists where they had to reject prior plans once confronted with the unpredictable complexity of others' reality in the field.

## Science

Anthropology should also reject a dated view of science as applied to the study of human beings. While Comte asserted that human societies could be studied for universal laws, comparable to gravity, Evans-Pritchard (1962) argued no one had come up with a single universal law about human behaviour.

Another view of science privileges notions of falsification and repeatability, but again, the philosophy of science provides precedents for a healthy scepticism for ethnographers. Contrary to Popper (1961), scientists do not follow the ideal of setting up theories put through rigorous procedures of falsification. Scientists also form interest groups with unifying paradigms (Kuhn 1962). The community of researchers works within these until a new paradigm emerges, again without falsification procedures. So, even in science, the idealized model of falsification is inappropriate. Scientists also have flexible practices. With massive ideological power in the public imagination, however, science holds its mystique regardless of informal accounts by its practitioners who challenge the imagined projection.

Byatt, the novelist, claimed that science 'brings the truth, while the arts is just a story'; however, the physiologist with whom Byatt was consulting disagreed: 'Science is also a story. It is the best story we have at the moment. Science is about change and about curiosity' (1996).

It is therefore absurd to demand of social scientists positivist procedures which others may have abandoned. Anthropologists do not waste time with falsification experiments. They are open to better explanations if they emerge as part of the intellectual enterprise. Anthropologists take others' field material on trust; however, this does not preclude detailed scrutiny. The material has to be presented in sufficient depth and with coherence. Anthropologists use acquired ethnographic sensibilities from their own fieldwork to make sense of fellow anthropologists' new material, from possibly the other side of the globe. Their suggestions may be provisional, but they have the power of insightful comparison and contrast.

Just as fieldwork involves an openness to anything that may shake preconceptions, so theoretical conclusions are open to refinement. It may be that the entire paradigm is overturned. The subjects of interest may have shifted. The historical context affects the intellectual questions. There may also be circumstances when the intellectual's enquiry is silenced. The State or the market may support only deceptive short-term aims proving counter-productive in the long run. Before 9/11 many Arabic and Islamic studies and university departments in the United Kingdom and the United States had been run down. They had been deemed merely 'esoteric' pursuits for gentlemanly scholars.

Given the provisionality of knowledge at *every* stage, the scrutiny of one's own or other cultures should be recognized as an intellectual adventure for its own sake. There are risks and surprises. Anthropological fieldwork has not been pedestrian data collection. But there can be fear of admitting it in print, lest joyful discovery be thought to undermine scientific enterprise (Okely 1996a).

## Universalisms and Specifics

There is a tension between examining the specific and seeking the universal. Universal aspects of humanity are not the same as universal laws. Social anthropology has had phases of examining universalisms, for example the incest taboo or the claim that everywhere societies distinguish between nature and culture (Lévi-Strauss 1973/1977: 321), subsequently contested (Bloch and Bloch 1980). Nonetheless, social anthropologists are cautious about world generalizations because their knowledge is steeped in the minutiae of differences and exceptions. Western psychologists, economists and some sociologists may assert universalisms which are in effect ethnocentric. The same applies to socio-biologists and popularist evolutionists. Symbolic-interactionists have also sought universalisms, so generalized as to be banal, while subtle differences are overlooked.

The privileging of the universal in knowledge quests has consequences for the recognition of cross-cultural examples with the potential for enlarging understanding. If differences are pushed to the margins, ethnocentrism retains its hegemony. Differentiations within the 'West' are also bulldozed in the rush for generalizations. Regrettably, anthropologists who insist that the discipline should be focused primarily on non-Western localities have themselves generalized about some imagined homogeneous 'West' (Okely 1996b: 5; Houtman 1988).

## Generalizations: Reliability versus Validity

Generalizations are a subcategory of universalisms. The standard quantitative critique of detailed field studies is that the material from participant observation is 'valid' but not 'reliable' because it is not generalizable. Reliability is associated with a 'measurement procedure', repeatability and numerical criteria (Marshall 1994: 446).

Social anthropological studies based on intensive fieldwork in a limited locality are then judged to be 'not reliable'. Seemingly, generalizations cannot include even neighbouring localities. This critique is fashioned for mass surveys and presumes that the research is confined to a single geo-political domain. Paradoxically anthropology confronts questions *beyond* any mapped locality or bounded domains to far reaches of the globe by comparison and contrast. The emergent knowledge raises questions which may be asked across space and time. Debates are triggered by the challenge of differences or similarities across continents. In contrast, quantitative reliability is culturally and geographically confined and its advocates necessarily parochial.

## Earlier Ethnography: Own Can Be Other

Understanding others beyond the familiar has centuries of history. Rosalie Wax (1971) brilliantly outlines this, moving from Herodotus in the fifth century BC through to the late twentieth century and the evolution of ethnographic fieldwork. Charles Booth's 1880s studies of English life mix statistics and participant observation with detailed descriptions. The Webbs studied the London urban working class. Ethnography has long been associated with the study of others; what is unknown or outside the regional context. The so-called exotic can be within the same polities, but across class, culture, the urban or rural. It would have been counter-productive to confront suspicious, often non-literate people with questionnaires.

Whyte's study of Chicago street gangs (1943/1955) with his 1955 appendix on methods was a landmark. Many of the Chicago school of sociologists confronted their white, male, middle-class identities and the unknown quarters of their own city. It should not, however, be concluded that such research should be confined to deviants and the underprivileged. It can and should be used for studying up (Nader 1974; Nash 1979a; Tett 2009). Nevertheless, such methods are easier with the powerless. The powerful by definition can block access as well as publication (Punch 1986; Okely 1987: 67–8; 1996b: 25–6).

## Numbers Unnecessary

On a micro level there are strengths from analysis which reveal a *system* where numbers become irrelevant for explanation and certainty. Edwin Ardener (personal communication, 1987) suggested looking at a room with multiple chairs. Someone could do wonderful charts recording the chairs in a certain position. The layout could be measured when in a circle, then in a square. The investigator could plot how the chairs were shifted during the week. But the quantitative data would ultimately be unnecessary. All could be explained by saying: 'This room is a dining room, sometimes used for assembly, sometimes for a dinner dance.' A qualitative study thus throws light on quantitative material when the *system* is revealed. Such arguments were made at a previous stage of early anthropological fieldwork practice (Kuklick 2011).

Similarly, Leach (1967), in a devastating critique of a survey-based study, argues that one in-depth micro study can best explain a mass of quantitative data. Long-term participant experience helps to make sense of even the most detached survey. Confronted with an extensive survey of landownership in fifty-seven villages in Ceylon (Sarkar and Tambiah 1957) Leach (1968) drew on his fieldwork in just *one* village to counter the interpretations of the statistics. The survey concluded that 335 households were landless peasants. From his detailed observation of inheritance practices, however, Leach revealed that over time a considerable number of the young would inherit land. Many sharecroppers were in fact heirs.

Leach (1967) argues that there is 'a wide range of sociological phenomena which are intrinsically inaccessible to statistical investigation of any kind'. Whereas the survey sociologist focuses on 'units of population' and 'individuals', by contrast, the anthropologist envisages 'systems of relationships'. Just as feminists pointed to the inadequacies of privileging 'the (male) head of household', Leach questioned the tradition of singling out one individual as representative of a household: 'The anthropologist . . . purposely chooses a small field within which all the observable phenomena are closely interrelated and interdependent' (Leach 1967: 87).

Leach argued that some of the interpretation in the study was convincing only because the main researchers, already familiar with the region, arrived inadvertently 'at their conclusions by intuitive methods' (1967: 76). I suggest that 'intuition' is acquired experientially, whether in one's own or other culture, after intensive fieldwork.

## Hypothesis-led Research

The emphasis on understanding a system contrasts with the unidirectional hypothesis. Leach's mentor, Malinowski, declared;

> Good training in theory, . . . is not identical with being burdened with 'preconceived ideas' . . . Preconceived ideas are pernicious in any scientific work, but foreshadowed problems are the main endowment of a scientific thinker. (1922: 9)

Another student of Malinowski, Powdermaker, insisted:

> A lack of theory, or of imagination, an over commitment to a particular hypothesis, or a rigidity in personality may prevent a field worker from learning as he stumbles. (1967: 11)

The privileging of the quantifiable comes from hypothesis-led research. Agar outlines the essentials:

> A hypothesis . . . has some predicted truth value . . . [and] states a relationship among a group of variables . . . To test the hypothesis, some kind of measurement is necessary. . . Defining how values are assigned is called an operational definition. (1980: 63–4)[4]

Operationalization is defined as:

> the transformation of an abstract, theoretical concept into something concrete, observable, and measurable in an empirical project. Operational definitions are . . . crucial to the process of measurement. (Marshall 1994: 368)

For anthropologists both hypotheses and their operationalization may be inappropriate and counter-productive.

## Neutrality

In much of the social sciences there have been presumptions that the researcher should be so neutral as to have no influence on the encounter. This is clearly impossible in anthropological fieldwork, where the participant observer must either be involved or perish. Survey research, in the quest for reliability, works with the metaphor of 'contamination' of interviewees or research subjects. Thus 'having once interviewed someone, a repeat interview may be contaminated by the earlier experience' (Marshall 1994: 447). The anthropologist, by contrast, needs to interact on multiple occasions with the same individuals in the field. 'Contamination' through daily contact is a sign of integration not failure. The subjects are implicated in the fieldworker's presence. Granted, some anthropologists have ignored or denied the implications of their presence. In practice there were always tell tale signs.

Scientists are themselves questioning the value placed on detachment and invisibility. It is therefore even less plausible that social scientists should cling to this in the name of what they imagine hard science to be. Social scientists are listening through keyholes and behind doors, the other side of which they imagine what scientists are up to.

Controversies within science challenge notions to which social scientists have outmodishly clung, including the contrast between quantum physics and classical physics. Only the latter is premised on the existence of a reality separate from the observer. The former confronts the role of the questioner. The study of humanity poses even greater complexity in that human beings can respond with infinite diversity and with relative autonomy.

## 'Reality', Othering and Autobiography

Anthropology has engaged with postmodernism and earlier misgivings about the fixity and objectivity of 'reality out there'. Labelled a 'crisis of representation' (Halstead 2008), this is not only an epistemological crisis but one based on political context. Post-colonial critiques confront the political history of anthropology, traditionally a study of 'the other' by Europeans and by non-indigenous North Americans.

The provisional character of ethnographies, scepticism about the existence of solid and external 'facts' as things, the constructed production of the published text (Clifford and Marcus 1986) and the specificity of the anthropologist as category (Okely and Callaway 1992) in relation to the people as research subjects: all these dilemmas have been widely debated. Nonetheless, fieldwork guidance in many textbooks continues only partially touched by these debates. Alternatively, they are used to reject the tradition of fieldwork 'in favor of mimicking textual analysts' (Borneman 2009: 9).

For a while, the standard monograph sidelined the innovative debates in articles or autobiographical accounts. Given the emergence of experimental texts, there often remains a curious split between the reflexive examination of field practice and other less personalized theoretical developments.

## Definition of Ethnography

Qualitative research's association with the word 'ethnography' has had potentially misleading consequences. In sociology there has been a strong presumption that ethnography is aligned to only one theoretical perspective, namely symbolic-interactionism, which tends to focus on the immediate minutiae of one-to-one encounters at the expense of any wider structure (Hammersley and Atkinson

1983; Silverman 1985). This is a betrayal of the pioneering Chicago sociologists who first created the term participant observation.[5] This does not mean of course that those who first devised the label were the first to practise the method (cf. Kuklick 2011).

The term 'ethnography' in anthropology has different meanings and history. Social anthropologists will have accumulated a mass of material from long-term fieldwork. It is this body of knowledge through which anthropologists may work for some years and continue to draw ideas. Ensuing monographs are also referred to as ethnographies. Ideally, monographs are both theoretical and rooted in fieldwork. The theoretical stance can be the full range, from Durkheim to Radcliffe Brown, from Marx to Weber, Gramsci, Derrida, Althusser, indeed as many of the theoretical perspectives as exist in the social sciences. Some lauded theoreticians, such as Foucault, have been most brilliant when combining historical ethnography with embedded theory, as in *Discipline and Punish* (1977).

Ethnography can also refer to specific field material. Anthropologists may ask of each other 'But have you got the ethnography right on that question?' or 'You don't seem to have enough ethnography to convince us'. It is assumed that the specific detail emerges from a larger corpus. Occasionally, it may be said that someone has some wonderful ethnography, but doesn't seem to know what to do with it. Accumulated facts are not good enough on their own. Theoretical issues are emergent as I outlined in the American Association of Anthropologists (AAA) Distinguished Lecture for the Society of the Anthropology of Europe (Okely 1998).

Anthropology's well-grounded ethnography has risked being downgraded by high theorists as 'just description'. For anthropologists however, anything 'descriptive' is already highly loaded and selective. Continuous choices are made: be it topic, locality, group, event or specific statements. Description may or may not render explicit the emergent theories. There is a major contrast with other social scientists' practice of separating so-called 'substantive' from 'theoretical' issues; something I was to discover among my then colleagues in a prestigious sociology department.

This is another legacy of quantitative empirical traditions where hypothesis as theory was separated, as organizing principle for the ensuing survey-induced facts. There are indeed vast divisions in sociology between theorists who are rarely involved in direct empirical research and those steeped in it. The former, I learned from Ted Benton and Ian Craib, my then colleagues at Essex University, may have greater intellectual empathy towards ethnographic approaches than quantitative empiricists. Although there may be chronological changes in emphases among anthropologists, where the monographs may be followed by more general overviews of the discipline, there is little place for the revival of the hegemony of the nineteenth-century armchair anthropologist.

## Holism

Malinowski's approach is close to an holistic tradition:

> the field Ethnographer has seriously and soberly to cover the full extent of the phenomena in each aspect of tribal culture studied, making no difference between what is commonplace, or drab, or ordinary, and what strikes him as astonishing and out-of-the-way. (1922: 11)

Ethnography, as understood and practised by anthropologists, often commenced as a detailed description of every aspect of a particular topic.

The significant contrasts between anthropological and sociological empirical research have implications for analysis (Okely 1994a: 18). The two disciplines came from different historical contexts. Sociology's empirical work was concerned mainly with Western societies of which the sociologist was a member.

Unlike the sociologist, the anthropologist could not take much as given. She or he could not isolate one theme extracted from a wider context since the society as a whole was largely unknown to the researcher and undocumented. Rigidly formulated questionnaires were inappropriate. The very interview mode is culture bound. The sociologist could afford to be more presumptuous in knowledge of the wider social context. Whereas Durkheim (1897/1952) could claim to identify and subclassify suicide in France, Malinowski (1926) had first to discover and then redefine such a practice among the Trobrianders. He had no official statistics, let alone context.

The historically divisive association of sociology with Western societies and anthropology with non-Western societies is no longer appropriate. Each discipline has strayed into the other's territory. While retaining its traditional methods, social anthropology can be used in the study of *any* group or society (Okely 1996b).

## Armchair to Verandah, Tent to Tarmac

In the nineteenth century so-called armchair anthropologists such as Frazer (1890) lived off the material brought back by Westerners who had travelled to distant places. Travellers, traders and missionaries followed the traditions of the explorers and conquerors. In the many myths of first encounters 'the others' were often accredited the inverse of the incomers' norms (Arens 1979).

The perception and selection of material were governed by the search for peoples allegedly at an earlier stage of mental and social evolution. Little thought was given to the notion that (a) the peoples had their own histories and centuries of transformations and (b) the peoples' own voices, in their own words, should be heard and listened to (cf. Tonkin 1995).

With the professionalization of ethnology, sets of questions were sent to local Western officials about a range of topics. This was possibly the initiative for *Notes and Queries* (1874/1951) devised by the Royal Anthropological Institute. Eventually it was recognized that secondhand information from non-scholarly amateurs, was untrustworthy. While this method had some similarities with questionnaires and pre-decided questions of relevance, these were not administered to the indigenous peoples but addressed to the Western outsiders, taken to be experts.

It was gradually recognized that ethnologists themselves had to enter the field for first hand research. Scholars, such as Haddon and Seligman, journeyed to New Guinea (Stocking 1983). Many of the early anthropologists were in fact trained as biologists, with a tradition of amassing observational material without too many pre-filtering hypotheses. The practice obviously excluded questioning the non-human subjects. Instead, biologists depended on grounded observation of the *total* field site for their study of the vegetation and wildlife environment, to anthropology's profit.

Thus the early ethnographers inherited the recognition of the total context, as opposed to extracting the individualized subject in 'uncontaminated' isolation. This prefigured what was to become the classical holistic approach in anthropological fieldwork. Sensitivity to the immediate wider context was thus fortuitously significant for the study of human cultures and actions. It does not follow that this methodological strategy in subsequent anthropological fieldwork is selected for the study of an imagined 'primitive humanity in its natural state' (Gupta and Ferguson 1997b: 8).

The pioneering scholars, driven by enquiry, snatched at any immediately available information, without prior language training. Thus what I label the 'verandah' anthropologists, as in the photo of Seligman (Stocking 1983: 82), depended largely on interpreters in extended and semi-formal interviews with indigenous peoples. Such bilingual intermediaries, even if they had a grasp of the indigenous language, might not make satisfactory translations.

Brian Morris, the first anthropologist I tape-recorded in this study, provides an excellent example of how, even today, an indigenous interpreter may mistranslate not just technical words but deliberately transform the cultural concepts in the interpretation of local medicine. In Malawi, Morris witnessed a Scottish botanist on a brief visit interviewing, through an interpreter, the local medicine man about his use of specific herbs. Morris, fluent in the local language, noted that when the herbalist explained that one herb was for dealing with 'spirit possession', it was translated for the academic as a 'headache'. When the medicine man was asked about the use of a very phallic-looking plant, he said it was for 'impotence' but the local interpreter translated this as 'stomach ache'. It seems the interpreter was *not* lost for words, but seemed determined to shield his people from being branded 'primitive'. Likewise cross-cultural knowledge and deliberate mistranslation by interpreters may also have affected the answers for the verandah anthropologists.

Those early researchers began to communicate in intermediary pidgin languages. Others came to recognize the importance of communicating directly. Malinowski (1922) presented himself as the originator of intensive fieldwork, whereby the anthropologist moved from verandah to tent, which he pitched in the centre of the village. Stocking (1983) argues that others before him pointed to this. In any case, recent anthropologists, guided by the celebrated Malinowski and his students, have taken as given the need to live alongside their subjects. In my case, motorway roadside Gypsy encampments with tarmac surfaces in the British Isles. This continuity through change should be celebrated rather than destabilized by a new return to the privileging of armchair theorizing over fieldwork, downgraded as seemingly quaint (Borneman 2009: 8–9).

## Holism Not Hypotheses

A significant methodological outcome of the earliest anthropological fieldwork was an approach whereby the topics and focus could not be simplistically formulated in advance. In the study of an unfamiliar, non-literate culture, with few if any written records, nothing could be taken for granted. Specific issues could not be privileged to the neglect of all else. Everything and anything could be relevant for recording and interpretation. Thus social anthropology was ironically saved by biologists from a pastiche of laboratory techniques (cf. Kuklick 1991).

Anthropological practice generates unique material. Despite months of literature reviews, possibly years of theoretical and comparative reading, hypotheses will be ejected like so much ballast. The people may not live as recorded. There could be famine, strife or abundance. Rituals may be missionized, nomads dispersed, documentation distorted or concealed from the outsider. The original focus may be an irrelevance, as chapter 3 documents.

As fieldwork traditions have developed, the anthropologist learns about the group or culture by immersion over an extended period of time. It has been generally accepted, at least in British anthropology, that fieldwork should be for a minimum of one year. Other traditions and new approaches have been embraced. Repeat visits are what Wulff has called 'yo-yo fieldwork' (2002). Fieldwork has not necessarily entailed fixture in one tiny location. Malinowski travelled from island to island on the celebrated Kula expeditions. 'Multi-sited' fieldwork has emerged as acceptable practice (Marcus 1998). Regrettably, some have interpreted this as being ever on the move. '*Do not linger* seems to be the motto' (Hammoudi 2009: 25). Many have consolidated their initial fieldwork with follow-up years (Kenna 1992, 2001a,b). In addition, anthropologists have explored return fieldwork and reanalysis through decades (Hirsch, James and Parkin 2000; Howell and Talle 2011).

Historical ignorance of classically a non-Western 'exotica' encouraged a recognition that ritual, kinship, the economy, politics, religion and many other aspects were to be comprehensively included. In this holistic approach a single custom or practice could not be torn from context. Holism coincided also with the rise of the more controversial functionalism as developed by Malinowski and Radcliffe-Brown. This had inbuilt problems, in that every custom and practice was deemed to be contributing to a balanced harmony from which conflict and change were banished. Moreover, Malinowski reduced social structures to the satisfaction of a few biological needs. Thus, although his ultimate theories may be challenged, Malinowski's holistic approaches have a fruitful legacy. His covert biological reductionism does not exclude others' potential privileging of the politico-economic base.

Given the flaws of functionalism, it does not follow that holism need also be jettisoned. There continues to be a vital case for studying groups or practices in the wider context and as much in 'the West' and the anthropologist's own culture(s). In my research among the Gypsies I found it especially important, thanks to Leach's influence, to be open to classical holism, thus studying the inter-relations of the Gypsies' economy, politics, kinship, ritual and travelling aspects of the community (Okely 1983). The holistic study, as examination of the total context, necessarily extended to relations with non-Gypsies, the wider politico-economy, as well as non-Gypsy ideological representations (Okely 2008).

Asad's critique of holism (1973) is misleading by presuming that it is necessarily limited to the micro. Holism can be extended to the global. It need not be confined to the imagined isolate of a bounded village, but should extend to wider terrains, be they national or global. Thus anthropology has moved beyond any earlier tradition which sometimes tended to construct isolates, regardless of colonialism and world systems. Anthropological research progressed from Frazer's armchair (1890) to verandah to tent and now tarmac, namely 'where my caravan was resting', or any location, urban or rural, and anywhere in the globe.

Regrettably, some social scientists have presumed that the overall anthropological concept of culture, which should include political economy, is as restricted as that defined by Spradley:

> The concept of culture as acquired knowledge has much in common with symbolic interactionism, a theory that seeks to explain human behaviour in terms of meanings. (1980: 8)

Perhaps that restricted definition explains some 1980s and later neo-Marxist hostility to anthropology (Okely 2007a: 240).

The rippling outwards of multifaceted holism is very different from the generalizability with variables of which anthropologists have been cautious. Agar argues that holism helps understand:

> why ethnographers are cautious with the idea of a variable. For what is a variable but something that can be measured in a standardized way across situations, across people, across groups, and even across cultures. (1980: 76)

For the anthropologist such variables, if they exist, can only be banalities if they extend beyond all contexts. Nevertheless, Agar, in 1980, regretted that anthropologists were increasingly moving towards 'hypothesis-testing methodologies'. He footnoted that 'many of the recent text books in anthropology emphasize quantification, standardization, and hypothesis-testing'. Thus the positivist pressure elaborated in the United Kingdom, after the Thatcherite threats to the Social Science Research Council, had already emerged in the United States.

Intensive research methods may have been adopted initially in classical anthropology's study of exotica for instrumental reasons. But these methods have force *anywhere;* in the anthropologist's own or another, less familiar, culture. Intensive fieldwork by one person, wherever the locale, throws up a special or different type of material. The theoretical and methodological approaches from anthropological participant observation can be pursued in literate and industrialized contexts, in the metropolis and all continents, as this book will demonstrate.

Any group, culture, area or subject can be approached as if all is strange. Anthropology's need for constant awareness of cross-cultural comparisons and its 'technique of estrangement' (Lévi-Strauss 1973/1977: 272) can be fully exploited, wherever the place. Inevitably, the very selection of a research area is a limiting act of definition, influenced by intellectual, political and theoretical concerns; even apparent whims. Within those bounds an holistic approach does not proceed by pre-selection.

An open-ended approach allows and encourages questions to *emerge* throughout the endeavour (Okely 1998). The material speaks for itself and to the researcher. It presents its own problems, which are unforeseeable. The people speak out of turn and as they are wont. Chapter 3 reveals the continuous and necessary responsiveness by anthropologists to the people's voices and concerns.

## Advance Knowledge/Theory

To reject hypotheses is not to abandon advance theoretical knowledge and a sense of enquiry. The anthropologist embarks on field research with all her past reading and intellectual instruction. The research is free to generate new theoretical problems rather than be constrained within old ones.

Seemingly, positivism lives on among some economists. As recently as 2006, I watched an Oxford development economics professor browbeat an anthropology postgraduate, insisting that she have a hypothesis before embarking on intensive fieldwork among nomads in the Middle East. Otherwise, he asserted, she would 'only drift'. No matter that she spoke the language and had spent some time with the people, yet wanted, and indeed needed, to find her way among them and on their terms.

An advance hypothesis is not the same as advance knowledge. Acquaintance with a wider range of knowledge will necessarily be advantageous. Agar suggests:

> When you attempt to describe some aspects of a group's life, you may be drawing from conversations, casual observations, twenty formal interviews, a previous ethnography, two novels, your general idea of the human condition, childhood experiences with your parents and who knows what else. (1980: 6)

The influences start long before the process of description, interpretation and writing up. The experience of fieldwork is also directed by the anthropologist's knowledge of the discipline. This includes admixtures of theory and cross-cultural comparisons. Agar, in Kentucky, found there were informative similarities with his previous work in south India (1980:16).

Similarly, the prior reading of details of the Trobrianders, the Azande or the Balinese offer resonances wherever in the globe the anthropologist may be standing. The quest is not for comparisons through quantifiable reliability, but critical questioning arising from the anthropologists' other cross-cultural possibilities. Both contrasts and similarities from elsewhere stir the anthropologist's thinking. Where the anthropologist is grounded, fieldwork has the potential for *lateral,* not just linear, knowledge.

## The Funnel

A potential fieldworker may be asked by non-anthropologists, what 'theory' she or he has adopted and is 'testing'. If the anthropologist admits to no such thing she or he risks being labelled a vulgar empiricist or someone concerned only with a-theoretical description. Agar, finding himself 'the lone ethnographer among sociologists and psychologists', was frequently asked, during his study of narcotics: 'Where is your instrument? What is the sample design? What is your plan of analysis?' (1980: 16). He suspected these were the wrong questions, yet was unable to explain why.

Agar offers a superb alternative metaphor for fieldwork practice. Somewhat mechanistic, it doubtless allays the worries of those wanting proof of research 'tools'; he calls it a

> 'funnel approach', with breadth and humanity at the beginning of the funnel, and then, within the context of that beginning, depth, problem-focus, and science at the narrow end. (1980: 13)

From the outset, the anthropologist adopts an open-ended approach to the full range of information and to all manner of people. The material and ethnographic concerns are not cut to size at the start. The people, as subjects, are themselves freer to volunteer their concerns in their own voice and context. All this has implications for the kind of material and field notes which the anthropologist is faced with when writing up.

Both during fieldwork and after, themes emerge. Patterns and priorities impose themselves upon the ethnographer. Voices and ideas are neither muffled nor dismissed. To the professional positivist, this seems like chaos but is creatively inevitable (Law 2004). The voices and material lead the researcher in uncontrollable directions. This indeed is *not* a controlled experiment. The fieldworker cannot separate the act of gathering material from its continuing interpretation. Ideas and hunches emerge during the encounter and are explored or eventually discarded. Writing up involves a similar experience. The ensuing analysis is imaginative, demanding and all-consuming. It cannot be fully comprehended at the writing-up stages by someone other than the fieldworker.

## Serendipity

Given this open-ended approach at every stage, the anthropologist is or should be 'disponible', a term I have borrowed from Breton (1937) and surrealism. The anthropologist is available for and open to what may come *par hasard*, however irrational and absurd at first encounter. Susceptibility to that which is above and beyond the 'real' is integral to anthropological experience. The ethnographer has, like the surrealist, to be open to *objets trouvés* (found objects) after arriving in the field. The anthropologist learns to abandon ethnocentricism and looks for the strange in the familiar and sees sense in the strange. She or he flies above the restrictions of realist banality and pedestrian common sense.

Knowledge is, at crucial stages, acquired through accident. We accept from childhood, stories about Archimedes' discovery when he was lying in a bath that a body immersed in a fluid shows a loss of weight equal to the weight of fluid it displaces. His famous cry 'Eureka!' has become a noun, meaning a brilliant discovery. We also learned the fable of Newton sitting under the apple tree, and comprehending the law of gravity thanks to a falling apple.

The great scientists were open to chance and non-directive thought. Moreover, many of their discoveries were made in moments of relaxation or dreamy contemplation; in the bath or under the apple bough. Likewise, anthropological practice includes moments of nondirective discovery. Lévi-Strauss (1955/1973) described how the anthropologist might spend days waiting seemingly doing nothing. As with Archimedes and Newton, anthropologists combine such 'drifting' days with months and maybe years of concentrated and diligent background work. Yet in social science adulthood, we are expected to put away childish things to see through a glass darkly. Knowledge, it seems in the training manuals, can only be acquired through purposive, cerebral intent and tunnel, not funnel, vision.

## Majority/Minority: Overt or Covert

Ironically, with the rise of neo-liberalism and the ideology of the free market reducing state welfare obligations in Britain and elsewhere, the need for majority-based policy research has diminished. Instead, statistical information may be laundered to reduce official unemployment figures and poverty levels. Qualitative research has taken on new significance in mass media contexts with the use of focus groups and the emphasis on 'target' minority groups; both rich and poor, powerful or peripheral. From 1997, UK New Labour spindoctors, following the practice of advertising, saw the relevance of qualitative focus groups. But again, the potential of detailed and in-depth ethnography was ignored. Decision makers with power have rarely pursued the findings from participant observation.

There has been one ancient exception; namely, its covert use in the long-established tradition of industrial and political espionage (see chapter 2). Here (Okely 2006b), positivist and number crunching criteria, too frequently demanded by government and other funders for social science, are recognized as utterly irrelevant. Cumulative anecdotes, which ultimately expose systems, are more informative than numbers, as Leach (1967) long ago confirmed.

Post 9/11, anthropology has witnessed new attention by the Central Intelligence Agency, the MI5 Security Service and the military. While the UK Research Councils continued to privilege quantifiable data and quantitative research methods, the centralized state apparatus is looking to qualitative methods and ethnography for political intervention, if not conquest. Numbers are good for public rhetoric and voter majorities. While democracy is seemingly displayed through statistical arguments, real power lies in systems. Ethnography finds these. And the powerful must know and command them. As I discovered through decades of research among Gypsies and government policy (Adams et al. 1975), and explored in the Third Eric Wolf Lecture (Okely 2006b), when it suits the state, ethnographic knowledge can inform and change policy. Other times, it will be abandoned or ignored if politically inappropriate or merely embarrassing.

## Writing Up

It is the practice for the anthropologist to be both fieldworker and analyst/author. Division of research labour into discreet tasks or between individuals is at a minimum. The anthropologist/fieldworker records, interprets and writes up her or his own material. For the anthropologist, the stages of knowledge as the research progresses are not sectioned between persons. There is no need for mechanical procedures and managerial instructions to ensure uniformity of perspective along chains of command. The anthropologist does not have to check and double check whether numerous assistants and interviewers have understood or even faked the collection of data, as happens in delegated questionnaires. She or he has instead to look to her- or himself and her or his specific relationship with the people who are the subject of study. The anthropologist becomes the collector and a walking archive, with ever-unfolding resources for interpretation (Jackson 1990).

By contrast, I recall a social scientist in my research centre in the 1970s asserting that in order to follow the correct scientific procedure to ensure 'objectivity', ideally someone other than the fieldworker should write up the final report using my field notes. The fact that I completed the task myself was seen uneasily as a form of intellectual cheating rather than a scientific necessity and standard anthropological practice.

Such a division between collection and analysis might be possible in a research tradition where the researcher delegates the 'data collection' to a reserve army of interviewers with pre-ordained questionnaire and clone like application. Thus the pre-selected choice of answers gives material which can be mechanically classified for the analysis (Okely 1987: 59–60). Anthropology does not work that way. Similarly, the multi-faceted anthropological approach permits variety and the full range of writing styles, now celebrated without apology (Clifford and Marcus 1986; Van Maanen 1988, 1995; Geertz 1988: 140; Sanjek 1990; Bradburd 1998; Beatty 2009). Malinowski (1967) spent hours reading novels in the field, and this showed in his publications. Literary, indeed poetic, traditions are just as appropriate for non-fiction. Anthropologists spend years with the full range of humanity whose many nuanced languages and experiences transcend banal reductionism and scientific pastiche.

Although the anthropologists in this study were asked about their recording, note taking, analysis and writing up, limitations of space preclude exploring this in detail (cf. Okely 1994a), but to be developed elsewhere, for example in Wulff (forthcoming). I also argue that issues of ethics rest mainly with what the anthropologist chooses to publish rather than pre-selection of questions and topics. The anthropologist cannot always extract her- or himself from witnessing controversy but she or he can hold back from individual identification (Okely 1999a) and full publication (cf. Okely 2005). Nevertheless, the broader political issue of the subject of research has been transformed and narrowed in recent decades to a bureaucratic controlling gaze, now labelled ethics (see chapter 3).

# –2–

# Unit, Region and Locality

Other disciplines beyond social anthropology have sometimes tended to thrive on a caricature that the discipline only studied isolates and cultures in a fixed place. The isolate is an imaginative fiction (Okely 2012). Place cannot be equated with culture. Groups may be flexible (Leach 1964). Fieldwork was never an isolate. Its limited location was a heuristic device. But movement and globalization may have been less a focus. Global links beyond fixed localities were always present in the subject of classical anthropology and early monographs, but not usually the prime focus (in contrast to *Notes and Queries* 1874/1951: 39). Urban locations were also problematized (Mayer 1961). In practice, the elaboration or even invention of isolates has long been discredited. There has been the recognition of movement, migration and transformations through histories (Hastrup and Fog Olwig 1997). Anthropologists have worked with other social scientists to examine the transnational family (Bryceson and Vuorela 2002).

Gupta and Ferguson (1997a,b) provoked brilliant debates. Unfortunately, on occasions, their critique of past practices depended on caricature and an ideal type, which anthropologists have long recognized as constructions. Both Evans-Pritchard (1940) and Lienhardt (1961) studied nomads where there was no presumption of fixed site. Additionally, many European anthropologists have done fieldwork among groups within their own or other national spaces in Europe, for example Frankenberg (1957), Segalen (1980), Kaminski (1980), Strathern (1981), Zulaika (1982), Okely (1983), Gullestad (1984), Zonabend (1984), McDonald (1989), Hockey (1990), Young (1991), Edgar (1995), Stewart (1997) and Stewart and Rovid (2011), or migration within Europe (Pero 2008; Oliver 2008), despite the denigration of anthropology in Europe as 'easy' and already 'known' by Bloch (Houtman 1988).

They did not, as Gupta and Ferguson (1997b: 8) contend, believe that the anthropologist necessarily had to travel elsewhere to find difference. Additionally, fieldwork is as appropriate for studying the cultural context from which the anthropologist emerged (Jackson 1987; Okely 1996b: chapters 7, 8; 2003b), including the United States by a 'native' (Sutherland 1975). A key anthropological field study in 1960s urban United States was that by Hannerz (1969) of ghetto culture, after the pioneering sociological participant observation studies by Whyte (1943/1955), Becker (1963) and others. Other anthropologists, originating beyond 'the West', have done fieldwork in their national space, for example Condominas (1965), Nakhleh (1979), Mascarenhas-Keyes (1987) and Talib (2010). Then there are examples of non-Westerners doing fieldwork beyond their own national space, for example Tamil-born Tambiah's (1970) work in Thailand, and Chinese-educated Xiang Biao's (1970) monograph on professionals migrating from India to Australia.

Some of us indeed travelled only a few miles from our universities (Okely 1987). Anthropology is not confined to what is labelled obscure (MacClancy and McDonaugh 1996). The limited zone is also a heuristic device (Okely 1996b), unlike the argument that anthropologists imagined their isolates. Methodologically, there were always reasons for limiting fieldwork to repeated day-to-day contacts and participation through time. The participant observer can only cover so much. There are groupings and clusters recognized as 'multiplex' relationships, which the people themselves form from face-to-face contacts. The long-term fieldworker taps into such complexities beyond simplex relationships.

Akira Okazaki, of Japanese upbringing, found that staying in one place, either among the Masai or later the Gamk in Africa, meant that he got to know the community in depth. It was little to do with the belief that peoples were isolates but that there were repetitive contacts:

> I wanted to be among the Africans because I could learn a lot of interesting things, maybe expand my experience, knowledge and my interest by moving from one place to another. But I am not the person to move all the time. I am always interested in staying in one place: a very closely knit relationship. If you move from one society to another your relationship with others becomes different. The kinship system is quite different, even between neighbouring societies.

The earlier field anthropologists privileged the local and small scale partly because huge sections of the world's peoples did not live in urban concentrations. These alternatives elsewhere had been dismissed by social evolutionists as mere 'left-overs' in Eurocentric, neo-Darwinian beliefs. Industrial development was previously and arrogantly conflated with intellectual capacity by Westerners. The outstanding ingenuity of peoples in varied conditions was overlooked. But social anthropologists who lived alongside peoples did *not* entertain such prejudices. Evans-Pritchard's (1937) study of the Azande contested Lévy-Bruhl's assertion that so-called primitives were 'pre-logical'. Instead, he explained the rationality of the Azande.

Granted, in the past some anthropology departments put up world maps pinpointing each named 'people', implying spatially, once 'racially' bounded cultures. These were illusory. Travelling Gypsies demonstrate the impossibility of locating a separate people and culture in a bounded space. They make their own symbolic boundaries, through notions of the body, their controlled interaction with non-Gypsies and the circular layout of the shifting campsites (Okely 1983: chapter 6). Gypsy 'culture,' moreover, I argue, is no isolate, but a continuously creative construct—a form of bricolage—selecting parts of the dominant society and rejecting others to form an internal, oppositional coherence (Okely 2010c). It is also regrettable that in the caricatures no account is taken of anthropologists who included the dominant context in their focus on minorities. Some did indeed address questions of constructed boundaries (Stolcke 1995).

The participant observer can only cover a limited territory, unless she or he experiments with displaced fragments. The very practicalities of fieldwork in a limited space may have inadvertently encouraged the anthropologist to appear to construct social and historical isolates. They are in recent decades more sensitive to colonial and capitalist interventions as part of the picture, as well as earlier migrations and histories. Globalization has made the notion of any bounded isolate even more untenable.

## No Isolate

There was always evidence of encounters beyond the groups, to varying degrees. Signe Howell, in tropical forest Malaysia, confronted the history of the Chewong:

> They hadn't been *isolated* for centuries. Somebody had always been trading goods. They needed knives, salt, and some cloth, but there are just a few people who would go out: a few men. They'd brought knowledge about the outside world back. They felt they were stigmatized. They were very proud of the fact that I went with them. Towards the end, [on] short visits, I left the forest to the Trading Station. I never went on my own. The Malays and the Chinese would speak to me in Malay. I would say: 'I don't speak Malay very well, I only speak their language.' They [the Chewong] thought that was terrific!

Despite this counter to the stereotyped isolate, the media still delight in presenting newly 'discovered' groups as being unchanged for 'thousands of years', as in the reportage by satellite of tropical forest Indians in South America as recently as May 2008.

Stephen Hugh-Jones, who studied tropical forest Indians in Amazonian Colombia, acknowledged:

> Today we who have studied groups within the western anthropologists' territory are finding out the rather shaky secret that those who studied exotica abroad were not ensconced in hermetically sealed cultures. Our scepticism is now confirmed from even the remotest tropical Amazonian forest. The assumptions of 'isolated' communities can no longer be sustained in any part of the globe. Anthropologists elsewhere are waking up to the fact that seemingly isolated peoples are not only affected by new invasions and changes, but also that they had a history. (Hugh-Jones 1989: 54)

By contrast at an earlier date, Malcolm McLeod was encouraged to assume he would be aiming at isolated fieldwork:

> I was brought up to think of fieldwork in the almost heroic terms emphasized by Malinowski and his pupils: going off into the bush and living miles away from anywhere. It was a very

inappropriate view going to work in Ghana in 1966, and particularly in Asante. Firstly, Ghana had regained its independence a few years before. Ghanaians were highly sophisticated and international. They were constantly coming and going to Europe and the States. Many had been educated in Britain. They had families in Britain. They were part of an international network then, as now. Secondly, in every village, there were people who travelled widely. People had radios, access to newspapers, books.

Europeans studying Europe, and other anthropologists studying 'at home', have long lived the paradoxes of fieldwork in geographically familiar but socially, psychologically unfamiliar places. The boundaries are constructed. I have placed aspects of the British upper-middle-class culture under the microscope, including my own (Okely 1996b: chapters 7, 8). As Rimbaud said '*Je est un autre*'. Europeanist anthropologists subverted the suggestion that anthropology is only non-Western exotica.

The anthropologists in this dialogic study include a number who have done fieldwork in Europe: Herzfeld, Kaminski, Kenna, Okely, Silverman, Wulff and Zulaika. Some have conducted subsequent research in Europe after fieldwork (Howell 2006).

While the field may be shifting and bounded homogeneous cultures illusory, the intellectual horizons have always ideally been unbounded. If we study in Europe, we take everywhere with us from readings in the vast cross-cultural anthropological literature. We take the world's differences with us. Regional specialisms were always problematic. The more complex question to ask is not where but *how* do we do fieldwork?

Gypsies are a case study of the new interest in hybrid border cultures. The tendency to use past voyages out as the only model (Gupta and Ferguson 1997a,b) is a straw/mud hut version, and is especially inappropriate among anthropologists, labelled—indeed denigrated—by some as Europeanists. Just a few miles from London, I occupied a caravan near major motorways. Anthropologists long ago moved from veranda, tent or sledge, now to tarmac (asphalt) and concrete, not wooded jungles. Fieldwork among the Gypsies was never a physically bounded place. Even the camps were ever open to non-Gypsy intrusion. Fieldwork consisted as much on routes traversed by everyone else and in public places, including government offices. Illuminating encounters took place on house-dwellers' doorsteps and in non-Gypsy courts.

The 'field' was always an imagined construction, created by the people I was with, including non-Gypsies. No permanent en-cultured space, a site could be abandoned then barricaded by council rubble or wooden posts. The physical field could thus be obliterated. Although I had to drive only a few miles up a motorway from my home and to territory visited in earlier identities, my fieldwork, when writing up, became a far away place.

## Movement: The Caricature of Non-Movement

Another caricature in perceptions of practice is that the peoples studied were also fixed. Yet even the quintessence of anthropology in Malinowski's *Argonauts of the Western Pacific* (1922) explored movement, as the very title confirms. The

Trobrianders took hazardous voyages from island to island. Malinowski may have pitched his tent in the village, but he also travelled by boat with the Trobrianders. He complained if they left without him (Malinowski 1967). Perhaps they preferred the *anthropologist* to stay put.

Subsequent anthropologists doing fieldwork on an island, seemingly as fixed isolate, were also studying movement. Margaret Kenna originally planned to look at inter-island communication in Greece but adjusted this when discovering she could look at movement by staying in one place, getting to know those who stayed or moved:

> The idea of moving away from the island was soon dispelled, partly because I was a young unmarried woman and the people who had time to speak to me were older women and older men. They were always talking about who had what names, what people would inherit when their parents died, what religious services were being planned for the souls of dead people, and therefore what objects had to be got ready for these religious rituals. All of that swam into my consciousness at the same time that I was taking notes about who was leaving, who was arriving for inter-island links. These began to seem more important than inter-island links because there were things that were in Campbell, in Friedl but not put together systematically.
>
> On Anafi it was clear that all three things linked together- family, property and ritual. That linked with the domestic cycle. Men were going off as seasonal migrants in the gap where harvest finished in June. They would go to Athens then come back when the agricultural year would start again. That was the way in which men got into seasonal, then permanent, migration in the city. In fact migration had always been a part of the island experience. Now it was transforming the island because, like a lot of rural Greece, it was depopulating. The young adult contingent in the age pyramid was simply not there anymore. It was all children, older people and the people who couldn't or wouldn't migrate.

## Nomadic Movement

Nomads are the supreme example of intergroup and spatial breadth. Anthropologists have been engaged with nomads for decades, for example Evans-Pritchard's (1940) celebrated fieldwork among the pastoralist Nuer. It was indeed insights from fieldwork with pastoral nomads, which presaged the notion of 'multi-sited fieldwork', now more fully recognized in a globalized context (Marcus 1998). But that in turn was perhaps influenced by fieldwork with nomads. Earlier pioneering suggestions by Dyson-Hudson (1972: 10) concerning nomads were already relevant for all types of fieldwork:

> Our analytic units need not be population aggregates of some sort: they can as well (and sometimes more revealingly) be segments of time or action, points of contact or separation.

But even in the 1970s it was rare to find such discussion of nomadic fieldwork. Anthropologists had the knowledge to bring a nomadic perspective, but this was methodologically sidelined.[1] Anthropologists studying nomads have also had to problematize the dominant settled society with whom often stigmatized nomads have to negotiate (Okely 2008).

Dyson-Hudson's emphasis on 'segments' and 'points of contact or separation' could as well be applicable to the subsequent study of 'non-places' such as airports by Augé (1995). My Algerian student Taleb (1987), initially sceptical of research beyond formal interviews, experienced a major breakthrough among Algerian migrants to France when encountering them on the ferry to and from Marseilles. They opened up precisely because they were in a liminal location. Meanwhile Halstead (2004) has contested that airports are culture free, being ritualized localities for culturally specific gifts from those bidding farewell to departing relatives.

## Change

We have tended to take on trust orthodox anthropologists' claims to heroic journeys into the unknown, isolated communities up the jungle and over the mountain ranges (Okely 1996b: 7).

It may be that earlier field anthropologists were under pressure to select places isolated from their *own* familiar. But the islands, villages, tropical forests and hills were never distant for the residents (Ardener 1987). Neither were they generally 'untouched' by outsiders, traders, missionaries and colonial officials (Okely 1996b: chapter 2). They had their own histories and experienced indigenous migrations and movement (Wallerstein 1974). World trade and interconnections existed in early times, as archaeologists confirm. Globalization's new character is merely adding high-tech privileged communications, multinationals and enhanced Western or Asian hegemonies to earlier interconnections.

Nevertheless, due recognition should be given to the anthropologists who, in the early twentieth century, moved from armchair or desk-bound traditions to find out things for themselves. Simultaneously, these voyagers rewarded themselves with a sense of heroic adventure. For the Westerner travelling afar, there is profound investment in the notion that he, less often she, has been where no one—that is no white man—has been. Lévi-Strauss was alert to the elaborate strategies that explorer/lecturers, with slide projectors, used to claim unique arrivals and returns from 'untouched' territories. In their lantern/slide shows he spotted external objects such as 'rusty petrol cans in which this virgin people does its cooking' (1955/1973: 39). The same confusions confront today's television viewers seeing football T-shirts, if not mobile phones, adopted by tropical forest peoples.

Granted, anthropologists today are more alert to global movements and influences sharpened by new technologies. Suzette Heald noted the transformations in her interactions with research associates in Uganda in the late 1960s, contrasting with her fieldwork extended over decades in Kenya:

Globalization has made a difference, as we're all now part of the same world, and this really hit home with me in 1994 when I first met Joseph. He was a schoolboy, but had imagined the West. Though he'd been brought up in rural Kenya, there was nothing I could tell him that surprised him. He had 'seen' it. He had read about it in books.

The greater visibility of migrants and massive refugee displacement around the world, made prominent through instant media coverage, has prioritized such issues. Thus funding bodies may also be more alert to migration and movement if perceived as local political problems.

## From Colonial Context to Globalization

Before the 1960s and decolonization, the discipline was indeed facilitated for Westerners by fieldwork in then-colonized countries. Entry by Western anthropologists often depended on access through colonial gatekeepers and indirect financial patronage (cf. Kuklick 1991). British and French anthropologists tended to concentrate on colonial regions in Africa and Asia under their nations' respective rule. By contrast, pioneering North American anthropologists engaged in research among their internally colonized indigenous peoples: Boas among the Eskimo/Inuit, Kroeber among Native Americans. Australian Aboriginals were usually studied by anthropologists of European origin and with ancestors who had appropriated Australia.

The acknowledgements in classical monographs reveal the vital role played by both funders and colonial officials. There were political gains for authorities needing to know more about the 'natives' under their control. Anderson (1969) and others highlighted the fact that Evans-Pritchard (1940) was officially funded to study the Nuer in the Sudan after the rise of charismatic prophet leaders. Evans-Pritchard was rebuked for merely footnoting the destruction, indeed bombing, by the British of impressive Nuer monuments. These were interpreted by the colonial rulers as symbols of increasing solidarity among once disparate and decentralized kin groups.

Gough, uncompromisingly and famously, asserted that anthropology was and is 'a child of Western imperialism' (1968: 403). Clearly, anthropology thrived in a colonial historical context (Owuso 1979). However, any monocausal explanation is simplistic. James (1973) argues convincingly that anthropologists considered that they had a duty to act as intermediaries against the worst ravages of colonialism which they believed, however naively, would be for the long term. Few, if *any*, knowingly acted as spies and 'lackeys' for the colonial rulers, although their interpretations were affected by their positionality (Kuklick 1991: chapter 7). There are ongoing debates today about development ministries and nongovernmental organizations employing Western consultants and others for narrowly defined programmes and, of course, Central Intelligence Agency (CIA) recruitment.

Thus, despite the independence of former colonies, there remain Western political priorities in international funding. The World Bank, global corporations and increasingly, counter-terrorist initiatives, may require 'local knowledge' to minimize political and economic risks. This is not knowledge for its own sake. As under colonialism, anthropologists and other intellectuals may continue to approach these issues with contrasting concerns. Despite some vulnerability, they are not inevitably branded as agents of a new indirect colonialism. Like earlier classical anthropologists, their concerns are not necessarily reduced to cynical career routes, but also to respect for varied humanity and the enlargement of knowledge. The examples in chapter 7, especially of Lindisfarne in Afghanistan and Wright in Iran, confront the anthropologists' political positionality.

## Colonial and Post-Colonial Context

Naïve or not, many anthropologists, both past and present, have been driven by a curiosity for *the full range* of humankind as the dialogues here confirm. This curiosity has a history. Colonialism may indeed have unforeseen counter-consequences for the very children of colonialism (Okely 2003a). During World War II, British men were recruited to fight for king and empire. For some their experiences evoked unpredicted challenges to any ethnocentric presumptions. After the war, Edmund Leach, Rodney Needham and Jimmy Littlejohn returned to live alongside and study peoples in either South East Asia or Africa where they had been stationed as servicemen. They turned to anthropology. Thus colonialism was subverted by inspiring the appreciation of difference.

In the United States, without the same formal colonizing history, anthropology emerged from other power relations, including genocide. The search for seemingly disappearing indigenous peoples, such as the Native Americans and Inuit, inspired Boas to salvage vanishing traditions. Although Boas did indeed live alongside the Inuit, the differing wider context for North American anthropologists may explain what I have discerned as a privileging of one-to-one interviews, as opposed to long-term participation observation. The dominant white governing class lived in the same nation. The indigenous were now minorities who, in contrast to colonized Africa and elsewhere, could never threaten independence.

Anthropology has never operated out of historical context. Whereas intellectually open-minded anthropologists once researched the colonized, by the early twenty-first century, a younger generation of anthropologists are drawn again to the dispossessed rather than to the powerful—in this case asylum seekers, diasporic children, the 'undocumented' and migrant carers, often with their children back home (Zontini 2008). As before, the vast majority of anthropologists find themselves as allies of their subjects. This does not preclude the findings being misappropriated beyond the control of the individual researcher. In-depth fieldwork can inform, not enlighten, policymakers seeking greater controls of moving peoples.

## Research Misappropriated

It is deeply disturbing that anthropologists' work has been misused, usually unpredictably, against the research subjects. Here the very power of anthropological practice is proven. States, fortified by military control, need espionage among the 'enemy'. Only long-term participant observation with linguistic and cultural intimacy can reveal the systematic working of group cultures. Horrendously, studies of the rural Vietnamese by earlier French or Eurasian anthropologists (Condominas 1965) were translated and scrutinized, without their consent, for the peasants' routines (Price 2007: 21). Fields were then bombed by the US military when the peasants were most likely to be working there. Village 'leaders' were targeted for assassination.

Research has been appropriated not only by direct rulers but also by 'neocolonialist' powers for indirect rule. Project Camelot (Horowitz 1967, cf. Jorgensen and Wolf 1970) exposed the extent of recruitment by the United States of potential intellectuals in South America, all the better to facilitate clandestine or even overt intervention and control (Huizer and Mannheim 1979: 481–94).

Price has documented how, among academics, anthropologists were systematically marginalized through the 1940s and 1950s and the cold war if deemed to be activists, especially for racial justice in the American South. McCarthyism penetrated the campus and research funding bodies. People were deprived of tenure and grants because sympathy for the dispossessed and even non-whites was dubbed anti-patriotic, if not communist (Price 2004). Thus the caricature, still propagated by other disciplines that anthropology was allegedly racist and that anthropologists were colluders with white empire is shamefully ignorant.

## Espionage and Overlapping Methods

In 2006 it was publicly revealed that the supposedly independent Economic and Social Research Council (ESRC), the Arts and Humanities Research Council and, more significantly, the Foreign and Commonwealth Office would be jointly funding a hitherto secret project called 'Combating Terrorism by Countering Radicalisation' with the sum of several million pounds sterling. Funding was to be donated with neither advertising nor interview selection. The programme had been developed 'without the scrutiny of the ESRC's various boards and committees' (Spencer 2010: S292). This broke the Council's constitution. Only after public exposure and debate, were these plans jettisoned. The President of the Association of Social Anthropologists, John Gledhill, objected that the financing of anthropologists as spies would endanger *all* anthropologists (Spencer 2010; Attwood 2007; Gledhill 2006; cf. Frean and Evans 2006).

The Association of American Anthropologists (AAA), especially since the disastrous invasions of Afghanistan and Iraq, has confronted State and military demand for anthropologists as embedded experts, if not spies. In 2006, controversially, the AAA's elected body consented to the CIA advertising funding for postgraduates on its Web site. This was subsequently withdrawn. At the 2006 annual meeting of the American Anthropological Association in San José these issues were fiercely debated.

A special session, not in the programme, was inserted, 'Practicing Anthropology in the National Security and Intelligence Communities' (17 November 2006, 12:15–1:30 pm). I attended. The opening, ex-military speaker introduced himself incongruously as 'having done distinguished service in Vietnam'. He declared that 'after Iraq', the military now needed people who understand 'culture'. New recruits, we were informed, would now be more likely to gain fast promotion if 'qualified in culture' (the subtext being Islam), and languages, rather than in engineering. He and other State employees present—with anthropology qualifications—were looking to recruit anthropologists. A woman speaker declared they were 'looking to British anthropology'. Seemingly, the speaker's notion was in a colonial time warp, embracing the very aspects which post-1960s critiques had abhorred.

As a stigmatized symbol of the military's current and outmoded (mis) understanding of 'culture', the Vietnam veteran projected on the screen an image of a donkey. As contrast, his ideal of ultimate sophisticated cultural understanding was represented by the image of a macho sports car. The presentation revealed *no* comprehension of the crucial economic role of the donkey elsewhere, let alone the biblical icon of Christ on an ass (Okely 2003a: 14–15). The sports car appeared to some, if not all the anthropological audience, as ethnocentric extravagance, fit only for US highways.

Present at this and advertised sessions were scholarly researchers of the US censorship of anthropologists through decades, including Price (2004). There were also long-term experts on Iran, Islam and the Middle East. Several anthropologists openly declared they were always willing to be consulted by the State and militia, but *not* signed up as spies, thereby losing total control of their research and publications (Price 2006). Moreover, to work as secret agent would publicize and jeopardize the identity, indeed lives of anthropologists across the globe. Already, after the attacks on the World Trade Center and the Pentagon, William Beeman had lamented:

> It is a sad feature of Anglo-American culture that otherwise well-educated people have little knowledge of other cultures . . . the anthropologist needs to do some ethnographic analysis of his or her own culture. (2001: 1)

Price (2007: 20–1) was later to expose the unattributed plagiarism and misuse of anthropologists' texts in a Counterinsurgency Field Manual. By early 2007 the US Department of Defense had deployed 'human terrain' teams to Iraq and Afghanistan. These five-person teams included anthropologists (Gonzalez 2007: 21).

The recruitment issues had already gained national publicity in the *New York Times* (Rohde 2007). The 2007 AAA meeting in Washington DC again had officially scheduled espionage sessions—some aiming to recruit anthropologists for the military, others critical. Here Beeman (2007), with long-term expertise in Iran, publicly declared he was willing to advise but not sign up as an employee; confining all information to the State's secret control. Anthropologists have already had to analyse and confront conflict and violence (Nash 1979b; Zulaika 1982; Jarman 1993; Nordstrom and Robben 1995; Ghassem-Fachandi 2009; Okely 2005). The knowledge is already there to read.

The study of the State's use of anthropology during World War II has been further explored (Price 2008; Keenan 2008a). The militarization of anthropology in continents beyond Asia, namely Africa, is also being pursued (Keenan 2008b; Besteman 2008). The general debates about the appropriation of anthropology have continued (Lutz 2008; Mahnken 2008; Gomoll 2010). Additionally the UK Arts and Humanities Council was in 2011 under pressure by the UK Coalition government to prioritize a Conservative electoral theme of 'The Big Society' (Boffey 2011), thus controversially challenging independent research.

Whatever the political controversy, the resort to the discipline of anthropology, based on intensive cross-cultural fieldwork, confirms the vital scientific importance of its research methods. This is despite the arrogant undervaluation of ethnographic discovery and analysis in quantitative social sciences and celebrity fiction writers. Moreover, the latter do not understand the concept of plagiarism (Armitstead 2008).[2]

Recent interest in Islam and conflict contrasts with the 1980s. Research Council funding for anthropological research in Libya (Davis 1987) was denounced as frivolous by members of Thatcher's Conservative government (Spencer 2010: S290). Zulaika, a pioneer researcher but non-activist among Basques, described how, long before 9/11, a military 'expert' refused to share a conference platform with him—an alleged terrorist. The context has now dramatically changed. Another of my interviewees was approached by the CIA. The anthropologist refused the lucrative offer. Whereas grounded knowledge of conflict was previously ignored or denigrated, official strategies to recruit embedded anthropologists, for Iraq, Afghanistan and beyond, continue.[3]

## Choice of Location

For the anthropologists I interviewed for this book, there were not only choices to be made of continent and country, but then specific field sites. The majority were not facilitated by colonial historical links. There was a variety of reasons for their choices. For some there was the quest for the elsewhere, precisely because these were far from their own identity and history. Howell, of Norwegian descent, selected tropical forest Malaysia partly through her supervisor's inspiration:

> I started my anthropological postgraduate studies not thinking about Malaysia. I was thinking about the Middle East. In order to be with a particular supervisor, I had to change my regional focus. He had worked in South East Asia. I wanted tropical forest people. He suggested the Malay aborigines. He had done some fieldwork there in the early 1950s. He had passed through the rainforest and tried to visit some of the aboriginal groups. He'd come across a couple of the Chewong. He said: 'Why don't you go and study them? Nobody knows anything about them.' There had been two small articles by a British game warden who discovered them in 1936.

For Akira Okazaki there was a search for difference. He wanted a culture and indeed continent, far from his native Japan. He was also inspired by French literature, including the poet Rimbaud, who had journeyed to North East Africa. Okazaki lived first with the Masai. His second choice, among the Gamk, emerged after years of saving money to return:

> From 1981 I decided to find another field. The reason why I tried to leave Masai land is complicated. The Masai are a Nilotic people and the Gamk (the name they call themselves but other people call them the Ingessana) are on the edge of Nilotic culture. Their language is a little different but they have a lot of borrowed words from Nilotic languages. The Masai are the southern-most Nilotic people and the Gamk or Ingessana are the northern-most. I have been asked many times why I moved. I wanted to change, partly because I had been involved with the Masai for many years; just to go and try new methods and new way of learning as well as just to get the stimulation from a new world.

Clough, of American and English parentage, and American citizenship, wanted specifically *not* to go to any part of the world with a history of US intervention—for example South Asia with the legacy of Vietnam and Cambodia. His Anglican identity being not so marked, the legacy of British colonialism was for him less problematic. He chose a region as far from US connections as possible:

> It was all pure idealism. I was living in Malta. I had a Peace Corps application. They wanted to send me to Melanesia. I didn't want to go because it looked like I was moving into an American colonial situation—American protected territories. I thought I wanted something genuinely different. Out of idealism, I started looking for jobs in Africa. There was an American Jesuit priest at a Maltese school where I taught who said: 'Write to the Vice Chancellor of Ahmadu Bello University.' I sent him this letter saying I wanted to be a volunteer teacher. That's how I got to Nigeria—another strange accident.

With a focus on agricultural economy, Clough also chose the rural because the majority of Nigerians lived there. After a chance visit to a supposedly 'isolated village', he found it was linked directly into international economic agricultural production.

Brian Morris, who had lived and worked in Malawi before studying anthropology, was advised by his department to 'extend' his expertise. But he had also to consider his familial obligations:

> Why I ended up going to India? I could only study the Kubu [in Sumatra] if I first learned Dutch. I had to go to a place where the background material was essentially in English. Back then I had three children, the oldest of which was seven. I was warned by Heimendorf that nobody but an idiot would take three young children to the field. The trouble was I only had one grant. I wanted somewhere where, if problems were happening, within a few days I could get back into a place where there was a hospital.

There were articles on the Hill Pandaram in India. Heimendorf had gone there for a short visit in 1953. They were obviously still living in the forests and still hunter-gathering.

Louise de la Gorgendière had already visited Ghana through her Canadian masters supervisor's contacts. Interested in local education, she chose a field site that was not too urban.

Herzfeld, with a degree in classics, had done earlier Greek folklore research. First political circumstances were relevant, then serendipity:

I had decided to work in Rhodes in a village that I had previously visited. This was the time of the military dictatorship in Greece, the end of 1973. I quickly discovered that I had already studied the major ritual. The villagers were quite adept at keeping me out of things. The focus of my dissertation shifted. Then finally I got the boot from the colonels in the wake of the Turkish invasion of Cyprus.

We found the Cretan village quite by chance. My wife and I went to Crete for a few days prospecting for a good field site. We went to the wrong bus stop, and as a result of a conversation we had with a man there . . . I said 'My wife's interested in local weaving, I'm looking for a place to study practices that have to do with where people marry.' I made it sound rather like folklore. He seemed to understand: 'Where you really want to go is up in [X].' He bellowed across at somebody. This turned out to be the bus conductor, who said: 'Well, I go to a village called X if you want to come and see it, come along!' What he *didn't* tell us, what we discovered at the end of the bus line that we were going to *his* village. We stopped in front of a coffee house, which turned out to be *his* coffee house. He ushered us in, and there was his father-in-law and his father-in-law's brother, both dressed in full Cretan costume. They made us feel very welcome and asked us what we wanted. I said something about practices of endogamy. He started to talk about their marriage rules. I asked if I could write all this down. He said 'go right ahead.' In the next hour or so I must have collected more information than I could normally get in a Rhodian village in the course of a week.

Okely's specific choice of locality in Normandy was also a mixture of chance then subjective recognition:

In 1986, I obtained a grant to do research in France—primarily among the rural aged. When I met a French geographer at a London conference, she offered to put me in touch with a professor at Caen University. He would *place* me in a village. Out of obligation to some notion of coordinated research, I went to the university. As I waited for the receptionist to confirm whether the professor was in, my knees gave way. My body and instincts told me that this was not what I wanted. I recalled an AAA paper by Susan Rogers who described a French professor treating researchers like 'sharecroppers'. I fled. Instead I drove around Normandy with Alan Campbell. I was drawn to certain landscapes. We would go to the tourist offices of each town and make general enquiries without revealing the details of my research.

In a market town we met 'Nathalie' behind the tourist information desk. Never revealing my research topic, I asked about the area and renting. At the end of her impressive public relations talk, she dropped her guard: 'There's just one thing wrong with this place—too many old people.' We went off to the central café to celebrate. A miniature electric train, full of elderly French, crossed the square. 'There are your informants', my companion declared.

Kenna, also open to study within Europe, chose a non-touristic Greek island but subsequently recognized it locked into a wider economic and spatial system, through migration. It was a matter of seizing the chance when faced with an impasse:

Paul Stirling, who had done his research in Turkey, was on his next generation of students, some of whom were going to work in Greece. Nobody had yet done a study of an island. The idea was I might do something about a fishing community and the links between a remote island, its larger neighbours and the mainland. I would go to Greece, to a particular island, then to the next, then the mainland and look at the links between the three. As it turned out, the island I had chosen turned out not to be suitable because there was a French anthropologist working there. The people who sided with her wouldn't talk to me. The people who didn't like her would talk to me. This was a ridiculous situation. The notary on that island said: 'I go sometimes to do dowry agreements and land sales to the island of Anafi. You've got the same combination of a smaller island next to a big island that's got more regular contact with the outside world. Why don't you try that?' He phoned Anafi and the man who ran a café with a room that the notary rented: 'I've got somebody who might be a nice little earner for you because she wants to stay for a whole year.' That's how I got to Anafi; a complete chance.

Susan Wright chose settled, semi rural nomads in Iran. She ignored her first gate-keepers, an Iranian urban elite who despised the non-metropolitan. They were less influenced by their own history than by a US education and elitism instilling an armchair disdain towards peoples in their own land.

Other anthropologists were not escaping, but instead seeking links with their own past. Hélène Neveu, of Franco-Senegalese parentage, returned to Senegal and childhood experience:

I'd been to Dakar about eight times as a child. I found myself gliding into the place much easier than I would have done otherwise. I remembered the feel of the city, the sounds and smells. It helped me getting started because it didn't feel as strange a place. I could still find my way around a little bit. The bulk of my memories were from the age of five from playing in the street with other children, going to the beach and smelling the rotten fish. All these things were still there. Of course, the city had expanded. There were more cars. It had changed. But some of the sensory impressions were still the same.

Joseba Zulaika, once planning to 'escape' to Africa, switched back to Europe and the Basque; his own people:

I wanted to study symbolic systems and was interested in going to Africa. Fernandez [Zulaika's supervisor] pushed me in to going back to my own culture. I was taken aback, disappointed. I thought about this for a few weeks. If I'm going to study my own culture I should take the one thing that is critical, the most traumatic, which is political violence. These guys are killers on the one hand but also heroes and priests for their followers. This was cultural anthropology with a symbolic bent. I had gone into anthropology as a way of escaping my culture and suddenly he's telling me this. I had no way out, as if the topic had chosen me, that platitude. I did not want to go back. I had dreamt of anthropology as something far more exotic. I had read Evans-Pritchard and that was for me anthropology. This was having to give up fantasizing anthropology in an exotic place and having to test it in a real political, ritualistic, initial Frazerian question of murderers and priests. I had no escape. Facing up to what had puzzled me had been a political and moral dilemma and one that confronted me with the history of crime of the twentieth century. It was a call to reality. Anthropology is not about evasion. It is about facing it.

Zulaika superbly articulates the core of the discipline that challenges the stereotype of exoticism for its own sake. He eventually moved to his own village. When studying a controversial subject as ETA (Euskadi Ta Askatasuna; Basque Homeland and Freedom), no one could ban him from his home place:

I started in Guernica, historically the heartland of Basque traditional institutions. Hitler's Luftwaffe bombarded the village and became Picasso's painting. This was a symbolically charged place for violence. I realized that people were suspicious of me, even if I was Basque. I wasn't from that town. I was asked to leave after there had been some protest in Pamplona. Some had been shot and killed by the Civil Guard. They became nervous and told me to leave. I decided I'd got to go to my own village and nobody can tell me anything. Everybody knows me. I have the right to be at home. I was a native. Fieldwork was a device not to be a native where I was a native—a device to distance myself from my own identity.

Helena Wulff (1988), of Swedish nationality, after her first fieldwork among teenagers in South London, revived a long-time interest and expertise linked to her biography. Having trained as a ballet dancer in Stockholm (before injury forced her to abandon this), Wulff (1998) embarked on a study of major ballet companies in Stockholm, New York, Frankfurt and London. As with Neveu, in-depth bodily training facilitated access. Again the notion of prior detachment is counter-productive and a legacy of scientism.

Autobiographical knowledge has potential for anthropological enlargement. Okely drew on participation in a past terrain: nine years incarceration in a boarding school (Okely 1996b: chapter 8; 2003b). The anthropologist drew on insider knowledge acquired as participant, before retrospective observation.[4]

For many anthropologists there were puzzles either of extreme difference or unfinished enquiry. Wright, after a passing visit to Iran, suggested:

Anthropologically, there were questions about 'how to study localities' in the early 1970s: the 'community study' as a little entity, was being questioned in anthropology. One way forward was to treat a locality within the wider context of the State, especially in places that were subject to modernization.

I was trying to study whether the State could transform local social organization. I wanted to explore when states were trying to settle nomads. My supervisor suggested Iran. Most of the studies were of the big and famous tribes. I wanted to study a less famous tribe.

I'd gone as a tourist to Iran in 1970 and hadn't been able to get outside the urban areas, apart from travelling between towns. But even within the towns the Shah's modernization process was really visible. I remember travelling through one of the towns in Kurdistan, northwest Iran. The Shah was putting a road through the middle of each town—that they could get tanks down. Also, so they could have a roundabout at each end, with a statue of the Shah on a pedestal. Going through Hamadan—the town is *centuries* old. Much of the early building there was by sun-dried brick. So it had built up a 'tell', an archaeological term, a mountain, a mound of previous generations. When you've got sun-dried bricks and a building collapses, it just resides there and the next building is put on top. They'd bull-dozed through this tell, through these generations, through the houses on top. You could see half houses left hanging over this cliff. People had draped a piece of cloth to try and make the missing wall of their sitting room or their bedroom. It stayed in my mind as an image of the power of the State. That he'd *literally* bulldozed through people's living rooms.

Mohammad Talib responded to a contemporary controversial topic in India, his own land. He described a 'media storm' when it was revealed that in a democracy there existed indentured labourers, namely stonebreakers. Based in Delhi, Talib moved to study these peoples not far from the capital. As chapter 3 reveals, the topic and focus invariably changed once the anthropologist opened him or herself to the concerns among the people encountered.

## Colonial Carve-up of Islands

Joanna Overing, like Kenna, confronted the fact that anthropologists had indeed 'carved up' research territories:

I originally wanted to work in the Pacific, either in New Guinea or Australia. The first grant application was for Australia. The Australian anthropologists had divided Australia up into little fiefdoms. If you wanted to work in Australia, you had to write and ask: 'Where can we work?' They wrote back: 'You can go to an island—but there are missionaries there. You have to first get their permission.' They wrote back: 'We already have our anthropologist.' David McKnight!

We had to transfer our allegiances somewhere else, quick. What was the closest was tropical forest South America. This was almost the summer before we were to set off! My ex, who wasn't my ex then, we worked together. Originally, we were going to work in Colombia, we were on a grant with someone else. He went berserk in the field. We came back. We had another grant. So, what's the closest? We go to Venezuela. We went to the Indian Commission, or an anthropologist who had once led the Indian Commission. He suggested the Piaroa because they were the people that could be reached at that time of the year—the river system was dangerous. It was dry season.

I was dreaming of one of the large villages in New Guinea, or large groups. What you get in the Amazon, instead, you're lucky to have 30 people in one spot. Except for maybe one period of the year, when they have grand rituals bringing together 300 people. Instead, you get a community in one large house. That was a disappointment. I was looking for a large community to entertain me. Instead, the anthropologist had to do a good deal of the entertaining!

## Scattered Moments and Clusters

The distortion that peoples studied are not only fixed but also harmonious, is also strong in non-anthropologists' claims. Malinowski (1926) already explored internal conflicts and forms of resolution. Nevertheless, there are not necessarily the same interconnections in metropolitan urban contexts. Anthropologists have addressed these issues decades ago (Southall 1973). Network theories emerged (Clyde Mitchell 1969). As the pioneering Chicago sociologists recognized, there are overlapping interest groups (Whyte 1943/1955; Becker 1963). Individuals come together as work colleagues, drug users, leisure partners, musicians, club members, prisoners and activists. Anthropologists need to locate these clusters, along with ephemeral encounters and momentary gatherings, as researchers of nomads had long argued. Nash (1979b) researched a passing but momentous event, namely revolution. The urban setting, less like rural locations, may more likely be the site of individual rather than geographical isolation. The home-less beggar, the fearsome drunk and the ex-mental patient may indeed have their own transitory networks. Such individuals have more anonymity than in 'remote' rural areas. The anthropologist has to find other ways of meeting scattered individuals or invisible networks. She or he cannot easily pitch a tent in the same visible community.

Marcus (1998) has named what is now increasingly accepted as appropriate practice that is 'multi-sited' fieldwork. This has been embraced especially for those studying migrants in several locations (Malkki 1995; Fog Olwig and Hastrup 1997). Wulff (2007a), when studying dance festivals in Ireland, using the airline's label for cheap return flights from Sweden, resorted to what she called 'yo-yo fieldwork' (Wulff 2002). Thus anthropological methods have proved flexible within time and space.

In the social anthropology I would defend, number crunching as large samples is not the core of our research. Although census returns may provide important context, even these are to be viewed critically and as social constructions (Hindes 1973; Irvine, Miles and Evans 1979). My own research unpicked problems (Okely 2006b) in the first census of Gypsies in England and Wales (Ministry of Housing and Local Government 1967). In-depth encounters over time in specific locations, either in a limited space or across space, give ethnographic authenticity, indeed social scientific truths, especially in view of enhanced movement and communication by virtual or actual travel.

## Entry

The anthropologist does not necessarily arrive as outsider in the midst of an homogenous society. There will be competing interests. Wright found permission to conduct fieldwork in contemporary Iran severely constricted, not merely because of a British legacy of neo colonialism, but because the Shah was seeking to control nomads. It was (rightly) seen that anthropologists might too eloquently give voice to these groups:

> The Shah wouldn't give me permission to do any fieldwork. They wouldn't give permission to *any* anthropologists. There had been an anthropologist who'd been working in Kurdistan, and the Shah was blaming him for an insurrection. No foreign anthropologists were being allowed. I went in June 1975. I got permission to start fieldwork on the fifth of November. So from June to November, I was stuck in Tehran. I had no money left by the time I got to the field. Going every day to the Ministry.

Wright described her attempts to gain access:

> I went to Shiraz, the provincial capital in southern Iran, where a lot of the nomads had been settled. The university had been set up to study the region. I went from department to department to try and find someone who was studying the tribes. I went to the regional development department. But (there) were lecturers from the States, whose PhDs were in voting patterns in Chicago, or childrearing in some other part of the world. Hardly anyone had any interest in what was going on in Iran *at all*. The man in the geology department was Iranian. Most of the Iranians had degrees in America. This man was ever so natty; these finely pressed trousers. Men dressed very flamboyantly under the Shah. He had this *beautifully* laundered shirt, and this lovely silk tie, with lovely colours, beautifully pressed. I went to talk to him about whether he did any field trips into the mountains. He passed his hand down the crease on his thigh, and let it travel down his leg, saying: 'It's dirt, it's fleas, and it's danger, and I advise you not to go outside Shiraz.'
>
> Here is the professor of the geology department, studying the geology of Iran from maps taken by American aeroplanes. I went to a little institute studying birth control amongst tribal women. It was mainly staffed by men who had lots of land rovers, lots of money and were very helpful. They were going off into the tribal areas, interviewing women on their birth control—which was a stunning thing for men to be doing. They were happy for me to tag along. It was the first breakthrough that I managed to get outside of Shiraz. Everybody was telling me: 'The tribes are dangerous and they're dirty.' 'If you don't get hurt, you'll get ill. Don't go outside Shiraz, it's too dangerous.' There was a siege mentality in the university. With these men I was able to get out into the mountains. Eventually, I found one of the students working in this unit. His hobby was walking in the mountains. He was Iranian. At his weekends and free times, he used to walk into the mountains. He'd been stunned by the poverty. So he'd started working with tribespeople, setting up development projects. He went to the area and asked if they'd like an anthropologist to come and help understand why, whatever they did, whatever development projects they set up, ended up in disputes.
>
> This was a real block on any development. Whatever they did, was ending up with big conflicts. He came back: 'They're prepared to see you.' We arrived in the village. He guided me. How they managed to interview me I don't know, when I couldn't say

anything, but they decided I could stay. That's how my tribal area was chosen. They said they would like to have an anthropologist around. It wasn't entirely serendipitous. I knew what I wanted to try and do. I was exploring one avenue after another, trying to find a way of doing it, until eventually I found one that offered an opportunity.

## Deliberate and Unconscious Factors

There are both deliberate and unconscious factors which draw an anthropologist to a specific location. It may be a sense of remoteness, familiarity or imagined belonging. These may counter well-made plans, as learned by de la Gorgendière who wanted to study schooling in rural Ghana:

> As for that particular village: I just drove around for ages, looking for a village that I thought I could get a handle on. I was looking for something that was fairly remote, close enough to an urban centre, and the centre of development—government structures, that it wasn't impossible to see it affected by government—as a real periphery. But also remote enough so I could understand the rural problems of having no water, no electricity, no transportation. I drove into this village. It did have an oil palm plantation at its entrance, but I was told there was nothing down the road besides the oil palm plantation—and found this village with a population of about 150–200 people. When I came into the village, I was instantly greeted with a cathedral-like ceiling of bamboo trees. It struck me as such a calm place when I entered, and the people ambling out of their houses to greet me,—I felt this was the place. It was some instinctive thing.
>
> It was almost like I had been there before, but I'd never been there before. I felt some affinity instantly. I had visited maybe thirty-five villages in a radius of about forty miles. I decided that this was the place. I felt the peacefulness under the bamboo grove. Also it was a village of a size where I thought I could get to know everybody.
>
> [Okely:] The irony was, that by choosing somewhere remote, that meant that the kids had to go to boarding school.
>
> [de la Gorgendière:] Exactly. If I had chosen a larger centre, where there was a secondary school, I would have probably been able to carry on with my original project.

## Establishing Rapport: Shared Interest and Expertise

After the anthropologist has chosen the locality, she or he has to find ways of establishing rapport. In Neveu's case, her shared prior knowledge and expertise were proof that she was not merely passing through as a tourist. This unexpectedly ensured a working relationship and shared trust:

> I kept thinking that there was something wrong with me, not being more aggressive about the interaction, not being more confident about what I was doing there. Some of the main informants I ended up having was a dance group who I went to see rehearse. I was introduced and I had a good chat with the choreographer.
>
> The leader initially was a bit suspicious because he'd seen many European people come and go, show a bit of interest for a while and leave. He wasn't particularly warm initially,

but polite. When he found out I was there with my husband and daughter, he warmed up a little bit. He invited me to come back and see them rehearse. I did that as often as I could for the first few months. Gradually we established some connection by me watching them, discussing their work. They could see I had the eye of someone who knew about dance. I could watch what they were doing with a technical eye and comment. We had some of the same references in terms of choreographers, the work of other dancers in Europe and America. I used that as a way of making the connection.

As with so many key aspects of the anthropological research practice, chance is crucial, and the anthropologist has to be open to recognizing what opens up unexpectedly. The anthropologist is ideally attuned to every potential nuance.

Clough recalled his eventual field site in Nigeria. It came:

purely accidentally. Between the ages of 21 and 26, I was unorthodox. I wasn't living in university accommodation like most of the other VSO [Voluntary Service Overseas] or young contract lecturers. I went native. I was living in the town of Zaria in various mud houses, beautiful compounds. I wore local gowns. I picked up some Hausa. Above all I had very close friendships with various Nigerians. Not by any means Hausa, they were often southern Nigerians. That's because in the early 1970s you're more likely to pick up friendships with southern Nigerians who spoke English extremely well. Then in my last house my neighbour was a young man of exactly my age, who became very close. He said: 'Take me to see my mother.' I took him to his village seventy miles away on the back of my motorcycle. I took him far into the bush and became fascinated. Here was something I always wanted to do. I wanted to live in a village. I was very familiar with urban Nigeria. But I was very conscious of the fact that perhaps 80 per cent of Nigerians were rural. I was missing out and it was through this accidental relationship with this young man that I found my village. The angels helped because it turned out this village was in the middle of a highly commercialized area selling a lot of food crops and cash crops to other parts of Nigeria and to the textile companies. So like pure chance, I lucked into the village which was appropriate to research on economic underdevelopment.

The role of chance in finding, then seizing a rewarding field site echoes the often crucial serendipity in comprehending and analyzing the research material. It is therefore regrettable that this should be denigrated as follows: 'The repeated narratives of discovering field sites "by chance" prevent any systematic inquiry into how those field sites came to be good places for doing fieldwork in the first instance' (Gupta and Ferguson 1997b: 11).

This chapter has explored how dialogues with anthropologists reveal that they indeed were often open to chance as to field site. Significantly, they were later able retrospectively to explain their imaginative and productive choices. But their initial reasons had been so submerged as to appear merely instinctive at the first recognition. After confronting problems of access or discovering the unsuitability of initial localities, they could use that very experience and acquired knowledge to make informed choices when chance came their way.

# –3–

# Choice or Change of Topic

## Questioning Fixed Agendas and Ethics Directives

Funding bodies and research committees in the United Kingdom and beyond have been under pressures from an audit culture and archaic methods with less trust in individual judgement. The researcher is expected to devise a pre-empirical strategy with fixed 'aims and objectives', and ideally predictable 'outcomes', to which she or he must rigidly adhere. The same strategies are expected in nongovernmental organization development research (Wallace 2009). In at least one Canadian university, prospective doctoral anthropology students are expected to present in advance the very questions they will be asking of informants. The latter are then to be presented with these for signed informed consent. All this presupposes advance and fixed topics, with no possibility even of follow-up. There is, moreover, no understanding that signing forms for non-literate individuals suggests that the researcher is a government official, if not spy. Thus the signed forms are perceived as betrayal, not protection of confidentiality. Additionally for some groups, as I found among the Gypsies, the very question mode is culturally inappropriate.

Unfortunately, recent scandals in UK medical research have resulted in the profession's notion of 'informed consent' being imposed, without comprehension, on social scientists. Yet the record of the most basic consent has been ignored. In the early 1990s one UK university medical department recruited an anthropologist to interpret data in what she was to discover was a grossly unethical project in Africa. Despite overbearing pressure, she insisted on whistle-blowing (de la Gorgendière 2005).

Unlike medical researchers, anthropologists have never gutted dead babies and stored their body parts in jars without parental knowledge, as occurred in the Bristol Royal Infirmary and Alder Hey, Liverpool hospitals in the 1980s and 1990s. After these scandals, I was lecturing in another UK university and discovered that social scientists were then confronted by the dominant biomedical committee's ethics form reflecting their ethnocentric model. Social anthropology masters students, embarking on fieldwork, were even asked if they were going to 'take tissue' from their informants! Anthropologists have confronted ethics with greater subtlety but increasingly have had to defer to such inappropriate review boards entirely ignorant of anthropological practice (Simpson 2011). As Caplan, in an excellent edited volume (2003a) and overview drawing on Mills (2003), has argued:

from the 1960s until the end of the 1980s, support for ethical codes was seen as support for a politically radical version of anthropology, while by the 1990s, ethics had for some become a politically conservative part of audit culture. (Caplan 2003b: 19)

Questions of ethics have indeed become disengaged from politics and the wider context of choice of topic and the anthropologist's role. An audit culture, claiming political neutrality, compromises anthropological practice and scientific enquiry (cf. Macdonald 2010; Simpson 2011). Others have explored varied dilemmas across disciplines, including those for archaeologists, also noting the disconnection of ethics from practice (Meskell and Pels 2005: 20). Anthropologists also bring ethnographic knowledge to expose medical mis-diagnosis (Okely 1999b).

## Original Curiosities and Subsequent Changes

In the majority of my dialogues, the anthropologists found that the main focus of their projected study changed once they were in the field. They had indeed done considerable pre-fieldwork preparation, reading the relevant, available literature. If they had geared their research aims to bounded hypotheses, let alone fixed questions as interrogation, they would have been stranded. Instead, planned or not, they drew on holistic knowledge and history when switching focus and topic. Anthropology had opened up the researchers to multi-faceted social and cultural contexts: the economy, political organization, kinship, symbolic classification, everyday practices, ritual and religion, art and material culture and, increasingly, gender categories and State intervention. While anthropology has more explicitly shifted from any suggestion of bounded cultures, the theoretical and methodological approaches developed in classical stages are still, indeed *more* relevant.

To appease grant givers and assessors, researchers may have to go through an elaborate exercise in deception, couching the proposal in 'applicantese' (Ditton and Williams 1981). In practice the researcher follows hunches. Things happen. Things change. The unplanned character of ethnography is *precisely* its value. Anthropological practice is open to change through its duration. In the final report, the researcher may feel compelled to reinstate the original plan. If not, she or he risks downgrading by the final assessors, jeopardizing future research applications (see chapter 1, note 1). Thus mystification is continuous.

The way out of the closed cycle of deception is to explore anthropologists' actual practices. Not only have some qualitative sociologists been intimidated into concealing their intellectually plausible research practice, so have anthropologists by default. Creative and contextualized initiatives in the field may be perceived as illicit deviations from the original brief instead of as inevitable, indeed necessary strategies. The researcher embarks on the project with multiple skills, talents and resourceful imagination. Otherwise she or he is lost. Those with rigid approaches may never come up with anything memorable, precisely because they have felt obligated to keep to their straight-and-narrowed initial path.

Malcolm McLeod confirmed the role of chance:

> Any fieldwork is a matter of accidents and opportunities, more than any ruthless plan. Or at least it should be. I've seen some terrible examples of people going in and saying: 'I'm going to do research on the X!' and they do it, whether the material is there or whether the material supports their ideas or not. They grab a mouthful and run off with it.

Many of the anthropologists interviewed had indeed some pre-existing interest, either in specific theoretical puzzles or world regions and groups. Some had initially been encouraged to pursue these by their supervisors. Others found their interests were triggered by a prior visit. In some cases, the anthropologists were returning to past connections. In the vast majority, if not all, of the cases, their focus changed during or even at the outset of fieldwork. Overing as outlined in chapter 2, had to change from New Guinea to South America.

Morris embarked on a field study of hunter-gatherers in southern tropical forest India. He initially hoped to assess Douglas's (1966) ideas about animal classification. Requiring a sophisticated grasp of linguistic nuances, he found he could not achieve this in a year. Instead, he concentrated on the more easily observable economy. Years later in Malawi, with extensive experience there both before and after fieldwork in India, he could pursue his interest in human ideas about animals (Morris 1998).

Some anthropologists have been drawn into the subject through fantasies and dreams. This should not discredit them. They merely adapted the dreams to a lived alternative reality. Invariably, the new reality was more interesting and fulfilling. It was the potent mix of ordinariness or familiarity, combined with unimagined difference in humanity across the world, which was so inspiring.

Anthropologists respond to what awaits them. They can do all the background reading and research on a theme, a people or locality. None of this is lost in changing focus. The anthropologist has to be open to others, while also drawing on his or her full resources; imaginative, theoretical and embodied. In the practice advocated by Malinowski long ago, the anthropologists responded to the peoples' *own* perspectives:

> This goal is, briefly, to grasp the native's point of view, his relation to life, to realize his vision of his world. We have to study man, and we must study what concerns him most intimately, that is the hold which life has on him. (1922: 25)

Falk Moore has recently acknowledged in a fieldwork retrospective:

> Listening to what people wanted me to know, rather than what I was trying to find out, was a large part of the fieldwork encounter. (2009: 169)

Parry in our dialogue suggested: 'Go for what grabs you.' What the people in northern India wanted to talk about was not politics for which he had prepared, but 'hypergamy', namely the practice of women marrying 'up', either into a higher-ranking descent group within their own caste, or into a caste above them. This very term, he admitted, he did not even know until someone suggested it during his first post-fieldwork seminar. For some, there were key early factors in the choice of topic and location that were later adjusted or changed. Howell, embarking on fieldwork in Tropical Forest Malaysia, did not find the expected systematic classification. Hughes-Freeland's previous trip with the Voluntary Service Overseas (VSO) to South East Asia had indeed alerted her to the significance of dance. This was not her original motivation for joining the VSO. Zulaika, wanting to study in Africa, changed to violence in his home place. Neveu was drawn through kinship connections and a return to her childhood. Heald scrupulously prepared a sociolinguistic study in Uganda, but when she arrived, she was unable to go to the appropriate area. She soon found her new topic when encountering institutionalized violence. Talib responded to the media scandal around indentured labour. Curiosity drew him, despite the devaluation by others insisting it did not fit their orthodox theory of class. Subsequently, he was also to find himself unexpectedly studying a Hindu temple constructed by the labourers.

Wright, on a previous visit to Iran, witnessed the Shah's destruction of towns for his roads and security policy. This inspired her to research political power, though at this stage at a general level. McLeod's concern with Ghana and witchcraft followed the apparent advice of a French anthropologist. A few weeks in the field, he switched to material culture. Overing's desire to study large gatherings in New Guinea had to change because all locations were 'spoken for'. The last-minute possibility was in South America and governed by seasonal access up river. Here, there were no traditions of large gatherings. Silverman was inspired by her interest as an undergraduate in Balkan music and dance, long before her doctorate. I suggested that her father's early skills as a jazz musician had left musical traces. She had to change plans for fieldwork in Bulgaria; because Roma music was officially banned under communism, she risked having field notes confiscated. Initially she researched Roma ritual and gender in the United States. Neveu's original plan to study popular dance changed to professional dance. My student Hesham Issa had for some time worked as a development officer on the settlement of the Bedouin around Cairo and beyond. This was his doctoral proposal. But he was later inspired to accompany the nomadic Bedouin into the Sinai Desert, focusing on Sufism (Issa 2005).

Political controversies in the media may inspire sceptical curiosity among potential researchers, producing a contrary effect. It is inspiring to note the new generation of anthropologists who, when confronted by racism towards Gypsies, Travellers or Roma, became curious as to the causes of such hatred. They were driven to seek the perspectives of the maligned, rather than merely reproduce the dominant propaganda.

## Control as Gendered Stereotypes in Research

The bureaucratization of knowledge, in research priorities dictated by the State and funders, is misplaced (Okely 2006a). Advance planning is counter–productive—a block to discovery. This might also echo gendered stereotypes in so far as masculinity is associated with control and advance strategic planning. By contrast, the stereotype of femininity is associated with receptivity, even sensitivity to others, before intrusion and control can obliterate the unexpected. Letting go of advance overviews imposed from above, gives way to attention to detail and grounded minutiae. Advance hypotheses privilege research as a mechanical exercise (chapter 1). The contrary approach is non-instrumental, indeed expressive and replete with emotions, inspiring theories and images. No wonder anthropologists were once loath to discuss their experiences and transformations, if mistakes were perceived only as failure. The tradition has been to maintain a mask of competence. Yet fieldwork may entail apparent loss of face while simultaneously bringing enlightenment.

When we proposed the 1989 Association of Social Anthropologists conference topic (Okely and Callaway 1992), critics in the open debate argued that auto-ethnography was 'navel gazing', 'narcissism', 'California speak' and a 'feminist plot'. It seemed threatening to confront social science with experiential narrative and revelations of loss of control. Delightfully, the classical anthropologists in the audience, Leach and Firth, both students of Malinowski, voted for our proposal. Years later, further details of self-revelatory and broader issues in new narratives are confirmed as essential.

The anthropologist, if open to alternative ways of being, by definition cannot know the system in advance. The anthropologist may only learn the rules when innocently breaking them. The attraction of anthropology is to submit to others' ways of experiencing the world. These are found in the crevices even of the cultures from which the anthropologist came. It is arrogant to declare that cultural alternatives exist only in pre-industrial, supposedly 'untouched' mythical places. There are always unexpected issues in the seemingly familiar (Okely 1996b).

## Travelling Concepts

Advance knowledge of the elsewhere cannot be presumed. Theories may travel but change on the journey. We accept that some linguistic terms may be untranslatable. Evans-Pritchard (1940) published the Nuer's 'Kwoth' instead of God in his text. Ethnocentrisms can also be dismantled in the same space. Stephen Rose (1997: 52–3) notes the shift in Western scientific metaphors for the workings of the brain, from industrial to computer, to managerial and even to chaos theory applied to stock exchange fluctuations. Emily Martin (1987) exposed how the medical image of the body as industry paralleled changing metaphors in research presentation.

Metaphor is disguised as science. Agar's (1980) funnel metaphor satisfied his interlocutors. It is open ended. Only gradually is the material sifted. The anthropologist is the funnel through which all material passes. An alternative could be a kaleidoscope whose disjointed fragments, if shaken and reconfigured, reveal patterns and repetitions.

Anthropological fieldwork has classically been described by the metaphor of immersion. This implies a riverside baptism, if not drowning. A milder version is tank flotation—being laid back. Whatever its tactical merits, Agar's funnel remains a technological trope and hardened object. Science is still conflated with hard implements, sensual bodily knowledge repressed. Although Agar offers an informed alternative, the body is still absent, partly because he privileges observation over participation.

Nevertheless, the funnel method stood me in good stead in Research Council applications when needing to convince sceptical committees of the credibility of anthropological methods. It appeals as phallic tool. It is ambiguous; either a probing invasive implement, in line with orthodox research procedures or, as perhaps Agar intended, a receptacle, like a mouth or orifice, rather than a penetration. But would I have obtained grants if proposing an 'orificial' method?

Another image is osmosis, bringing the body back. We do not just absorb material through talk, but through the senses (Stoller 1989). Absorbing experience through the very pores of the skin, involuntarily, without conscious awareness, is part of anthropological practice. It happens beyond our control; also fundamental. Agar valued pre-fieldwork openness, bringing a fulsome range of prior reading and experience (1980: 6, see chapter 1). It is best to bring all the intellectual, aesthetic and poetic baggage you can. My prior knowledge when arriving in Normandy included the following:

Earlier studies at the Sorbonne, memories of impressionist paintings, nineteenth century novels, as well as material on the aged, Michelin guides, tourist booklets, maps, historical background, census returns, photographs and old remembered films. I had also read the key ethnographic literature on France, in addition to a full range of anthropological texts. (Okely 2001, 2010b)

As for pre-fieldwork theory, anthropologists may advisedly devour any available 'literature' before geographical or psychic embarkation. All is excellent preparation, even when, upon arrival, the anthropologist finds the people have vanished, they don't speak the language she or he had learned, or what seemed a major concern, now in context, is irrelevant or non existent, as the example of Lindisfarne will confirm below. The narratives of McLeod, Parry and Overing also show how the pre-fieldwork proposals and readings represent only 'as ifs' and explorations of what might be. Precisely because the readings are so wide and free ranging, they carry multiple openings and opportunities.

## Holism: A Creative Interpretation

Unfortunately, holism has come to be associated with a discredited functionalism or with the accusation that anthropologists ignored macro perspectives (Asad 1973). There are, however, creative legacies in the holistic tradition. Nothing is excluded, neither in advance nor during the process. This openness is now extended to history, global influences, local documents, media representations and *all* persons encountered during fieldwork, that is ethnic minorities cannot be studied as isolates, any more than the Trobrianders can be studied to the exclusion of missionaries and traders, or Gypsies without non-Gypsies (Okely 1996b: chapter 2). The 'field' is more than a demarcated geographical place, if it ever was.

Pre-fieldwork theory is pluralistic. Theory also emerges from ethnography and the 'anecdotal', a concept shamelessly denigrated in pseudo-scientific discourse. Openness can be another route to general ideas rather than re-reading preconceived abstractions. In the field, this extends crucially to others' priorities, as the anthropologists' experiences illustrate. The anthropologist is open to the peoples' preoccupations, their concerns, not those of the incomer. Flexibility and surrender (cf. Wolff 1994) allow the subjects, topics, puzzles and reworked theoretical concepts to emerge from difference or similarities.

This sensitivity to the people as subjects discredits the notion of the fieldworker as isolated observer. The anthropologist was never the lone scholar, but interacting with many persons, some of whom become friends. There are indigenous intellectuals and potential research assistants in a shared enterprise (see chapter 7).

As suggested in chapter 1, chance and serendipity are significant. *Disponibilité* extends to place, people and subject. Overing succinctly declared:

> You have parameters—things you like, learn before you go. The best advice I ever received was: 'Study what the people have passion for. What they're interested in.' You don't know that before you get there. If they're interested in digging the ground, you study digging the ground! I happened to be in a place [where they] were fascinated by jaguars and anaconda. I was fortunate to be with a group who were so verbal. The Piaora are known as the intellectuals of the Orinoco. What we didn't have was all this ritual. I wasn't expecting to have to work on kinship and I hated kinship. It turned out I couldn't do my study without becoming knowledgeable of the kinship system before you could talk about the relationship with the political, the religious or cosmological or anything. It was my disappointment that I became known as a kinship expert for the first ten years of my career!

Okely asked what other advice Overing would give students before going into the field: 'Change if you have to—quick! Change groups. Change people. Change wherever you are. Change topics.'

## The Flâneur

There has been a revived interest in the notion of the *flâneur,* the nineteenth-century dandy who strolled the Parisian streets in pursuit of superficial encounters (Tester 1994). The flâneur was the 1990s replacement for the bricoleur. Benjamin (1992) elaborated on Baudelaire's flâneur, subsequently elevated to the ultimate postmodern figure. Feminists have noted how the flâneur is primarily a male figure with free movement of the streets, without harassment (de Beauvoir 1949, 1958; Okely 1986; Wolff 1990).

Similarities between an anthropologist and the flâneur (Gibb, personal communication, 1996) lie in the latter's free-ranging curiosity, open-ended agenda and desire to 'wallow in the rush of sensate information' (Shields 1994: 73). There are also clear contrasts:

> The flâneur is the embodiment of alienation . . . he loses contact . . . even in the process of participating in the crowd, because his sense of 'being there' is withheld. (Shields 1994: 77)

The anthropologist, by contrast, works to overcome alienation and distance from others. Similarities concern the experience of strolling 'at an overtly leisurely pace, allowing oneself to be drawn by intriguing sights or to dawdle in interesting places' (Shields 1994: 65). In contrast to the survey researcher, with fixed agenda, the anthropologist does not appear to be 'doing' research; just hanging around, loitering with intent. The anthropologist's free wandering ultimately finds its directions. The search is on for 'contact'. Integral to fieldwork is the consolidation of relationships. Fieldwork is *with whom*, as well as *how*.

I draw on a literary concept from the surrealist André Breton. His *disponibilité* (1937: 41) is linked to wandering without express and pre-formulated aims. It is also, although not exclusively, associated with love. Anthropological practice has resonances with Breton's emphasis on being *disponible*—being accessible, open to events, people and objects, while in search of encounters. Breton writes that in 'this thirst for wandering in search of everything, I shall be sustained in mysterious communication with other available or *disponible* beings' (Breton 1937, my translation).

Breton's readiness for *la rencontre* included the celebrated *objets trouvés* (found objects), myths, words and revelatory signs. He went on the prowl through the streets and flea markets, *disponible* to events, people and objects whose meaning he understood only in fragmented ways, until it eventually crystallized. Whereas Mauss (1954) and Lévi-Strauss (1949/1969) argued that objects or persons can be exchanged. I argue that foci, like objects, can be found, gradually incorporated and made sense of. The arbitrariness of the encounters may eventually disappear. There is of course also exchange and reciprocity because the people give the anthropologist the subjects and topics.

Relevant aspects which can be drawn from Breton's work include:

1. The notion of *disponibilité* to unexpected encounters with persons, objects and events. An encounter cannot happen everyday, but the seeker must be ready (*guetter*), in a state of attentiveness.
2. The privileging of the fortuitous encounter with hitherto unknown persons who allow the seeker to go beyond (*dépasser*) his or her presumptions.
3. The subterranean signs to which the anthropologist is sensitive may be apparent only through retrospective interpretation. Unlike the surrealist, who imposes meaning on the meaningless, the anthropologist theorizes and unfolds meanings, possibly hidden both to outsiders and insiders (Eco 1998).

Openness to ideas, people and to other cultures entails the *very opposite* of planning. The anthropologist cannot dictate his or her terms of entry. To be *disponible* is to be free to wander where the people and context take you. Likewise, anthropologists cannot dictate those who might become their closest associates. There is necessary serendipity to these attachments. The anthropologist is merely receptive to potential collaborators. Subterranean factors draw us to some individuals and them to us.

## Normandy Fieldwork

I returned to Normandy some months after my original exploratory trip preparing for a study of the aged. After dictating the concluding paragraph of my book on de Beauvoir (Okely 1986) from a public phone booth in this tiny market town, I was free for my formal entry. By chance, there was a public ritual on Armistice Day where I would meet elderly participants. Midday, I stood hesitantly outside the town church, watching the flags and be-medalled octogenarians. A woman was walking toward me. I asked her disingenuously if it was okay if I, an English person, could participate in the service: 'Of course' she said: 'You are welcome.' A member of the choir, she went off to her allotted place.

After the service and wreath laying, a procession, with band, passed by. The same woman spotted me: 'You're coming with us.' I was swept off to the town hall and the *vin d'honneur* (celebrity reception). She, Madame Matthieu, was married to the adjunct mayor. Revealing my interest in the rural aged, I was introduced to the mayor. I received a flowery speech and welcoming toast to *une Anglaise* and ally. Glasses were raised by the dignitaries, octogenarians and all. Madame Matthieu invited me to lunch with her husband at her sister-in-law's house. I was then given a tour of the locality in their car and, after another generous meal, was finally deposited at midnight at my farmhouse *gîte* (lodgings). Thus my fieldwork was launched, thanks to a tentative approach to the first person I the flâneuse encountered.

Another example of *disponibility* comes from Lindisfarne on her first visit to Afghanistan in 1968:

> We almost turned into ethno-musicologists, though we were completely untrained for the job . . . We spent a week in a small town, listening to music—long story songs about local history. The first time somebody sang one of these, we watched as half the café got up and left. Other people were enthusiastic, so we kept on taping. The next day somebody came along and said: 'Get your tape recorder, I want to sing.' He gave the opposite ethnic group's accounts.
>
> These story songs stood us in good stead for the rest of fieldwork—important information about the ethnic dynamics. We realized that it was so safe a way to discover a lot about people. They were pleased that we'd taped the songs. We learned for the rest of the trip that a good question to ask wherever we went was: 'Who plays good music?' It took us to unexpected nooks and crannies or to cafés that we wouldn't have found. *It was a thread which created a lot more spaces for us to meet people unexpectedly. We weren't directing what happened.* (my emphasis)

Inadvertently, Lindisfarne, through anthropological receptivity, had encountered the drama of long-standing local ethnic rivalries at the very beginning of fieldwork.

There are creative, methodological consequences of classical anthropological fieldwork having been *elsewhere,* therefore unknown and unpredictable. Anthropological practice has recognized and embraced uncertainty. While Beck (1998) and others have associated uncertainty with the crumbling of predictability in a postmodern age, uncertainty and creative chaos have been integral to anthropological practice. Decades earlier, Salvador Dali, also associated with surrealism, declared: 'The certainty of chance'. Because other systems and spaces were unknown or unfamiliar to the researcher, by definition knowledge is acquired through chance. Fieldwork is non-linear.

The approaches from elsewhere, the voyage out and chaotic vastness of an openness and vulnerability to strangers—in whose hands you rest, upon whom you depend for cooperation, whom you cannot control—these approaches are applicable in an unpredictable flux anywhere. Chapter 2 already reveals that location may also be subject to chance and the anthropologist's intuitive readiness.

## Further Examples of Changing Focus

Morris shifted his focus from classification:

> When I got to the field, I got more interested in their economy, their social life, and some of the things that I'd learnt about hunter-gatherers generally—why they lived in small groups. I started to make enquiries about what they ate and didn't eat, but that became secondary. I focused on where they lived, their kinship structures, family life. The thesis ended up on socio-economic life.

Wright, choosing Iran, revealed that, unlike most anthropologists in this text, she held to the initial and vast overview, but the means by which she studied the power of the State changed:

> Those initial ideas were so big that they didn't change. But the way I went about it changed. I'm trying to write about how these people were responding to, and trying to shape the State, and now with the comparative change in between the 1970s and the 1990s, born out of the Revolution. My research focus has always been the same. Given that, I didn't know where I was going to do this, or how, it was a case of being very flexible about the way that I might find an entry.

Howell had completed a library study on the existing anthropological literature on the Aboriginal peoples of peninsular Malaysia:

> I knew roughly what social organization I could expect, what subsistence activities. The group hadn't been studied before. I was *very* interested in classification. I was hoping to do a study on shamanism and animism. But I didn't seem to be able to find the material. I managed to come back to some of my original themes, but in a very different way. There were no ready, graspable social institutions. Their kinship system was very loose. The political system was extraordinarily loose. I couldn't get at the model of their reality. In the end I found it in day-to-day, mundane activities, full of meanings.

Helena Wulff's initial idea was do fieldwork in the American South, especially with African Americans. Then Sandra Wallman, as visiting professor in Stockholm, suggested London. Wulff (1988) switched to fieldwork among West Indian teenage girls in South London:

> But then I discovered London teenage girls were in mixed ethnic groups. I also found second generation West Africans who were hanging out with mixed groups. One parent was Finnish, another Irish/Maltese. It didn't take many weeks to realize I had to include the white girls and those of West African origin.

Lindisfarne, returning to Afghanistan, found that, despite detailed advance source work, the specific pastoralists she and her husband intended to study were no longer there:

> In 1968, we went to Afghanistan for the first summer, which is when we discovered there were no Turkic pastoralists left. I spent about six months, doing the ordinary homework for northern Afghanistan, and looked at sources, including Russian sources. Everything suggested they would still be there. They were there in the nineteenth century. When we got there and travelled around, it was patently obvious that they weren't there any longer. So we changed ethnic groups.
>
> The next year I researched the history of the Pashtun. I had already learned a whole lot about the region from doing the earlier work. We were interested in the comparisons

in terms of pastoralism. It's funny, isn't it? One justifies the fact. So began the bane of my life; too many languages!

Herzfeld found another topic towards the end:

> Every now and again somebody would make some allusion to animal theft, but it was always about something that had happened in the past. What I was getting was the official line. That this doesn't exist anymore. I didn't really focus on it. Until, two days before we left. We were sitting with the village secretary in his office and two young men walked by—again, dressed in full Cretan costume. I asked: 'Who are these people?' He said: '*Aroti khtadhes*'. [Men who visit their kin and ask about missing animals (Herzfeld 1985: 175)]

Change of location inevitably requires change of topic, as Overing and Heald had to confront. When Overing returned to Venezuala in 1977, she was not allowed into her former field sites:

> Again, I wasn't able to work with the women. All the shamans and young men came to our hotel room. It was great, because they were from all different sections of the Piaroa. They argued with each other. It was marvellous. But it was not what I wanted. I was dreaming of escaping in the jungle.

Parry deliberately switched to death rituals in his second fieldwork and in another locality, namely Banaras. He emphasized the 'irrationality' of choice as well as the direction by the people:

> In doing fieldwork, *it is such a peculiar kind of commitment, that at some deep level, one has to choose one's field for completely irrational reasons as to whether it 'grabs' you* [my emphasis]. In both the Kangra and the Banaras case, I felt that I was given leads directly by my informants. What they wanted to talk about that immediately grabbed me as being something that they were highly preoccupied about—hypergamy in the one case, and gifts in the other—that was intrinsically interesting. Then one simply follows one's nose, and pushes and asks more and more questions, and is attuned to people talking about that topic.
>
> I had spent a long time writing up my Kangra material. If I went back and did fieldwork in Kangra, I felt that I'd go on agonizing over the same problems—caste and kinship. I decided that I should make a move. The way that Indian studies were going, the focus was on what Betéille would call a 'sociology of values' rather than a 'sociology of interests'. There hadn't been a lot of work done in that context, at that stage. This major centre of Hinduism appeared to be an interesting thing to do rather than death per se.
>
> It's terribly easy to think up incredibly worthy and important issues to investigate. But you've got to want to go live there for a year. And live with the material for several years.

Given the need for adaptability and flexibility once in the field, the anthropologist may find relevant literature on the selected topics *after* fieldwork, not in advance.

Parry described how in his first fieldwork he changed his advance topic entirely. He was not embarrassed to reveal his prior ignorance of a classical concept in anthropology:

> What I thought I was really interested in was in micro-level politics. I was in that village for about two years, and in India for about two and a half years—I did devote quite a lot of attention to this interest in political factionalism. But it's nothing I ever wrote up because I found it very difficult to get any analytical handle on it. It didn't seem to be nearly as interesting as what I did wind up writing about, which were classic topics—caste and kinship, particularly the marriage system. I had absolutely no intention of writing about hypergamy and marriage alliance because although I had, through my undergraduate training, some vague notions about marriage alliance, I'd never even heard the word hypergamy. It wasn't until right at the end of my fieldwork, when I gave a paper in a seminar at the Delhi School of Economics, that somebody said: 'What you're describing is a system of hypergamy!' Which is a symptom of my appalling ignorance.
>
> In the Banaras case, I had a very general idea about what I was interested in—the symbolism of mortuary rites. . .the division of rites presided over by different kinds of caste specialists; all of which I wound up doing. But there were aspects that—with hindsight— shouldn't have come as a surprise, and that I've subsequently spent a lot of time writing about, but which came as a revelation—ideas about the poison in the gifts that the priests receive in remuneration. Gifts help to rid the body of sins of karma, which get dumped on the priests, causing terrific moral angst. When I got back from the field, I discovered that there's a considerable literature that talked about these ideas in classical Hinduism.

Again, Parry responded to the interests and concerns of the people whom he encountered:

> I soon found that people were endlessly telling me that they were receiving all these gifts— that terrible things were going to happen to them as a result of receiving them. This immediately grabbed me, as something that seemed extremely significant to the people and also seemed intrinsically interesting.

Parry's third fieldwork was in the iron and steel industry:

> With the Bhilai fieldwork, and I hadn't realized the importance of it before, there were variations between public-sector and private-sector employment. You're far more likely to be working alongside your own kinsmen and caste-fellows in the private sector than in the public sector. Public-sector employment creates a melting pot. The world of industrial production in the public sector is far more of a space that is secularized, a disenchanted world, than the private sector, where ritual observances on the shop floor are much more overt.

As in his previous field sites, Parry, the anthropologist, listened to what the people volunteered, not what he had necessarily predicted:

> The thing that immediately struck me the very first day. I was asking: 'When the steel plant came, did you immediately want to take the jobs?' Somebody said: 'No! We were

frightened then! There was all sorts of reasons why we were frightened, but we thought we were going to be sacrificed.'

I was endlessly being told that initially when the steel plant came, people wouldn't go and work in it because to get this plant into production, it is necessary that thousands and thousands of workers be sacrificed to make the machines work, the foundations solid. So there were those ideas about sacrifice which led into other ideas, about the mystical causation of industrial accidents, for example. I didn't know whether those themes were going to have much of a role in the way people think about industry.

Parry's observations could serve as key advice for any anthropologist approaching fieldwork:

One has to go with the grain of the culture. One has to talk about what people want to talk about. Trying to ask all sorts of questions in which they're not very interested doesn't get you very far. *The most important thing is to pick up on what people do want to talk about* [my emphasis].

In Bhilai, my experience was very different. Both in Kangra and in Banaras, people were very keen on telling you the cultural rules. You have to know people quite well before they start producing cases. Whereas in Bhilai, I found that people were much less interested in giving me rules, and endlessly interested in giving me gossip about the actual instances.

McLeod's choice of Ghana was through a mishearing:

I'd been working as E-P's [Evans-Pritchard's] research assistant, doing work on his Azande materials, which he was then republishing in book form. Obviously, if you were working on the Azande, you got interested in witchcraft. There was a visiting French anthropologist. E-P said to him: 'McLeod is interested in witchcraft. Do you know any societies in Africa where witchcraft is still going on, and where there's a good amount of written documentation, so there's some historical depth?' This guy said: '*Oui*. He should go to les Asante. *Il y a beaucoup des sortilèges*.' I listened politely and went to see Peter Sarpong: 'Peter, this guy says the Asante have got witchcraft, is it true?' Peter said: 'They're all over the place! People believe it very seriously.' I looked into the literature, and there was loads of stuff on Asante witchcraft, so I did my B.Litt. on it. It seemed natural to follow it up, so I went to Ghana. I came back about two or three years later, and this same French anthropologist was in the pub. E-P said: 'You remember McLeod, he's come back from Asante where he's been working on witchcraft.' The guy said: 'What do you mean, you went to Asante? I was telling you to go to Azande.' This is absolutely true—the thought that anyone could actually advise someone to go and do Azande witchcraft when E-P was sitting next to him still baffles the mind!

But, despite all the preparation, like so many anthropologists, McLeod switched focus once in the field:

I quickly realized that witchcraft was even more contentious than I'd expected. It would be inappropriate, or impossible, to do a great deal of work on that. So I gradually widened my interest. I got more and more interested in the material culture of Asante, and the wider question of the spread of so-called modern, post-1900 cults and religious movements.

Thus McLeod went for what drew him, what caught his attention and what stood out, namely material culture:

I got interested in material culture because it is impossible if you're working in Asante not to be aware of the enormous elaboration of things, which came about because of a centralized society. Particularly the material culture that you find in use around the major chieftaincies, and the King's court in Kumasi: tremendous textiles, woodcarvings, and especially gold-work. At that stage very few people had taken a great deal of interest in that. It seemed such an exceptional culture, by African standards, in terms of the elaboration of material culture, the sheer richness, the sheer quantities of gold that were still being used.

Okely noted that all this resulted in McLeod becoming Curator first of the Museum of Mankind, linked to the British Museum, and then the Hunterian Museum, Glasgow where our dialogue was recorded. It was indeed the Asante who set the agenda for McLeod:

The nice word is a dialogue between you and where you're working; in some people's case it's more a conflict. You get pushed and shoved, you do a bit of pushing in one direction and society pushes you back in another.

I have been interested in material culture, and I've ended up in museums. Certainly, a lot [of previous museum work] was despicable, intellectually contemptible, because it never had any consciousness of theory. Although it purported to be interested in other societies, it tended to be interested only in the things they produced, not why and how in any seriously analytical way. I've always felt that anthropology could contribute an enormous amount. When I was at the British Museum, I was keen to get good social anthropologists appointed.

McLeod also revealed his openness to yet another entirely new research subject, once in the locality:

The wider question of modern religious movements and cults is such a striking phenomenon in West Africa, particularly in Ghana, with Christian churches springing up; traditional priests possessed by their gods, operating side by side with breakaway Muslim groups, Christian groups, Jehovah's Witnesses. There's a maelstrom of religious activity. These things were continually poking you in the eye. It would be madness to ignore them.

Suzette Heald was initially interested in sociolinguistics. Her husband agreed to accompany her as schoolteacher in Uganda. At the last moment he was assigned to another area where a different language was spoken:

I went out to study one thing in one place, and ended up, like lots of us, studying something else in a different place altogether. I read Benjamin Lee Whorf in my final year as an undergraduate, and was entranced. It changed my vision of what anthropology could be. I did one year studying linguistics then framed a proposal in terms of sociolinguistics, to go and study either Acholi or Lango, both Nilotic speakers, in northern Uganda. The whole project made sense in those terms. We chose Uganda because Don insisted that there should be a decent university there. We were assured that he could be posted to a school in those areas. Three weeks before we left, they posted him somewhere altogether different, so I ended up in Bugisu. I'd had just about enough time to read up a bit about it.

Heald changed her topic within a few weeks. As a young English middle-class woman, with a sheltered naïvety, she was driven by genuine intellectual, yet innocent, curiosity:

I was only twenty-two. I did experiment with the idea of studying another Nilotic people. There was a small enclave about thirty miles away. After three or four weeks, it didn't make sense to commute. I started thinking about learning Lugisu. But it was a totally different language, Bantu not Nilotic, and the study just wasn't transferable. So there you were, an anthropologist, searching for a topic, as usual.

Like other anthropologists, Heald changed topic. For both practical and intellectual reasons she chose:

Very quickly, violence. I'd had a very middle-class, English upbringing in the fifties, where personal security was absolutely taken for granted. There were two events that focused me. One was coming across a party of men one morning armed with knobkerries and pangas. Knobkerries are sticks with rounded heads, and pangas are called machetes in other places. These men were quite heavily armed, and me saying: 'Where are you off to and what are you doing?' and them saying: 'We're on the tracks of a thief.' Me: 'What are you going to do with those implements?' 'Oh we will kill him of course'—just absolutely straight. That shocked me. Then very soon afterwards, a witch was killed, an old man, fairly near where I was living. I was immediately challenged by this violent side of Gisu life.

Like Heald, anthropologists, such as Zulaika (1995) and Okely (2005), may not specifically set out to study violence, but if its use and management are integral to the society or group, the anthropologist cannot ignore it.

Heald acknowledged the second interlinked research imperative as due to:

The way they filtered information. Because of the way reputation worked in Bugisu everyone knew the identities of these deviants: the witches and the thieves. That was public knowledge. It provided a focus; because whatever you were going to deal with in Bugisu it was going to have to do with this high murder rate. Even if you were studying something like kinship, it was going to have to deal with murder at some point or other. So why not make it a central focus?

In her more recent fieldwork in Kenya during 2001–2002, again studying violence, Heald used a known contact:

In Kuria in Kenya, where I've been working since 1984, two months or so of every two or three years, so not intensive, unlike my doctoral research. It was the only way to combine fieldwork with a teaching post. I'd had a letter from a Catholic Priest that they'd started *Sungusungu*, a vigilante movement, borrowed from Tanzania. He wrote that 'Kuria had gone rough on their thieves'. A number had been killed and a lot more severely beaten up. I had to go back and study this. I knew that I would be able to get access because someone I knew would be bound to be in one of these groups. Someone I knew would be bound to be in one of these groups.

Chance, or the readiness of the flâneuse, provided the opening:

Within the first week I went to see someone I was very friendly with, and turned out to be the treasurer of the local group. He introduced me to the committee and they agreed that, as a member of the community, I could come to all the assemblies. Then they said: 'You must meet Mathias Mwita'—the man who started it all. He was the Secretary of the very first group. It was pure chance.

I happened to be living at that time in this area where it had all began. Mathias had kept minutes of the first five months of all the committee meetings and he gave them to me. That is serendipity. Fortunately, there was a trail of trust. If I had just met him, that wouldn't have done. But I came recommended and via links. I was a known entity; someone they could trust and he could trust. The trust has continued to develop since then.

In some instances, random commonalities link the anthropologist in assumed shared identification. For Ignacy-Marek Kaminski, of Catholic Polish identity, a neutral, detached stance was inappropriate. He later drew on commonalities between himself and his subjects:

At the beginning, accident plays a most important role. I concentrated on the Gypsy groups divided across the borders, Czechoslovakia first, then East Europe and Scandinavia. Anthropologists have, because of their backgrounds, a different sensitivity. Some people cannot see the very clear opportunity. They are not prepared to recognize, take action and be involved, because they are overcome by 'methodologists' saying that we should be neutral participants. To some extent you can be when you are in Poland. You could be neutral. But when I was in Slovakia, and dealing with that fight, I can hardly be neutral [see chapter 7].

Then when moving to Scandinavia, I was a refugee myself. There is no chance that I can be a neutral observer. I am involved, studying refugees. My sensitivity to things which other Swedish anthropologists couldn't notice is because of the position I found myself in, as an individual first, and anthropologist second. But not everybody can interpret that chance as an event.

Contrary to any research application demanding fixed aims and objectives, the anthropologist is best advised to 'let things happen', as Hughes-Freeland recounted:

I let things happen. That's when things went well. I'd seen a lot of dancing. Everywhere I went there'd be some sort of dancing. It struck me that there was something going on here that seemed different from what I was used to. When I saw the court dancing in Yogyakarta, I thought it was extraordinary and beautiful. I wondered how on earth it kept going. I couldn't relate it to this highly materialistic society I'd been living in, in East Java, after becoming an anthropologist.

The people themselves may decide whether access is possible. The anthropologist adjusts. Hélène Neveu explains:

My initial idea was to do work on popular dances in Dakar, Senegal. I changed radically because I found myself doing most of my work with professional dancers and musicians— which wasn't my intention initially. But that's where I had the easiest access because of my background as a dancer. What I thought would be a side-interest ended up being the central interest. I just followed people I'd met and related well to people with whom I could connect because we had similar interests.

Chance events opened new possibilities:

I was in the field when the main professional dance association was starting up. When Dakar's big international dance festival was going to run for its second time only, [it] was serendipity. People gave me the opportunity to become closely associated and help organize the festival. I was there at the right time. That contributed to making me focus on professional dance.

The anthropologist may not only have to change research plans but also face stigma from close family, as Neveu discovered:

Traditionally, performing in public is the domain of a caste of praise singers, *griots*. Although that's changing, there's still a perception that anyone who performs in a public space and for money belongs to that caste or is associated with it. Women performers are perceived as quite loose. There is the caste status and a sexual stigma to the trade, which makes it unacceptable for high-status families—descendants of Wolof aristocrats, as my father's family perceive themselves. They couldn't quite make it fit with the idea that I was studying in England and going to have a degree.

Paul Clough changed disciplines from sociology to anthropology. He had initially been influenced by general theories concerning capitalism, with complex Marxist arguments:

My interest in going to live in a village in northern Nigeria was due to the fact that I was teaching for six years, in university in northern Nigeria. I got interested in political economy and Marxist ideas of the economy and underdevelopment. It was the early 1970s these ideas were abuzz in universities everywhere, also in Ahmadu Bello University in northern Nigeria, then the only full university in the Muslim Hausa-speaking northern part. I was looking for a niche: 'I'll look at marketing and trading networks, to see if we can chart the growth of capitalism in northern Nigerian agriculture.'

In my former pilot research: only eight weeks on study leave, I focused entirely on traders. Thereafter I resigned from Ahmadu Bello University, used my savings to begin postgraduate studies in sociology at Oxford under Gavin Williams, who was then a Marxist sociologist in underdevelopment.

I had a perfect scheme whereby what was going on is that your ordinary village farmer was selling grain at very low harvest prices to village traders operating with funds of much bigger patrons, then having to obtain loans and go deeply into debt so that much later they became trapped in a permanent cycle of debt. I was postulating that eventually they would have to sell their land in order to keep their whole cycle of spending going. It was a polygynous society. They were marrying twice, or up to four wives.

It was the act of living as participant observer for extended, shared time that transformed Clough's focus entirely. Changing from sociology to anthropology, he emerged with an entirely different interpretation of the empirical material through practice. Micro examples overturned his previous macro economic theories:

In these two years my ideas changed. My whole scheme was far too perfect, too schematic. It was not at all as simple. It was two years of great confusion. When I went back, not as a university lecturer, but as a 28-year-old, rural sociologist who lived round the clock with these people, their whole relationship to me changed.

In my pilot research they had treated me as a guest with great hospitality because of my contacts through sons of the village, my personal friends. When I went back, I was living with them permanently. They began to doubt my presence. The famous anthropological syndrome; they started to worry whether I was a spy for the government, prying on their income. They had been subject to a lot of extortion from the Hausa hereditary ruling class. I faced increasing distrust in my research and, paradoxically, increasing friendship as a person. They liked me but were suspicious of my role as a researcher. Through all the confusion the evidence was beginning to pile up which didn't support my theory. Two things happened.

One—I increasingly came to admire these traders, to know them as individuals, to know their lives. I didn't live with a family, inside the house. But because I was beginning with the traders, I decided to stay in the same warehouse of the leading village trader as I had stayed in my eight-week research. Gradually, I used to pick up his conversation, his thoughts, his worries and his fears. I used to learn about him from his younger brothers who were in a fraternal, traditional farming unit with him as senior brother and patriarchal head. I picked up an increasing friendship with his oldest son. Through him I got to know other traders and began to admire their intelligence, their acuity, their involvement with local affairs.

The second problem I faced with my scheme—I found these very traders were not making a big profit from trade. True, they were investing some of their profit in land and in part-time wage labour. But they were diverting a great amount of money into marriage ceremonies for themselves and for their children.

What seemed to be going on was not a growth of capitalism, but a curiously hybrid development in Hausa-speaking northern Nigerian agriculture. Here were a group of very innovative traders, closely linked by marriage ties, client/patron ties, friendship and neighbourhood ties with ordinary villagers. They were propelled by polygyny and what I call the ethic to remarry.

So what had begun as a fairly economistic schematic approach to traders as the brokers between two modes of production, turned into a village study in which you have a village alive with people, buzzing with gossip about marriage alliances. Divorce was easy.

I began to see that the marriage dynamic was crucial. It took years to become close to several of these traders, but from a close study of several traders, I came to the view that they weren't incipient capitalists. I ended up with a big problem. *I could not explain my evidence in terms of the model I began with* [my emphasis]. I ended up by arguing that what was going in Northern Nigeria was what I called a trajectory of non-capitalist accumulation.

I ended up with the argument that capital accumulation is constrained by cliental accumulation and household or polygamous accumulation. We have an overall trajectory enjoined by local indigenous society and by the recent conversion by people to Islam. There's innovation but it's not capitalist. We need to understand a fascinating indigenous African phenomenon. My supervisor picked up very strongly the idea of Polly Hill that peasants need to be studied for their own sake—highly intelligent people. They should not be regarded by economists as somehow backward nor as passive objects of study by an economist or a sociologist.

As chapter 2 revealed, Kenna found specific reasons to stay in the one place, while also studying movement:

The people who had time to speak to me were older women and older men. They were always talking about who had what names, what people would inherit when their parents died, what religious services were being planned for the souls of dead people, therefore what objects, items to eat, had to be got ready for these religious rituals. That began to seem to be more important than inter-island links—for example, how children are named, parents' obligation to provide a dowry for their daughter, the way in which a son will inherit from the parents either when the father is very elderly or has died, and the cycle of rituals. It was clear that all three things linked together. *So I could link family, property and ritual* [my emphasis].

Kenna vividly described the constraints of 'applicantese':

I find it an enormous problem if I'm writing a research proposal. How do I know what it is that I want to write until, through the exercise of writing, I find out what it is that I'm going to write? I'd say in a research proposal, this is what I'm hoping to do but the research might take another turn altogether. I may go somewhere to study agricultural statistics and a cupboard opens and somebody's diary falls out and a box of photographs and the life of that person is much more interesting than the agricultural statistics that I said I was going to study.

Indeed the latter did occur. Kenna (2001a) was to rescue a hidden part of the island's history. She, like Lindisfarne with music, had to become acquainted with something then outside her expertise, namely the interpretation of the visual image (Okely 2001).

Akira Okazaki, like others, was driven to the elsewhere, but once in place, changed to something very different:

> The first time I went to Africa I wasn't an anthropologist. I was there as a hitchhiker and a traveller. I found myself living among the Masai. I started to be attracted by their way of life centred on age groups, but I didn't have any way of knowing or understanding their way of life. The early 1970s was the time of something hopeful for Africa, the age of Africa. I had been disturbed by language and particularly written forms. I had been studying French symbolist poems, critique, and philosophy always dealing with what is writing, like in France at the time, the way we were talking '*Qu'est que c'est l'écriture?*' was common.
>
> So a written form of language has something to do with my own perception where we experience things and ways of seeing. I was interested in Africa because I thought that some people there are not disturbed by that written form. My interest was in how they could see the world, landscape and other people without being disturbed by *écriture.*
>
> But after I arrived and several months living among the Maasai, I completely forgot the initial reason of going to Africa. I found something totally different and another new question coming from that experience. That is, how can I understand?
>
> In French poetry, people are talking about what is truth in poems, like the title by Verlaine, *What is the truth of the poem?* I was a master in that discourse, unable to think about any alternative way of looking at the world. From 1972 and after 1980, many times I returned to Maasai land. In total I spent two/three years there. Now I find I'm recovering my initial approach. The poetic approach is more interesting.
>
> From 1981 I decided to find another place for my fieldwork, to try new ways of learning the stimulation from a new world. I was unemployed for 10 years or even 20 years, doing fieldwork with my own money, gained by manual labour because I wanted to be among the Africans and because I can learn and get interesting things. I found one community in the Gamk area.

Okazaki, on first arrival, was treated as outsider with seeming advantages, but later, he discovered disadvantages:

> There is an area for visitors or guests. There are many local traders moving around. Settled traders usually give accommodation and hospitality free. Later I realized this is the common way for northern traders and people who call themselves Arab. They regarded themselves as different. Local people—they've never been given that hospitality. I'm a foreigner from far away—entitled to be given that hospitality and I didn't even realize. I was given that hospitality for traders. I started to visit villages or local homesteads, and tried to learn their languages.

The breakthrough towards full sharing came unexpectedly after illness, departure, then return:

I returned after less than one year and the people's attitude was so different. They all knew I left because of sickness and I came back because I love to stay here. The people started saying: 'Don't stay with these traders. Why not come and build your own house in the village?' I was forced to build a house. I was already interested in how people make houses by cooperative work. Finally I have a house and I settled there.

Okazaki spoke of the value of unpredictability, which he argued effectively depended on having prior assumptions to be challenged:

During my fieldwork always there is something new. Amazing things happen. Not in terms of spectacular things. Just tiny things like the way a ritual is so different from what I know—some new word which they use when they are doing rituals. That new word at the beginning is difficult to understand but after, I talk to the elders and many people and alter my previous understanding.

If I have no prejudice or even if I have no expectation, it can't happen. Always I have some so-called prejudice or expectation or my own existing knowledge or maybe because I know a little about this culture. That means I can predict something happening. But that is always denied by new movement or a new word. It is inter-subjectivity created as knowledge.

The Gamk are always a people who try to make jokes with others. Always when I meet people, all come out with just a joke or something.

Having changed country, locality and preferred topic, there may be further changes for an anthropologist. Joseba Zulaika even switched his choice of continent at his supervisor's instigation. But he did not follow the suggestion of cultural tropes and symbolism. Zulaika's topic was triggered by an assassination before fieldwork. Like Heald, he focused on violence. Zulaika could not escape a topic which was part of his ethnic identity: 'My own experience pushed me into this.' Zulaika was drawn by a puzzle; more specifically, by an exceptional event and conflict:

When you're doing fieldwork, things interconnect in ways you didn't expect. The whole history—it was there when you unearth it—things that you hadn't suspected. There is so much in a small village of a few hundred that it made me worried that anywhere you start digging you find all this interconnection between families and between events.

I had been invited to join ETA [Euskadi Ta Askatasuna; Basque Homeland and Freedom]. I said in horror: 'My God, I don't want anything to do with ETA.' I would have never joined ETA for a political cause. Yet I felt that as a writer I could go into this excess of witnessing their lives. It went beyond my conscious decision. As if I had some secret guilt for not having joined ETA when it was the justified and the heroic thing to do in my youth. Writing was for me a way of compensating for that guilt, not because I would join them as a political cause, but as an intellectual cause. All this contrasts with so-called terrorist experts whose discourse rests on the demonization or pathologization of activists from whom they have maintained so much distance that no rationale can be presented for their actions and beliefs.[1]

If I'm going to study my own culture, I should take the one thing that is critical, the most traumatic of the Basque society, which is political violence. These guys are killers but also heroes and priests for their followers. This was cultural anthropology with a symbolic bent. If there's anything symbolic, ritualistic, this is it. It was a challenge for anthropology. I went into it ignorant as to what I could come out with.

Fernandez, who was my supervisor, would have preferred if I had studied this versifying, improvisational, troubadorial singing. He loved that topic when I wrote about it. He would have been happy if I had studied Basque traditional culture, mythology. He was into tropes, expressive culture and animal metaphors. He, being a symbolic metaphorical analyst, still thought that it was okay for me to do that. Later, it evolved. Maybe it went beyond what he thought I would be doing.

My own experience pushed me. I had known a few people from ETA.

When I was in London, suddenly I was teaching the Basque language in the apartment of a guy on a hunger strike—100 yards from where I was working. Initially, I didn't want to know anything about that. I evaded them. I had gone to London for a year. The last thing I wanted was ETA people on hunger strike in Trafalgar Square—100 yards from the old Charing Cross hospital. The initial days I didn't want to salute them. I would pass by and obviously look at them until they called: 'You are Basque'; 'Yes I am Basque.' I could not get away from them, from my own society. I had known these ETA people.

Then in my own village a few months before I went to do my masters in Canada, the police informer of the village was assassinated in the bus in which my own mother was present. I had known him when I was a child, 10, 12 years old. He had taught me dancing, been a counsellor how to study. In the politicization of the village, he became the bad guy, police informer, the traitor. I know also the good guy, the two heroes of my ethnography. If I was to write about this society, these were real murderers in stark opposite terms, from different perspectives. It was calling for interpretation, the foundational morality of a society.

It was '75. I had gone to study anthropology. I was in Princeton two years later, when Fernandez was telling me to go back. I could not be writing on something peripheral when this was happening. That is how I decided to take this topic. Suddenly I am in my village. I have this friend of mine who had been in ETA. I come back to do my fieldwork '79/'80. In the meantime in a small village, we are a peer group, we would all be in the fiestas, a single group even if they were younger. They had kidnapped a couple of people. They had murdered one. They had been in prison. They expected execution or many years in prison. Franco had died. They had come out from prison in the de facto amnesty in '77. They were back in the village. They were my friends from school days. These were people that we had idolized. They were anti-fascist freedom fighters.

In other cases, a media and political controversy can awaken the curiosity of the would-be fieldworker. Talib based at the University of Jamia Millia Islamia, embarked on a study of stone quarry workers in New Delhi during 1984–1987. He was driven first by the media storm and then by specific political questions:

Why is it newsworthy, but not part of a political mobilization? That was my puzzle. Here was a group of people, and if you spoke to a number of workers, they were living their routine life, they had some misgivings, but the organized movement was not in place. There were very few articulate workers, but the large majority of them were not bothered, they were just doing their work.

The stone quarries south of Delhi are the margin of physical geography of Delhi, but also the margin of society. This was the area which even the census didn't venture forth. They were not counted—the area in which all the official institutions, State apparatuses, just didn't want to implement their regulations. It was left to the contractors and the lease-holders of the stone quarries.

Why did I select this theme? The department of sociology at the university I worked in was pursuing sociology and anthropology on the margins of world capitalism, and this particular location was really on the margin.

Talib's research focus reflected the political and academic context of the time. But as with Okely, confronted by sociologists of the early 1980s, the emphasis was on pre-selection according to the current preordained theories and subjects deemed relevant. Talib commented:

Why did I choose class or workers? Partly because that was the 'in' thing on university campuses—to pursue Marxism. In the early 80s, if you were a good anthropologist or sociologist, you would be working on something revolutionary. Therefore I opted for this theme. But it was not a very 'appropriate' theme. I was told that if you are really looking for a study of class then this is a bad example because no left political party was successful in this area. They don't have a trade union movement. It's a scattered lot. Therefore what are you going to show? Do you have any theory of social class, to understand the absence of class in a community?

Okely commiserated:

I had a similar thing when, in a seemingly radical London research centre, but devoid of an-thropologists, the traffic planners and other social scientists said: 'Why study the Gypsies? This is lumpen-proletariat. They are not organised. They are petty traders. They should be integrated into the class system.' A delegation of 'radicals' went to the director objecting to 'their' money being used for the study of Gypsies. A now-celebrated geographer told me: 'After all, they are *only* a minority.' I was shocked.

Talib continued:

This was exactly my plight. In my panel of selection for PhD candidates, one of the pro-fessors asked could I tell the conclusion of the study. I was very shaken because I had no intellectual resources to counter this kind of thing. But my supervisor, Bikram Nanda did his thesis on the tribals of Orissa at Keele and was a student of Ronnie Frankenberg. He was into rethinking class, saying that this notion of a very polished, organized class, where position and disposition link up in a very intelligible fashion is not true and that one has to account for a lot of mess in the field. But I did not have the required language of descrip-tion at that point. Much of the later data arising is not part of my early thinking, when I was about to leave for the field.

Stone cutting workers in the early 1980s created a media storm, because the issue of bonded labour was raised in the newspapers. There were politicians who had to explain to other party members why this is happening. It was unfree labour in free India. That was the problem. If a labourer, a stone quarry worker is employed by a contractor, he was usually indebted and it was the bonded system where this labourer would not be allowed to change his employer unless he clears the debt. Sometimes this debt would go on for generations. I wanted to know: 'How is it that this marginalized class is entrenched, besieged in that situation? Why is it that organized left parties are not doing anything about it? Why is it newsworthy but not part of a political mobilisation?' That was my puzzle.

A human rights organization, People's Union of Civil Liberties, had organised a trip to a quarry. This is how they described it: 'We'll take some university students and teachers who would like to go, to be sensitized to human rights violations.' I went. What added to my puzzle was that if you spoke to a number of workers, they were living their routine life. They had some misgivings, but the organized movement was not in place. There were very few articulate workers. The large majority of them were not bothered. They were just doing their work.

As with the most successful practices, Talib the anthropologist gradually let things unfold:

I did not see class in organized institutions. There was no salient trade unionism. But I found these to be sites of contestation: school, the temple, and the folk tale sharing. This helped me evolve, or document, the world in a symbolic sense—the worldview which the workers were projecting.

Thus Talib (2010) persisted against the fashionable theoretical grain and also found himself researching a range of topics, all of which gave inside and unpredicted perspectives.

Louise de la Gorgendière also acknowledged transformations once in Ghana and the field:

The project was changed considerably. I had initially planned to look at the education of youth in villages and see how parental attitudes affected that education, and subsequently how parental attitudes towards education could affect development. When I got to the village I found out there were no *youths* being *educated* there because they all went away to boarding school!

*I had no intuition as to what would unfold but I thought let me just hold my curiosity in abeyance, and just shut up and be with them* [my emphasis].

De la Gorgendière changed focus in part to life histories and education in the past, rather than locate to a new locality:

Although I had planned to look at the education ministry and the formal programmes for education, I was keen to understand—particularly how women in Asante, because of the matrilineal ties, viewed their children leaving for education and the role that education could play in their lives, their children's lives, and perhaps the life of the village. But since the children were already gone—that was an impossible study. I ended up looking at education more generally, not focusing on one specific age group. I looked at education in the village as well as education of older people, how this had affected their life past. I collected a number of life histories and how it affected the village. Then I did a major survey of education in urban and rural areas.

De la Gorgendière confessed to her mistaken advance assumptions:

I should have been aware. I was looking at the Canadian model, of kids going to school locally, and didn't realize that secondary schools were so removed from the villages that children would have to commute, or live maybe twenty miles away from home.

Carol Silverman followed an interest originally linked to seeming leisure activities and music. Unlike Talib, who first confronted a politically explosive topic then moved to additional themes, Silverman had no premonition that a seemingly benign topic would prove to be politically controversial:

I started working with minorities in the Balkans not out of an idealistic, political analysis of minorities; rather, I happened to like the music of the Muslim minorities. I was working with Bulgarian-speaking Muslims. They were not allowed to wear their costume, practice their religion, or perform their songs. Their names and the names in their songs were changed to standard Slavic names. People took me in to their homes. I saw their costumes, very Turkish influenced, and none of this was allowed in a public bus or market. I stumbled into a very politicized topic through music. This was while in I was in grad school. I formulated my ideas in process. There would have been no way for me to formulate a hypothesis, read the Bulgarian literature and try to tease it out, because Bulgarians were not allowed to talk about these topics. *This was an invisible topic that I reached through a back road- a very winding way* [my emphasis].

The power of Bulgarian voices—it's amazing. That's what made me go to these villages, to hitchhike on trucks to get there. It became my passion; my hobby turned into research.

My first theoretically sophisticated analysis was through my idealistic and romanticized view of music. These minority groups had preserved older layers of music. I was after these incredible songs. I arrived at politics and gender via these routes. The gender roles were interesting because the unmarried Muslim women were most of the singers. After marriage, singing was frowned upon. But some resisted. In general, their songs were contested by the State. Since the women were the performers in folk festivals, they had to bear the brunt of State policy. The men did in other ways.

At that time, when I was working in Bulgaria, there were horror stories about anthropologists, folklorists, ethnomusicologists not being able to take their materials home because of the socialist government. I decided to look in the United States for something related to the Balkans.

It was through chance, then recognition of its potential that Silverman focused not just on the Balkans but specifically on Roma in the United States:

That's when I switched to a Romany emphasis, because by accident I was exposed to a Romany school, a temporary school in Philadelphia where I attended graduate school. Rena Gropper also helped me with contacts in New York. So I ended up doing fieldwork in the United States for my PhD. Having started in the Balkans as a hobby and having written many graduate school papers on the Balkans, I ended up doing my fieldwork in the US because of the political climate. A number of people had said: 'Don't take the chance of going to Bulgaria for a year or two and then having all your field notes confiscated.'

No one can really explain how somebody is drawn to something they love passionately, in terms of music or dance. I cannot tell you *why,* but *how* it happened. I was an undergraduate at City College in New York and I was exposed to the folk dance scene: Americans getting together in clubs, learning Bulgarian, Greek, Macedonian, Bosnian dances. It was a young social scene. I happened on it. I totally fell into it. Every night we would go folk dancing with a group of friends.

We would go to the Columbia University folk dance club, another other night at NYU [New York University] and some private clubs. We were exposed to this music.

But we weren't exposed to any real Bulgarians. That's when we decided to make our 'summer pilgrimages' to the Balkans, the source of this incredible music and dance. I got interested in the singing and learned the language through the songs. We were a pioneering group of Americans, three to five women, who learned the village music of Bulgaria and Macedonia—very esoteric, rural music. We spent hours transcribing. We would go to the Balkans and find these isolated villages. That was my hobby. But it provided an incredible foundation for later academic study.

My undergraduate degree was in English literature and film studies. Then, when I became involved in the Balkans, I found out you could study a field called folklore or cultural anthropology.

Thus contrary to state or market-led short-term initiatives, Silverman confronted the unconscious, as well as conscious factors, which, as for many, draw the anthropologist to specific themes.

Similarly, the topics which drew some of my students were all self-selected. They included: the Womens' strike in Iceland (Johnson 1984), Algerian emigration to France (Taleb 1987), Ageing and community in a post mining town, northeast England (Dawson 1990), the police force from the inside (Young 1991), a cross-cultural study of Kemalist feminists in Turkey and British suffragettes (Durakbasa 1991), Masai women and gender roles in Kenya (Knowles 1993), HIV and drug users in Edinburgh (Foster 1995), Symbolism and history in Maltese social identity (Mitchell 1996), AIDS and the construction of knowledge (Huby 1998), television advertising in rural India (Mitra 1999), Anti-Nationalist Resistance in former Yugoslavia (Jansen 1998, 2000), Nationalism and belonging: English speakers of Montreal, Quebec (Doyle 2000), Invisible lives of Gypsies and Travellers (Clark 2001), Place and identity in a Greek mountain village (Malenou 2001), Anti-racist movements in Paris (Gibb 1999, 2003), Bedouin in the Sinai Desert (Issa 2005), Retirement migration in Spain (Oliver 2008), Greek male homosexualities and the military (Dendrinos 2008), and a Care home in Saudi Arabia (Elyas 2011). Others anthropologists have demonstrated new ventures engaging with migrants from around the globe (Lewis 2007; Pero 2008; Zontini 2008), including the Cuban diaspora (Berg 2009, 2011). Anthropologists have not, as too often claimed, confined themselves to the powerless, but, while recognizing greater restrictions on access, have also selected the relatively privileged, for example Nash (1979b), Goodman (1990/1993), Hendry (1992), Okely (1996b: chapters 7 and 8; 2003b), and Tett (2009).

Knowledge emerges and is sustained, not simplistically from reductionist utilities and power trips, but sometimes from political questioning, unclassified passions and intellectual quests, all of which humanity may share. What initially may seem obscure and idiosyncratic is later confirmed as profound discovery with long-term consequences. Keeping to the UK Haldane principle, topics and advance agendas should not be dictated by governments or others. Trust should be placed in the intellectual curiosity of the potential researcher where practical utility may emerge but cannot be predicted.

# –4–

# Participant Observation: Theoretical Overview

## Methods by Committee

Even in the 1970s, there were few if any discussions of field methods. When I studied for an introductory postgraduate degree at Cambridge, there was no textbook, let alone any course on methods. When approaching fieldwork among the Gypsies, I bemusedly consulted the 1967 edition of *Notes and Queries* (1874/1951), the only guide. I had already learned more through unofficial fieldwork in the west of Ireland (Okely 2009a).

Devised in the 1880s, that text was revised into the 1950s by an RAI committee. Despite notable contributions, a committee consensus belied the inventive practices buried in the monographs of Malinowski (1922), and his pupils, including Evans-Pritchard (1937, 1940). The committee, as recorded in *Notes and Queries,* advised:

> There may be some hardy individuals who can undertake to live as the natives do, but for most investigators, especially in tropical areas, this is not practicable. (1874/1951: 31–2)

There is no mention of participant observation in the index, although there is some discussion of observation. The manual oscillates between positivist objectivity, confused with geographical distance, and some participation. It is possible that the committee was hijacked by cautious armchair members. Certainly, it carries the classic failures of committee consensus. Generalizations take little account of the unpredictable variety of contexts. My dialogues with anthropologists reveal both differences and commonalities, irreducible to banal injunctions. Nonetheless, the book is remarkable for the range of topics and themes considered. This emerges from holistic traditions and fruitful aspects of functionalism.

## History of the Concept

The term 'participant observation' was first defined by the Chicago sociologists in the interwar period. Earlier, Malinowski (1922) and others had been doing participant observation but without this now-celebrated term. Stocking (1983) has contested the Malinowski claim to be the first to pitch his tent in the village. Anthropologists were already finding their way to learning the indigenous language and living alongside the different peoples. Knowledge is indeed not merely the outcome of individual 'genius', a Western ideological construct (Battersby 1989).

For both anthropologists and empirical sociologists, research subjects initially entailed the relatively unknown 'other', whether in New Guinea or among marginalized Chicago residents. Such groups were unfamiliar to white male researchers who could not approach them as formal interrogators. In Whyte's (1943/1955) classic appendix, added in 1955 to his original monograph, Doc advised him *not* to ask questions, but to 'hang around'. Malinowski (1922: plate 1:16), unlike verandah anthropologists, did likewise. He warned against merely looking for the strange but additionally the 'imponderabilia of everyday life' (Malinowski 1922: 18). As with Doc's advice, answers and themes emerged with little if any emphasis on the quantification of practices (cf. Leach 1967).

Powdermaker, like Leach, a student of Malinowski, describes, 'the heart of the participant observation method' as:

> involvement and detachment. Its practice is both an art and a science. Involvement is necessary to understand the abstract reality. (Powdermaker 1967: 9)

She acknowledged insufficient knowledge about its practice:

> Field work is a deeply human as well as a scientific experience . . . Yet we know less about participant observation than about almost any other method in the social sciences . . . Most of the discussions of the actualities of field work have been limited to private discussions between anthropologists, and these usually touch only high spots or amusing anecdotes. (Powdermaker 1967: 9)

In this volume I interrogate such anecdotes. Powdermaker (1967), alongside Malinowski's *Diary* (1967), encouraged me to pursue the scientific discussion of fieldwork (Okely 1975, 1987, 1992, 1994a, 2008).

## Detachment/Objectivity or Involvement

The earlier assertions suggest that full participation risks being unscientific. Detachment is conflated with objectivity. *Notes and Queries* suggests that if the investigator becomes:

> a participator instead of an observer; this cannot but influence both his emotional and his intellectual outlook, and completely change his methodological approach. (1874/1951: 31–2)

This perspective was clearly not followed by anthropologists such as Evans-Pritchard (1937), yet it is still found in some social scientists' discussions. Moreover, distanced surveillance constructs the outsider as threat. Paradoxically, the detached observer may be *more* likely to transform contexts. She or he is threatening precisely because she or he is not involved, appearing as voyeur and critic.

Alternatively, if the anthropologist joins in she or he may cease to be intrusive. Additionally, the fieldworker as participant is open to learning beyond the verbal and cerebral. Participant observation involves more than co-residence, verbal interaction and observation; it also involves knowledge through the body, through all the senses (chapter 6). There is a difference between doing something and asking someone how they do it, as Deutscher (1970) earlier exposed. Malinowski argued:

> To study the institutions, customs, and codes or to study the behaviour and mentality without the subjective desire of feeling by what these people live. . . . is . . . to miss the greatest reward which we can hope to obtain from the study of man. (1922: 25)

Participation through shared action brings vital insights and instrumental acceptance among the people themselves. An outsider abroad may undermine or subvert stereotypes (see McLeod in chapter 5). The researcher is 'mucking in', as the Gypsies appreciatively told me. Participation, however incompetent, can be interpreted as respect.

Regrettably, Henrietta Moore, with an archaeology doctorate where classically participation is relatively marginalized, has implied that 'conventional anthropological accounts' convey experience as, ' "soft porn" or even soap opera' (Vines 1994: 21). When the interviewer noted: 'Her text deliberately conveys little about the nitty gritty of daily life of the Marakwet' (in Kenya), Moore argued:

> I want to distance myself from conventional anthropological accounts, and to stand at a distance—not to claim a spurious connection on the basis of experience. (Vines 1994: 21)

Unfortunately this echoes a postmodern fashion whereby 'knowledge from encounters is replaced with the use of what we call surrogate ethnography, puppeteering, and textualism' (Borneman 2009: 8).

In contrast, this volume argues that narratives of participation and their analysis are crucial for the comprehension of anthropological practice (Turner and Bruner 1986; Hastrup and Hervik 1994).

## Craft and Bodily Knowledge

Craft and bodily knowledge confronts misconceptions and limitations of verbal knowledge. It can integrate the two. Participation necessarily involves confrontation with the researcher's incompetence in contrast to others' long-term embedded skills. Instead of the fear that the individual be 'contaminated' by involvement, it can be argued that total immersion brings unique knowledge. My Durham colleague David Brooks would set an essay question: 'In order to observe you need to participate' (Okely 2007a: 235–9). The consequences of the researcher's presence are confronted and resolved through reflexivity (Okely 1992). Brooks (1993), when dangerously ill, was later to publish a poignant article about his experience as patient.

Participatory approaches have resonance with feminist structuring of knowledge:

> The feminist standpoint epistemologies ground a distinctive feminist science in a theory of gendered activity and social experience. (Harding 1986: 141)

Hilary Rose (1984) argues that some women scientists' 'inquiry modes are still "craft labour" rather than the "industrialized labor" within which most scientific inquiry is done' (cited in Harding 1986: 142; cf. Rose 1983).

> Feminist concepts of the knower, the world to be known and processes of coming to know reflect the unification of manual, mental and emotional ('hand, brain, and heart') activity characteristic of women's work . . . in opposition to Cartesian dualisms . . . and Enlightenment legacies. (Harding 1986: 142)

Rose argues that the 'domination of reductionism and linearity must be replaced by the harmony of holism and complexity' (Harding 1986: 144).

This is uncannily like anthropology's tradition. Anthropology is also a craft, using 'hand, brain and heart'. The fieldworker works through the body, emotions not cerebral distance. Beyond such divisions as 'both an art and science' (Powdermaker 1967: 9), I argue that the notion of science should be broadened as knowledge (Okely 1996a). The discussion about feminist standpoint, methods and definitions of science are finely discussed by Stanley and Wise (1990: 6–27).

## Going 'Native'

One consequence of participant observation is that the fieldworker may be confronted by the clichéd controversy as to whether to go 'native', also a legacy of colonial discourse. Even in 2010, I was asked about this 'risk' by confused social scientist postgraduates outside anthropology.

The fear of total participation is the fear that observation will cease. Yet there is always the need to take notes, although not necessarily in the middle of the action, just as soon as possible before the memory filters and fades. If note taking and the relevant anthropological analysis cease, then so does the research. The main problems for the participant observer are time and energy. To participate, then write field notes into the early hours or for days at a stretch, involves a double work shift. The self-conscious quest for some elusive 'objectivity' should not preoccupy the anthropologist in fieldwork's hurly burly.

The word 'native' has both a relatively benign meaning but also a racist history (*Chambers 20th Century Dictionary* 1983: 842). Going native is a leftover from colonial times, when it was feared that the white European could become too sympathetic to the colonized (O'Reilly 2009: 87–8). This legacy has been passed on to anthropologists seemingly to avoid alignment with indigenous peoples, even after political independence. Thus 'going native', emerging from political dominance and partiality, is negatively transposed in the name of impartiality and 'science'. Occasionally the term is strangely replaced by 'over rapport' (O'Reilly 2009: 87–8).

Hughes-Freeland reveals the legacy in Voluntary Services Overseas:

> VSO made you come home at the end of your second year to stop you going native. They had this funny idea that, if you've stayed longer than two years, you would be irredeemably lost.

I might ask what is wrong with leaving a past identity. If individuals choose to abandon their origins, nationality and culture, they may indeed choose to be lost to the discipline. The implication is that empathy and total participation are dangerously seductive. The possibility of never returning to a previous culture and finding peace elsewhere should be the least of academics' worries. If individuals so choose, so be it.

In a few cases, the researcher has joined the community, perhaps marrying into it and never returning, let alone writing up. This rare choice is no tragedy. In some cases, the researcher has married into the group and returned 'home' with a spouse, posing more problems of inclusion for the migrating partner than the anthropologist (Kulick and Willson 1995). It can also offer creative collaboration when the anthropologist meets a fellow intellectual beyond the groups being studied, but in that locality, as with Gigengack and Alonso in this volume.

## False Continuum: Participation/ Observation

Standard sociological textbooks repeat a typology with participant observation on a continuum: extreme participation at one end and observation at the other. Contrary to the previous discussions, it is believed that observation excludes participation and vice versa. This misleading continuum is rarely accepted by those who have practised long-term, anthropological participant observation:

> There is all the difference between a sporadic plunging into the company of natives, and being really in contact with them. (Malinowski 1922: 6–7)

The continuum also presumes the now-contested subjectivity/objectivity dichotomy. David Brooks's brilliant suggestion above provides the counter argument. The textbook continuum implies that observation, an activity which privileges the gaze, is the major scientific source of knowledge and critiqued by Fabian (1983). Participation is deigned too messy, indeed dangerously carnal, reflecting the Cartesian mind/body bipolarity, and the privileging of panoptican surveillance (Foucault 1977).

The continuum presumes that participation, as active body, entails switching off intellectual capacities. On the contrary, the anthropologist as participant also learns cerebrally in action and understands in retrospect, through the body, with mind, imagination and intellect intertwined. Moreover, I have argued (Okely 2001) that observing as 'looking' does not include the multi-sensual act of 'seeing'.

## Participating in Order to Observe and Understand

Subjectivity should not be conflated with the act of joining in and becoming an insider. Long ago, Maquet (1964) warned that distance should not be equated with objectivity. Unfortunately, participation has been inhibited by the put down of subjectivity. But in the broadest sense, scientific research is not suspended when the fieldworker tries to join in activity rather than act as spectator. Inevitably, membership of some sort may be impossible and inadvisable. Participation is not necessarily membership.

Ultimately, knowledge can be acquired through the total experience, not primarily through the role of detached questioner. The researcher may learn through becoming inconspicuous, eradicating any image as alien. Greater invisibility may be achieved by participation, rather than distancing. Anthropologists, in some descriptions of fieldwork practice, appear to have been plagued by the Protestant work ethic. Powdermaker (1967) could not make up her mind whether to take notes during a ceremony. She felt guilty if she put her note pad away, as if such an action were a lapse of the research role.

If the research is concerned with intelligibility and meaning, the participant observer may be best able to explain the otherwise unintelligible by also making the actions meaningful to himself or herself (Evans-Pritchard 1937; Okely 1994b). You cannot know in advance, nor from the outside, the meaning of what you are observing, unless you attempt to participate from the inside. Ultimately, the total meaning may never be full articulated by the participants. Indeed, their statements may be mystifications to themselves. In subsequent analysis, such contradictions may become apparent to the participant, now writer, but aided by participation or vicarious knowledge, however transitory (Okely 1994b).

Participation may not always be pleasant. Lévi-Strauss wanted ethnographic proof that the tropical forest Indians ate *koro*—grubs found in rotting trees. But since non-Indians had jeered at the Indians for eating them, they denied the practice when Lévi-Strauss asked. Ultimately, the only way to confirm the rumour was for Lévi-Strauss to profess a desire to eat them. After one blow with the axe, an Indian revealed:

thousands of hollow little chambers, deep inside the tree. In each was a fat, cream-coloured creature, rather like a silk worm. I had to keep my word. While the Indian looked on impassively I decapitated my catch; from the body skirted a whitish, fatty substance which I managed to taste after some hesitation; it had the consistency and delicacy of butter, and the flavour of coconut milk. (Lévi-Strauss 1955/1973: 160)

This can be seen as an analogy for anthropological fieldwork. Participant observation can require eating the worms; the unfamiliar or that which once seemed repellent. Lévi-Strauss made sense of this in terms of other familiar food. In the event, the experience is rendered less strange and intelligible through the bodily tasting. That is what participant observation entails. The example reveals how even the most vulnerable and isolated individual will not give way to pressure to give away secrets unless the interlocutors indicate a desire to participate fully and share.

## 'Naturalism' Parody

Extended participant observation has been misleadingly constructed by some sociologists as a commitment to a stigmatized naturalism, as if the researcher becomes the invisible 'fly on the wall', acquiring information in a 'natural', unchanged setting (Hammersley and Atkinson 1983; O' Reilly 2009: 182). Rightly this is a fiction. An anthropological counter argument to this invention and critique is that the researcher's presence and positionality must be confronted.

Anthropologists cannot become entirely invisible, although their presence may eventually be taken for granted. Even in physics and biology, it has come to be recognized that there may be no complete separation between the observed and the objects of research, in contrast to what was once postulated. Even less than physical sciences, can the social sciences maintain any pretence of a researcher's objective stance. Participant observation directly confronts this impossibility.

There is an extended parody that anthropologists have advocated dialogue in the indigenous language merely because it was 'natural', again with the implicit critique of naïve self-deception. By contrast, dialogue in the local language is a means of direct communication avoiding the ethnocentric commonsense presumptions of intermediaries and interpreters who themselves may convey the specific as universal and thus 'natural'.

The long-term experience of events and repetitive daily practice, have identified the ordinary and the mundane as crucial. Prioritizing the sensationally different is thus avoided. But there is again disagreement within the social sciences. Sociologists have tended to argue that participant observation is merely one ingredient in a repertoire of methods, which include surveys and statistics. Participant observation, from assertions by sociology colleagues, needs back up from other so-called 'objective techniques'. This mechanical notion of 'triangulation' postulates that a variety of methods will produce the correct 'facts' by homogenization of overlap. Yet each method may be revealing *different* things. If there is inconsistency, this is something to work with, rather than prioritize the greater number of methods. The sociologist Newby, in his study of farm workers, confessed:

> Not only did the participant observation crucially affect my theoretical understanding . . . but also. . .where survey and participant observation data conflicted I instinctively trusted the latter. (1977b: 127)

Strangely, Newby's final monograph 'contains little of the material gathered through participant observation' (1977b: 127). However, as argued in chapter 1, in-depth research within a micro area can both explain and even correct a mass survey (Leach 1967).

## The Anecdotal

Malinowski emphasized the importance of every day happenings as central to research as participant observation: 'events usually trivial, sometimes dramatic but always significant, formed the atmosphere of my daily life, as well as theirs' (1922: 7).

Just as participant observation has been caricatured incorrectly as naïve naturalism, so its emergent material risks being denigrated as producing the 'merely anecdotal'. This concept is, even in the twenty-first century, seen as a sufficient put down. Yet the anecdote, the ongoing narrative, is the very stuff of the enquiry and long-term engagement. One anecdote may throw light on an entire system. Even sociologists have pointed to eureka moments when everything falls into place with just one passing remark or incident. Newby (1977a) describes how, witnessing one incident in a fête in East Anglia focused his entire argument, namely the notion of deference among people whom he would later entitle *The Deferential Worker*.

Similarly, I was struck by the passing anecdote from one Gypsy woman who bemoaned non-Gypsies' stigmatization of the *outside* of Gypsies' homes on encampments, whereas Gypsies were shocked at the *inside* of non-Gypsy houses. Suddenly the division of inside/outside fell into place. Then a passing anecdote, as mere footnote in an article by Thompson (1922), provided the explanatory clue to Gypsies' animal classification (Okely 1994a).

## Survey or Participate

When social science departments have to prove scientific respectability, the anthropologist may be under pressure to posit not only slick theories, but also to manufacture quantities of numerical data, gleaned from a greater geographical space than that which the participant observer can cover. Numerical display and geographical mileage may be considered the only means towards generalizeable observations, when the intensive study of a single locale may explain and be applicable to places and people far beyond the anthropologist's stride and the quantifier's territory. Some social scientists from the 1970s, in a travesty of Marx's original theories, reduced materialist explanations to statistical correlations, overlooking the fact that *Das Kapital* (1887/1961) is *replete* with ethnographic examples and case studies.

The State and development agencies, in the name of democratic, majority rhetoric, may demand research with numerical mass and electorally relevant opinions. This insidiously sets the tone for academic grant-giving bodies, obliged to prove their immediate utility. The emphasis on 'users', and now 'income generation', covertly privileges the powerful, not the powerless (Okely 1987: 66–7; 2006a).

## Questionnaire versus Participant Observation

Malinowski long ago saw the limitations of 'survey work':

> there is a series of phenomena of great importance which cannot possibly be recorded by questioning or computing documents, but have to be observed in their full actuality. (1922: 18)

For questionnaires, the 'issues' and concepts are decided in advance. A pilot study is insufficient to produce unsolicited information; it only means refinement or elimination. The questionnaire is potentially authoritarian (Omvedt 1979). The subjects' replies are constrained. The questioner cannot learn as she or he progresses through the interview. One question must follow the other in ordained succession. Anything the questioner learns or wishes to follow up on cannot be done in that context, but either as an internal dialogue in the research retreat or in some follow-up where the subject may have lost the thread of his or her ideas. There is little place for volunteered information. What can be conveyed is a static purely verbalized description. Dialogue is destroyed. The positivist extreme has been critically challenged and demonstrated as counter-productive (Oakley 1981).

There are several compromises—informal, unstructured or semi-structured interviews where there is room for volunteered insights and comments. But they may still be out of context and in a one-to-one exchange. The interviewer remains depersonalized and formally framed. A male researcher for whom I and another female employee once administered questionnaires around Cowley, a working-class area in Oxford, confided that he was too 'embarrassed' to conduct the interviews himself. Such research delegation and distancing of the self are not available to a participant observer who must confront the consequences of intimate enquiries and be exposed to similar scrutiny.

The contrast between questionnaire and participant observation is most relevant in discussing fieldwork in the West, where sociological and survey traditions have privileged the latter. Anthropologists and others who have done research in tropical forests are rarely, if ever, confronted by such methodological dilemmas. They may be struggling with the language, without even a recorded vocabulary (Campbell 1995; Howell, Overing and Morris dialogues this volume).

Nonetheless, these debates may be equally relevant to contexts around the globe. The process of data collection in questionnaires has been separated from the analysis, and in a hierarchical system, with an intellectual and often sexist division of labour. The questionnaires in Britain at least, have invariably been administered by females and written up by desk-bound male 'theorists', with little or no contact with the research subjects. Unforeseeable responses during the interviews are filtered out and rendered unavailable to the theorist-analyst (Okely 1987: 59–60). By contrast, the participant observer, with no such separation between theory and practice, is able to revise his or her ideas and concerns at *any* time during fieldwork.

It is important to distinguish different kinds of participant observation. Like the word 'ethnography', participant observation has different interpretations for different disciplines. The ideal and traditional practice for social anthropologists is at least one year of shared residence and 24-hours-a-day presence for a total participation and joint living. This differs from intermittent spells of what other social scientists have called 'PO', and transitory visits, where the sequence of events are lost and where there can be no chronology of understanding and trust. The casual and occasional participant observer may elect to leave when things become too hot to handle. The subjects may also be able to maintain a performance throughout the duration of merely occasional visits.

## Questioning within Participant Observation

Those anthropologists who depended more on question-and-answer exchanges without participation could well be criticized for reductive verbalized accounts. Nevertheless, participant observation as shared life cannot eradicate the anthropologist's position as intruder researcher. She or he will want to ask questions. The viability of this form of communication depends on the cultural context. In contrast to de-contextualized interrogations and volunteered statements, answers to questions in the middle of the action are more acceptable and vividly enhanced. The shared context among co-participants is a crucial trigger.

Questions of law may be rendered intelligible for the researcher witnessing a dispute. Ideas about an after life may be elaborated at a funeral. Questions and answers become focused. Discussions in context may thus be more revealing when the researcher is a co-worker, fellow mourner or witness. Verbal descriptions, explanations or simple facts emerge from the stream of events and activity.

In my work among rural inhabitants of Normandy, people were pleased to answer many questions once acquaintance had been consolidated. Semi-structured, taped interviews were extremely productive with people known over many months or several years. They were not strangers and I had a rough idea what their views were on specific issues. The appearance of the tape recorder gave the chance to record their testimony, and I had the gift of their exact words and the minutiae of their comments. It was most rewarding to record dialogues about agricultural production with Madame Grégoire in her stable, while she was hand-milking her cows, and after I had myself been apprenticed through months of milking (Okely 1996b: chapter 10).

If the group is stigmatized and persecuted, outsiders may find the asking of questions virtually impossible. That was my experience among the Gypsies who, among themselves, also tended to avoid that mode of communication (Okely 1983: 45). However, it was, on occasion, possible to raise specific questions when out calling with Gypsies as fellow workers and sharing stigma on the doorsteps (Okely 1996b: chapter 1).

Similarly, other anthropologists have found variety in the appropriateness of the question mode. Esther Goody (1975) has suggested that question asking, any mode of interrogation, may be culture specific, and in some contexts entirely inappropriate. Overing also declared that she never conducted interviews. She describes her months of questioning the Piaroa as discussions.

Answers to questions may be deliberate lies, especially to the incomer still identified as stranger. Answers may be what the interviewee considers the questioner wants to hear. They may be unintentionally incorrect or misleading explanations—crucial mystifications to the actors themselves. Such mystification will be informative to the researcher, but at the level of ideology. The mystifications are different kinds of social facts. Despite their caveats, there is the suspicion that some anthropologists obtained their information in the field from just a few 'informants' to whom they fed tobacco or supplied machetes in exchange for information. We do not know.

Questions may also be answered after extended time and trust. Initially pertinent questions may invite automatic denials or diversions. In New Guinea, Powdermaker (1967), on first asking, was told that garden magic did not exist. Later, she learned of its existence after it was realized that she would not mock (cf. Lévi-Strauss 1955/1973). Similarly, Gypsies first denied to me that ghosts existed. I was later able to elicit positive information about their existence when I expressed a personal fear of them.

Empathy, complicity and the accumulation of shared experience may unleash the long-sought knowledge (Young and Goulet 1994). There may be added worth in prolonged, more abstracted, exchange with specific specialists and indigenous experts, visionaries and intermediaries.

## Autobiographical Narratives

Anthropologists back from the field are in a position to articulate and analyze, as well as simply describe the vagaries of their blunders and achievements. The disjointed incidents and peccadilloes, just like fieldwork jottings, throw up repetitious themes and similarities across cultures, thus giving generality to the individual anthropological fieldwork. Shared knowledge, if not dream work (Edgar 1995), brings coherence to what anthropologists might sometimes experience as incoherent sleepwalking.

There is room for thinking through the stream of events via 'free association' to disentangle the submerged significance of what emerge as crucial incidents (Freud 1900/1954; Okely 2010b). These are not necessarily the great public occasions. An anthropologist might have a people's worldview or a theoretical explanation crystallized by a casual aside, a seeming banality, or one anecdote—yes, the world in Blake's grain of sand.

# –5–

# Participant Observation Examples

## Embedded Theory

Participant observation, as outlined in the previous chapter, means more than co-residence. It entails sharing space, events and day-to-day living. The incoming anthropologist is repeatedly positioned in unexpected ways. This chapter allows the voices and examples of the many anthropologists to unfurl. Narratives carry important and varied experiences. Theory is embedded if the readers and listeners are open to finding it. Nancy Lindisfarne volunteered the core of anthropological practice:

> The importance of the ethnographic method is *this intimacy of detail* [my emphasis]. Which, even if it doesn't make it into the writing, is informing. Even the most banal or the most cold, distant description is still informed by having been there.

In so many examples, the anthropologists learn to go with the flow, not only through intellectual knowledge, but also through the body, moving through space. In the first example, Sue Wright, among settled nomads in Iran, reveals how frequent interaction brings trust and unique contextualized knowledge such as kinship allegiances, rivalries and conflicts in social relations. The only way to learn fully about the social interaction was through the kinship structures. She was invited to view the physical layout of the houses as kinship interests and to watch for social manoeuvering, as expressions of kinship rivalries or allegiances (Wright 1981). She could only understand the politics through genealogies and could be trusted only when she learned them:

> There'd be all these different interpretations of what had been going on, nobody was quite sure, because every single interpretation of these little tiny events was a question as to whether that person was going to go onto that side, or this person was going to go on that side, and whether they were going to fight.
>
> So that became learning; how to use space; learning what movement I could be allowed without incurring danger for myself, which really was a danger for my hosts. Little boys would take me.
>
> We stood on a rooftop, looking over the houses. I was trying to understand the kinship relations, how they worked spatially. Someone said: 'It's all my kin.' He started giving me genealogies. We spent hours in the evenings. He would give me all the kinship relations— I ended up with everybody in this village of a couple of thousand people.

I had to learn it all. So when I met somebody, I would know who they were. I had to have a spider-map. You had to find the innocuous issues to be pleasant about and to know what the danger signals were. I never got as versatile as any of them.

The schoolteacher said: 'There are bad houses there.' I'd got this contradiction between his telling me that things worked according to genealogies, reflected in the literature, and yet obviously didn't work in that a lot of his closest kin, he was calling 'bad houses'. Until I had that genealogical knowledge I wouldn't know which could be a 'bad house'.

When I'd been to a house, talking with the women, and maybe the man would come in and we'd talk too. I had to treat whatever they said, however seemingly innocuous, as confidential. I was absolutely watertight. I would go back. People would ask me questions. There was no way I was ever saying anything about anyone. I got a reputation for being completely discreet.

Eventually I stayed with different families, and lived the other side of the village that was in conflict with the side that I'd started off on—so managed to move over all these boundaries.

When visitors from the Ministry of Health arrived, Wright helped the women wash the tea glasses in the yard, then was invited to join the meeting as a respected, though junior, visitor sitting as honorary male in male space.

Participation as shared labour also brings trust and insights, sometimes across gender boundaries, as Wright discovered:

There were certain things I wasn't very good at. No one would let me cook rice on an open fire. But manual women's labour, I could do. I was always gendered as a woman, but I was moving through different tasks they were doing.

I was able to go to the fields and I went with the young men up to the mountains, to collect firewood. That was very dangerous. The forests had been nationalized. You weren't allowed to cut green wood. They used to patrol the mountains, and anyone collecting even dead firewood could be imprisoned. They let me go with them one day.

Extended co-residence in limited space may have its relative constraints. Movement provides another perspective. When Wright went up to the mountains with her companions she found:

Just the freedom to walk out of that tense atmosphere of the village—to walk in the mountains—the first time after six months. When they were harvesting, I spent a day working with the men threshing wheat. They had donkeys and horses going round in a circle crushing the grains, to separate from the straw. You had to rake the untrampled wheat back in the path of the animals. They gave me that job which was backbreaking in this intense heat. Male labour was hard to come by. That I could do men's jobs gave me a different access to the men. I was working with both the men and the women in the rice harvest. That I had experienced it meant they talked about things in a completely different way.

As confirmed in many examples, thanks to participant labour, the anthropologist found that information flowed easily. Wright was given massive detail about agricultural arrangements. Where previously there had been mistrust, now information was forthcoming. This contrasts with 'data gatherers' who stand back from bodily participation in the name of 'objectivity'. Wright was given all the information, and indeed more, through shared context:

> Once I'd worked on the threshing-fields and passed all the different threshing-fields, it became a very detailed knowledge—a much more open knowledge. Previously they'd been worried about what kind of information to give. Once I'd been part of the harvest, it totally changed.

There are no blueprints in fieldwork. It also depends on individual inclinations and potential. When working with Gypsies at scrap metal, calling at doors or attempting to hand-milk cows in Normandy, I could not match their skills. I learned also that it did not matter. My efforts were appreciated, indeed exaggerated. Before long, I was introduced to new Gypsies as: 'She can break up scrap metal like the rest of us,' This eased new contact.

Participation as a skilled worker is rarely achieved by the stranger anthropologist. The anthropologist through his or her very incompetence learns about others' skills by living the contrast. In Afghanistan, confronted with her own clumsiness, Lindisfarne, among Pashtun nomads of Afghanistan in the early 1970s, appreciated their manual skill. She decided not to attempt activities where she remained incompetent, so prioritized others:

> There was a way in which being there, because of the intimacy, the visibility of a domestic setting, you were always a participant. At the same time, I was more observer than participant. I used to be the standing joke. I could not roll yoghurt balls! I was cackhanded at rolling felt. I tried a lot of things and was a failure, which rather annoyed them because women's physical workload was considerable.
>
> I wasn't going to be a Pashtun woman because I could not churn butter. I decided that if I had a sense of how arduous a job was that was enough. I didn't even try my hand at weaving, but I spent a lot of time talking to them about weaving.

A different knowledge emerges through shared movement with nomads seated on animals. Such lived physical experience is very different from that dependent solely on interrogation torn from context. While horse or camel riding, Lindisfarne experienced the integration of bodily movement and the people's lives. The full implication was only recognized retrospectively when watching her filmed footage:

> Women could ride. But I was the only one that was regularly riding a horse. It puts you in the middle of the dust. On the steep passes, you have to get off and lead the animal. I was very conscious of feeding it, because there was so little fodder. It's unthinkable not to have had that intimacy.

We have a short piece of movie. It was spectacular, so evocative. If you're watching the camels, and this amazing back and forth movement, and you're in a line of camels, and everybody's going back and forth. I was overwhelmed the first time I saw the movie, because it was bringing back everything. How could you know that, if you didn't do it? What it means is something about the impact of the migration, the loss as they settled, in terms of the stunning movement through unbelievable scenery, that they had to face when they also became refugees. It's also an aesthetic thing.

I asked:

Supposing you went to those refugee camps, if you were trying to write an ethnography of their way of life, and you depended entirely on interviews and you hadn't been on the migration, what would you have lost by depending on so-called discourse analysis?

Lindisfarne responded:

You might as well forget it. You might have some documentary records of people who called themselves the Ishaqzai, lived in an area called Saripul until 1979. 'Some of them had lots of sheep. Some didn't. They grew some crops. They went on migration'—but it would be as flat as that.

Attempts at skilled labouring or craft may reverse stereotypes of the foreign in-comer. Just as Hilary Rose (1983) emphasized the dimension of craft as scientific practice, so the anthropologist can, through conveying some knowledge of crafts-manship, however basic, challenge stereotypes of the ignorant outsider. Malcolm McLeod, through a seemingly simple gesture, revealed some expertise in pottery:

I've always found making things—in Ghana, that people are extraordinarily surprised that any European would want to do that and that they have any technical skill whatsoever. In a small area market, I walked round one day picking up pots and just pinging them with my knuckle. If you ping a well-fired pot, it makes a nice sound. If it's cracked it gives a *thunk* noise. I heard people say: 'My God! He knows how to hit pots!' This is a realm of knowledge which Europeans are incompetent to have!

McLeod also learned, through the making of pottery, aspects which other material culture specialists might never understand:

The Asante make terracotta figures for putting as memorials. I found a potter who still made these figures and I made one. Again, people were fascinated. I just followed what she was doing; that's real participant observation. 'You do this thing. I'll try and copy it and you can correct me.' When you're making things, you learn all the things you can and can't do, which are not obvious from examining the finished specimen. There's an awful lot of theorizing by material culture specialists, about how things were done. If they'd only try themselves, they'd realize you can't get it to do that.

The terra cotta figure I left to be fired, saying I would go back in two or three months, when it had dried out, to collect it. I was prevented from going back as soon as I'd wanted and discovered that a European dealer had turned up in the village, and had bought it, claiming that he'd been sent by me! So somewhere in some museum or private collection, preferably in North America, is this really appalling terracotta that I made in 1968.

## Commensality and Reciprocity

Michael Herzfeld reveals in a different context the value of going with the flow of the local culture. His gender was crucial as to where he could gain access, namely the Crete coffee house culture. He spent hours, days in shared commensality, gradually alert to the customs of hospitality when visiting another village with his companions. He was sufficiently confident, after extended participation, to take the initiative in adopting the customs of 'his' village and outdoing their rivals. This public statement would further legitimize him among those in the village he had come to know. An act of 'joining in', however small or infrequent, has long-term effects in becoming an appreciated participant. Herzfeld explained:

I spent an awful lot of time in coffee houses because you could sit there. As a man, I had no difficulty in legitimizing my presence. They would treat me, sometimes, as a way of putting me in my place. I would then treat them, as a way of claiming a quasi-local identity. Once I insisted on that right, they became very friendly, because I had shown that I'd learned their ways.

There was a very funny moment, quite late in the fieldwork when my wife and I went with the son of our landlord to get firewood from another village that was notorious for its lack of hospitality. Somebody rather grudgingly treated us. We raised our glasses and toasted that man. Then I did what in my village would have been normative. I said to the coffee house provider: 'Treat everyone! Treat the shop.' He looked surprised and said: 'Everyone?' I said: 'Yes, go ahead!' This got back to our people: 'You've learnt our customs . . . showed those people what's what!' One does make contacts in all sorts of ways, but the coffee house was very important, because it is a place for male sociability.

Whereas Herzfeld could take the initiative in being generous, he could not adopt other very different practices:

The least successful thing to do with anyone, almost always, is to confront them. That's tough in Greece, because Greeks tend to be rather confrontational.

Joanna Overing regretted the pressure to obtain sufficient material for her doctorate. Her publications confirm her depth of material, but she had not been encouraged to go with the flow of events in the way she later wished:

I would do things very differently nowadays. One of the worst things is to be thrown into a situation like that. All these years are for naught if you don't end up with what you need to write a PhD. Imagine, if you're in a place: you don't understand a word of the language—how completely useless you feel—this horrible stress. I would take much more time playing with the children. I didn't work with the women. That's what I wanted to do. That's what I was planning to do (later) in 1977. That's when we weren't allowed to go into the jungle (permit refused).

## Acting Native

The anthropologist adopts or retains the practices with which she or he feels most at ease. It may depend both on the people's expectations and the anthropologist's personality. Overing decided to keep her Western clothes:

> I thought it would be pretentious to run around in a loincloth. Besides, they are very expensive. They have to be made. I never would have 'gone native', in that sense.

Whyte (1943/1955), in his 1955 appendix, described how he tried to integrate so well as to adopt the swear words of the Chicago street gangs, but he was reprimanded. They wanted him to retain his middle-class WASP image. By contrast, a Gypsy woman advised me to adapt by not wearing trousers, exposing hips. I had to wear a long tunic, certainly not my usual mini skirt and tight tops. I was also congratulated for adjusting my middle-class accent (Okely 1983: 43).

Overing adjusted to other practices, while sensitive to scarcity:

> We were brought into the distribution system, for things from the jungle. You'd wake up and find a pineapple from old gardens and other fruits from the jungle. Everybody would have their share. I didn't want to impose us on their eating. So I brought in a lot of pasta and sardines and did my own cooking. We would send in big boxes of sardines as our share. During the rainy season, they didn't like to hunt, so we'd give that to the chief to distribute.

Anthropologists Christine and Stephen Hugh-Jones, who did fieldwork among tropical forest peoples in South America, were forced by necessity to earn their keep by offering their labour and submitting to the peoples' orders. I recalled:

> I remember Stephen Hugh-Jones describing how he and Christine travelled with a boat with all these beads and things as gifts. Then the boat turned over. They arrived with nothing. They had to pay with their labour. The Indians had this wonderful experience of telling the white man: 'Go there. Sit there. Do that.' That's partly why they got involved in the pounding of the manioc and hunting. They hadn't planned it. That was an accident.
> [Overing:] I never knew that story.
> [Okely:] I asked Stephen to give a talk at Durham in the late 1970s. They adjusted. But it was hard work. They had to learn to hunt a monkey to get their food! Thus they had a completely different perspective. Those hours and hours of pounding, Christine learned through doing that.

Felicia Hughes-Freeland did indeed take seriously adjusting her attire. This quickly alienated fellow Westerners:

> A friend came to see me from my VSO [Voluntary Service Overseas] days. He was going to take me out to lunch—a very glamorous Canadian. I was wearing what I knew to be a nightdress, probably the same one I'd worn to see the Prince. I'd mended the tear in the back because I didn't have enough money. I had my hair tied up in a rag and was washing the bedroom floor. He came unexpectedly, took one look and left. It looked so funny. That was my high point of being a participant observational anthropologist who had irredeemably moved beyond the pale for her previous Western friends. I didn't get on so well with my former teacher colleagues. They all thought I was too much going native.

Hughes-Freeland had a later experience on the same theme:

> During postdoc fieldwork a year after the ninth Sultan of Yogya's death, I was invited by court friends to join them in a ritual visit to his tomb in the royal hillside mausoleum. Waiting our turn, all the women sat together on the steps wearing the required court attire of *gelung tekuk* [a type of chignon], breast cloth and batik sarong, when a group of Australian tourists who'd got in despite the mausoleum being closed, came up and jeered at me: 'You'll never be mistaken for a Javanese.' That wasn't the point: to participate I had no choice but to dress like that. Afterwards in my field notes I wrote that 'I felt my sense of me as Felicia slipping.'

In some cases the anthropologist in a highly stratified society may be expected to conform to the attributes of the high-status group. Here respectable non-manual attire and demeanour may be valued, along with a full grasp of linguistic nuances. Parry, in caste-structured India, faced this:

> In Banaras, the idea of visiting scholars is not peculiar. That I could speak Hindi and knew how to handle myself quite rapidly distinguished me. I always made a point of dressing conservatively and respectably, clean shirts, whereas a large proportion of the tourists visit the cremation grounds dressed in ragged Indian clothes.
>
> One is participating, simply by being around. In Bhilai this guy Somvaru (as I've called him in publications)—I'd go off with him to his fields. I'd do some reaping and ploughing the odd furrow, to everybody's amusement. But I didn't spend whole days in the field cutting the paddy.
>
> One of Somvaru's great problems, particularly with his youngest son, is that they all now want to be industrial workers. His youngest son wanders around, boozing and playing cards, and never goes to the fields—completely despises agricultural labour. He thinks it's for hicks. The fact that this long-trousered, white-collared professor came and reaped in his fields was something that he could reproach his son with. 'If he's not too proud to do it, why the hell can't you?' I remember trying my hand at ploughing in Kangra, and this causing great consternation because 'People like you—respectable people—don't plough.' They were Brahmins.

Parry found other ways of helping in Bhilai:

> Writing letters, petitions—I tried my hand at a machine for fun. But nobody was going to have me buggering up their machinery! Employment law wouldn't allow it. So what I was able to do in the steel plant was to shadow workers.
>
> One lives as near as possible to the same kind of life. I think that even untouchables in India, if you were studying sweepers and you went out sweeping, the sweepers would be as scandalized as anybody else. The most successful method is consistently hanging around with the same people. People produce more and more. Having a certain number of informants that you personally get on well with, you like being with, who begin to trust you, and who begin to have some vague empathy. That it's fun to talk to you and will say: 'Ah! That would interest you!'

## Risks in Participation

Helena Wulff (1988), among South London teenagers, had to adjust in multiple ways. Her main arenas were the youth club or the street corner 'where on a low wall you could sit with legs hanging, flirting, gossiping. This was the only arena without adults.' The mixed-gender club was 'tougher. Things happened with drugs and knives. Boys threw smoke bombs into the basement.'

Taking participant observation seriously brings risks, whether in Europe or beyond:

> In the summer we were meeting at a street corner. We were walking across the Common. There was this wall. We climbed over and some took off their clothes and went into the public swimming pool (then officially closed). Some boys threw in a bench. Someone shouted: 'Police!' There was panic. Everyone ran. I found myself running away from the British police. I could see the car. While I'm running, I'm thinking: 'If I'm caught, I'm allowed one phone call.' They got one of the boys. You don't know what the police do to black boys. I realize I could be thrown out. For my visa I never said what I was going to do. I was an alien and never said I was doing research. This incident helped. Someone said: 'Helena has guts.'

This example, where the anthropologist flees with the transgressing individuals from the law-making authorities, can be compared to that of Geertz observing an illegal cockfight in Bali. He and his wife ran away with the Balinese participants when the police arrived. His instinctive response earned him acceptance:

> The next morning the village was a completely different world for us. Not only were we no longer invisible, we were suddenly the center of all attention, the object of warmth, interest, and most especially, amusement. Everyone in the village knew we had fled. (Geertz 1975: 416)

## Shared Pain through Barefoot Pilgrimage

Kenna took seriously full participation when undertaking a pilgrimage in Greece. While Turner (1969) has written imaginatively on the symbolism of the practice, Kenna studied it through individual action:

> The first time I walked barefoot to the shrine of the island's patron saint I did it with no Greeks around. There was just the shepherd family who looked after the monastery. It took me about an hour to walk barefoot up this track because my feet were very tender. It should have been silent but I was making remarks because it was so painful. Having presented my votive offering to the icon, when I came out of the church I burst into tears. It was a very powerful experience, almost like Wordsworth: 'Thoughts that lie too deep for tears.' I don't know why I cried. All I can say is a Greek expression which is 'A burden was lifted from me.' I'd discharged my vow. I felt as much like a Greek as I could ever feel. On other occasions I was one of many, but people were saying: 'Look, the foreigner is doing it,' but I never again experienced that activity with the same degree of intensity that I did the first time. That was a totally physical experience.

## Routine Adjustments

Participant observation may entail adjusting to very different rhythms and a different sense of time, as McLeod articulated from fieldwork in Ghana:

> You never learn in fieldwork preparation to be patient. All these inexplicable things are happening: people don't turn up, or it takes three days to do something which should only take half an hour. Instruction on fieldwork should concentrate much more on giving people a sense of time. So they're not trying to impose their own rhythms. One is always taught to try and understand local society through its own language and behaviour. One of the critical things in our own society is the fact that we've got watches, schedules and events, whereas in other societies, to a greater degree, time is invented, or created by events themselves.

Co-residence leads ideally to showing shared enjoyment and acquiring empathy. McLeod, emphasized that, again in contrast to intrusive interrogation, quiet and respectful observation was rewarding:

> You have to enjoy being there. One of the keys to getting good information and understanding is, just to be able to show that you're enjoying it—that you respect the people. That you're willing to sit quietly for long periods, without interrupting, and just let things happen in front of you. Patience and quiet observation are highly valued in that society. For outsiders to show even the rudiments of that does make it easier to find things out.

McLeod also elaborated on the necessary limitations for participation when confronted by local micro politics. Here, being perceived as and remaining an outsider can indeed bring added dimensions:

If you're operating in another political system, you can't really participate in any major way. I would not want to get involved in Asante politics. Being an outsider is very useful. You can move from side to side, and find out things from different groups, without participating fully in their activities and stance.

## Participation through Dance

Mutual recognition through bodily participation is especially succinct when studying dance. Again there are different aspects and unique potential for mutual recognition when contrasted with cerebral exchanges. Hélène Neveu, in Senegal, found as such:

> The main way I used participant observation was by dancing with the people I was doing research with. That made a big difference. I did dance with the professional groups. One day I'd come to see one of the troupes rehearse. They were improvising, trying out new things in neo-traditional style. There was drumming, all having great fun trying various steps and dances. The choreographer shouted: 'Take your shoes off.' I didn't understand and sat down as I usually did. He said: 'No, don't sit, take your shoes off. Come over, just follow' and I started dancing with them. They really appreciated that.
>
> The next time I did it, they asked if I could help them warm up, so I gave them some ballet warming up exercises, which were new to some of the company. Initially I didn't take it very seriously. I thought: 'OK, let's warm up together.' I showed them a few things. The next time they were waiting for me to arrive. It changed the way they perceived me. They realized I had a body and I was able to move as well. That I was able to understand some of the things they were doing technically.

There are parallels with Wulff (1998) when she studied several Western ballet companies. She had a welcoming entrée, having trained as a ballet dancer. She shared a technical eye, which the dancers recognized.

While Neveu and Wulff restricted past expertise to back stage, there can be limits to total participation. Hughes-Freeland was confronted by exclusion from public performance, partly because of her visibly foreign status and self-acknowledged lack of skill:

> I participated in dance classes incessantly in a group at the beginning. Then I had private teachers when I got fed up with being the idiot in the back row who couldn't do it properly. The dance teacher wouldn't even let me do the exams. I had the costume. I had a little top made to do the exams. When I turned up, all dressed, he said: 'What do you think you're dressed like that for?' I said: 'For the exams'. He said: 'You're not going to do the exams.' I'd memorized everything. But I was never going to perform.

## From Disco Dancing to Danger

The anthropologist must be *disponible* to what is out there. Forget the initial research plan, if exposed as inappropriate. Anthropologists must trust their inner judgement.

Thus Zulaika, choosing to study terrorism in his own village and country, found the most productive access to be through helping initiate a discothèque. Then, faced with few customers, he had to convey confidence and act the star turn night after night. Zulaika makes a strong argument against any bureaucratic call for advance accountability in anthropological research.

I decided to carry on a normal life in my village as I had done when I was a student. I would stay home for a period, read and then go out when there were things happening, particularly with my youth group that were friends. There was this cultural activist group raising money for the local Basque school that was still private, not state-funded, so it needed to get organized festivals and music events. They decided to turn an old stable for cows and animals, into a discothèque. They thought I was the guy with more free time, so they put me in charge. A good part of my fieldwork was turning that stable into a discothèque; putting in the electricity, finding the carpenters, the music system, the lights.

Every day I was in hours of conversation with these guys who had been in ETA [Euskadi Ta Askatasuna; Basque Homeland and Freedom]. I could hear all their stories. They trusted me. They had no secrets from me. I knew exactly, mentally, the painful experience they had among themselves after ETA. They diverged politically. That became terribly painful. Finding how they had gotten in to ETA, how they had lived, what it had meant when they had murdered somebody—the torture in prison—their splitting politically. This is what made me know these ETA events there.

[Okely:] This is serendipity. They needed the disco and you seized the chance.

[Zulaika:] I was pretty much doing research on political terrorism and 90 per cent of all I did was organize this disco, which I added as an epilogue, dancing in an empty discothèque. I learnt through these guys, through this more than in any other way. I felt I needed to take more field notes. But in the long run probably it was the right thing.

For Zulaika, this was perfect reciprocity, giving his labour and skills proved to be thoroughly ethnographically productive: 'The real content of information I got was by just working on this discothèque and the hundreds of hours we spent together building that and then promoting it.'

His insider status and active engagement ensured integration:

The fact that I acted as a villager and took part in all the activities as somebody who had to take responsibility for what they were doing. I was just one more villager taking part and responsibility for it. I was, on the other hand, taking notes at the same time. It entailed a massive near full-time commitment in terms of time and energy.

Faced with possible failure, Zulaika found himself obliged to act as promoter:

We made the disco. Then nobody would come. So I had to become entertainer. There's nobody dancing. Many times I had to be there. There was another massive disco 100 yards away that was full of people and nobody would come to our disco. It was like we had done social work. It was indecent to create a disco. People preferred to go to this capitalist guy who was making tons of money. But to come to this socially minded type of discothèque, something funny was happening. Initially, we had problems in filling the place, so I had to be there, drinking and dancing until three or four in the morning most weekends. I think nobody did more than me for that year.

We were ten people. Somebody had to give the impression there was something going on. Many times, I was the disc jockey, the dancer, and the bartender. We had huge debts. Instead of making money it was losing money.

When we said to the hell with it and we didn't care any more, people started to come in droves. It became very successful after I went back to Princeton, after a year or so.

With his in-depth 'native' or local knowledge as member, rather than outsider, Zulaika then helped initiate cultural transformation, synthesizing specific Basque ethnicity with contemporary music beyond:

We followed the musical scene. These are former ETA members. In that year rock 'n' roll music was all in English, so we created a competition for young Basque rock 'n' roll music groups singing in Basque, which became a fashion. It became corrupted by the Basque radical youth, very much politically in ETA's way. So we were on the one hand bombed by ETA and on the other, we created a new musical form. This Basque rock 'n' roll, we created, we contributed to. Until then, rock 'n' roll had been seen as a foreign invasion, as American. It suddenly became Basque radical rock. So it contributed, this small village, significantly to the creation of this new musical form that then became a significant phenomenon in the late 1980s, as an expression of political protest, with musical forms that you could find in London.

As anthropologists have risked elsewhere, intervention, however well intentioned, may provoke controversy, sometimes violence. Zulaika described:

This disco was obviously a centre of fun, diversion, and a place for all sorts of young punks. So ETA put a bomb in this disco. The youth of the village, we got together, and we made a statement.

Thus participation as political intervention could also be extreme engagement as opposed to distancing observation, as Zulaika discovered:

Somebody from the village was kidnapped by ETA. It was a Basque family who had established the first nationalist locale. I am a villager so I thought it was totally inappropriate, unwarranted. It had no justification. I wrote a leaflet, made copies put in all the bars (saying) that I thought that had no sense. This was a family who was Basque nationalist. That ETA should do this was against all logic. This was an act that I, as ethnographer, was condemning what part of the village approved of, that whatever ETA was doing was alright. I knew I was going to anger, as I did, some villagers. So even if the fieldwork was a distancing, neutral device, there were situations where my being a native took the upper hand. I showed I wouldn't go along with everything that was ETA doing.

In contrast to McLeod, who convincingly recognized it was inappropriate to engage in micro politics as an outsider, Zulaika, as a local Basque, was in the thick of political disputes, engaging with his fellow villagers:

> I remember writing for the media that, with the youth of the village, we had built this disco, all of us together. We were shocked that ETA would go against our project. We as a group were very much in the orbit of ex-ETA, or still pro. Yet ETA was bombing something that we did from inside the nationalist community. We were subverting from inside ETA's regime from a village that was very much ETA. In that regard ethnography's activities were subversive. I was caught in these dilemmas in which, on the one hand, my writing task was not being the policeman, nor being a counter-terrorist. Yet from inside the village I found that the village's political rationale should be critical of things. I acted by myself or as we, the community—critical from inside.

In a far more timid context in England, I found it necessary to intervene when I was set up as a means of shaming a Gypsy involved in a conflict, resulting in murder. Here I, the outsider, in contrast to Zulaika as insider, was the non-Gypsy 'stalking horse' for punishing a Gypsy for past misdemeanours. I had to take imaginative action through playful charade (Okely 2005: 707–8).

## Exchange and Mutual Interdependence in Crisis

In some cases, as with Hugh-Jones, the anthropologist is especially vulnerable and dependent on not only acceptance but also basic needs. Akira Okazaki, among the Gamk in Sudan, found himself and his family in a period of famine, something he had not anticipated when arriving from Japan. He had returned with his wife and three children who posed added problems of access to food. Thus, participation became a necessity:

> Without participation I can't survive. It's not a matter of whether anthropologists should share food or not, we have to share, otherwise there is no way. There's no proper car there. Even if you have a car, there's no petrol—so the people were just walking. Even to keep a donkey is very difficult because I have to look for food for the donkey. All that means that participation is different according to which kind of place where you are doing fieldwork.

## Active Involvement in Charitable Distribution

An example of direct intervention is found in Talib's active involvement in an organization distributing bread among stone-breaking workers near Delhi. Paradoxically, in the early 1980s, fellow academics queried this as being insufficiently politically interventionist:

I spoke to this person: 'Could I be your helping hand?' he said: 'Yes'. Some of my friends raised issues of ethics here saying: 'Clearly your politics did not allow you to be part of that venture and you legitimized, in the eyes of the workers, a very non-political intervention.' I said: 'Yes of course'.

But the only consolation was that I'm not going to harm these workers and something useful is going to come out. I was not part of any sponsored research. This data is going to remain with me or with the workers. That was my only face saving. I became part of this organization distributing bread among the workers. This used to happen every Tuesday and in the process I made a lot of friends.

I befriended Raja Ram who was a student of social work. He knew the situation. He had the vocabulary to explain. I was also a kind of a social worker. I had tried this kind of participant observation that you suggest but it was not very easy, because the site of stone breaking had the worst air pollution.

## Co-Residence as Health Risk

As chapter 6 will elaborate, participant observation may expose bodily vulnerability. Confronted with the health risks of co-residence, Talib chose to commute:

I didn't live in that community. I wanted to. There were two things which scared me—one, the mosquito. There was rampant malaria and there were ways of protecting oneself. The other was this silica dust pollution. My colleagues used to tease me, some of my radical friends, saying: 'What is this? You've got scared of these little things.' I felt that since I was just thirty miles away, it was possible to return to my field as and when I wanted.

It would work out thrice, four times a week. I would meet workers, not in their work time, but when they were out of it or when they were idle, when the work was not available, or not well, just lying on the bed. They would be available for some conversation, some chatting. Thursday was their off day, it was a forced, unwaged Sabbath. It was declared a holiday. But they were not paid for it.

I couldn't use participant observation in the sense Whyte uses the term. I assumed a role that came very close to that context but it was not really part of them. I was still seen as an outsider. Of course I befriended some of them and that was very useful.

## Questions Emerge in the Process

Like so many anthropologists, Talib found advance questionnaires inappropriate:

The use of questionnaires was very limited and some of the questions emerged from the conversation, from the field. The questionnaire is a very unilateral tool. It was never feasible. If I would imagine a questionnaire I prepared and the fate of it in the field there was an interactive relationship between that tool that I carried in the field and what came out of it. It was a completely transformed tool towards the end of the exercise.

Carol Silverman confirmed emergent knowledge through participation:

> I got some analytical categories very early on. Not from a fieldwork manual, not from the Bulgarian literature, not from the American folklore or anthropology literature either, but from the practice of being a field worker. Then I was able to reformulate many things on a grander level.

## Specific Interpretations of Participant Observation

Roy Gigengack, as Dutch 'gringo' in Mexico City, mingling with street children, had of necessity flexible roles. Participant observation he interpreted as hanging around. But his other forms of participation are also consistent with roles which a variety of anthropologists may adopt when appropriate:

> I used three roles. These all had to do with a degree of intervention of myself. In Plaze Giribaldi with a lot of youth delinquents, they didn't need any intervention from my side. I was busy keeping them off my side. I also had to protect myself. This was more what anthropologists call participant observation.
>
> With another group, called the Booker Boys, quite young boys from eight to twelve to sixteen years old, they wanted me to act like a street educator; bringing them to a shelter or saying that they should not use drugs. It is the things that they like to hear from an adult who cares about them. They wanted to hear that taking drugs wasn't good for them, that it was wrong. Of course they wouldn't listen.
>
> There were also kids who asked me to be their father, which I could not do, but they do look for a father figure. Another thing that street educators do is play football at night. We were there playing football with them or me acting as a referee.
>
> Then a third role was that of human rights activist; one who arranges a priest when children have to be baptized or who talks on behalf of them to the policeman. They would say: 'Roy, it's better that you talk to the police because you are a foreigner and they will listen to you.' It is these three roles: doing nothing—participant observation, street educator and the activist, all dependent upon the group.

Gigengack elaborated the complexity of the children's status and his own family links:

> Many street children are not homeless. It's complicated. Many do have a mother. They see their mother frequently, it means a lot to them. Once my mother came to visit us. I brought her to the street children to see my *compadre* when he was shot. That was something they appreciated because they didn't do that. You don't bring your mother to the street children. But I did it. They remembered afterwards: 'Yes, I even know his mother. Can you imagine that, remember that you brought your mother here and that she had to see this?' Something they really appreciated.

Gigengack linked this appreciation with his self-revelation:

> It's through participant observation that you show that you are a human being, that you have family members too, that you have a mother too, that you also have your own problems that you can talk about.

## Routines and Nearby Residence

Gigengack and his partner Raquel Alonso Lopèz described their daily practice:

> We were living in an apartment quite near the places where we did our fieldwork. We could walk to the wastelands and to the *plaze*. It also has a lot to do with serendipity because when we did fieldwork in the Plaze Giribaldi we walked down to it. We had to walk around and see what was happening. Very often there were no street children there. You had to wait, then come back and finally find somebody who wanted to talk with us for a while. But they had lots of things to do. They have to go after what they called their business.
>
> They were always busy. They wanted to talk with us and have fun. But often after ten minutes they made it clear: 'You have to go now.' That was one of the good things, that we were doing it together, because when you're doing it on your own, it can be quite lonely. Then we walked to another group. Actually we were travelling the whole day. That was one of the reasons we did research among twenty groups. You also had the obsession: 'When I go home I have to have information. These guys are not there, so let me go to another street corner where perhaps a gang is hanging out.'

## Outsider Participation beyond Expectations

Louise de la Gorgendière, in an Asante Ghanaian village, was so fully active as participant, that a neighbouring villager came to check this out:

> I chopped firewood. I husked corn, went to the field and planted maize. I collected water. I ate with people, had conversations while they were braiding each other's hair, went for walks with people, just sat around and drank white palm wine.
>
> When I first got there, I was a novelty. After a period of months, I was just there. I was Akwiya. They went about their ordinary business. One day there was a man from another village, the son of the old chief. He had left the village a number of years ago, supposed to have been very intelligent, nicknamed Socrates. After about six months, he sat down beside me, and said that he had been hearing about this white woman who had come to the village, and was asking people all sorts of questions. That she wasn't just any ordinary white woman because she was just like them. There were no pretensions. I could actually communicate with people. There was no distinction in status. I was sitting eating their food, talking with them, going to farm with them. He didn't believe the stories. He wanted to see for himself. For a morning he observed me, and at the end came up and told me what he was doing: 'People were right. You are very down-to-earth. You can engage with these people. I didn't think you'd be able to. I thought that they were lying. But they weren't.'

## Participation Reveals Superior Local Knowledge

Paul Clough in Nigeria expounded in graphic detail the inappropriateness of World Bank recommendations. He learned this only after being encouraged to farm by the local hamlet head. This confirmed the relevance of practice over interrogation which interrupted the farmers, and proved uninformative:

> There was pain in being seen as rubber handed when it came to doing local things. When I look back, I see how much they guided my research. I regarded, from a Marxist perspective, my Zaria friend as being exploitative because he was the hamlet head. He was the local representative of a hereditary ruling class. When I think back I realize how solicitous he was. He came to my mud room in the warehouse: 'Paul, we're all farming, why aren't you?' There I was, trying to follow them around. I'd interrupt their farming by asking questions or just observing. He said: 'You must farm.'
>
> Belatedly, I began to farm and made a cock-up of it. I had to qualify my original classical Marxist thesis. They were hiring out their labour to each other according to their particular family cycle needs. Like others, I hired labourers. I hired my friend to help me plant things. I hired oxen and plough. I rented the farm, as they did, on a yearly basis. They moved from one farm to another. I farmed late. Stupidly, I didn't realize this. Because I began a month late, my ultimate harvest yield was going to be much poorer.
>
> It's a silly little story. I had a very scientific plan. In this part of northern Nigeria, food crops were cash crops. Although they sold a lot of cotton, their main crops were sorghum, known in West Africa as guinea corn, which is a wonderful grain crop, and maize. It was a modern, high-yielding maize, introduced by the World Bank Agricultural Project. I sectioned my slightly more than an acre into four sections: one section of maize with fertilizer, one section without— one section of guinea corn with fertilizer and one section without. I told the various villagers I was going to test the difference. I was careful with the amount of fertilizer I used, along World Bank recommendations. I would show the villagers how they could compare the use of fertilizer with the non-use. I ended up with the most miserable yield because I started too late.
>
> Then there were the local circumstances. The farm I rented was free. The farmer was happy because it had a huge tree in the middle. It was only at harvest that I realized monkeys had been in the tree and eaten my maize. When I took my crop to market I couldn't sell it. It was small enough to be carried on the back of my motorcycle. When I got back, one of the villagers wouldn't stop laughing, seeing me come back from the market eight miles away with unsold grain. So I began to learn in all kinds of ways just how expert they were and how little I helped.

## External Expertise Inappropriate

Participant observation, for Clough, as learning or attempting to farm in a supposedly systematic way, exposed the value and superiority of local knowledge and practice:

> I learnt because I used to ask a lot of questions and talk within a growing circle of friends. That's another aspect of fieldwork—the branching method. As you make friends, you're

branching out from the small group of friends to more and more people. When I started to ask about the fertilizer, I had another theory, which again related to the ideal amount of rice. They said: 'You don't realize that fertilizer is too hot for rice. Use fertilizer very sparingly.' They had been told about the recommendations, but had learnt from many decades, centuries, that you don't talk back to representatives of the government or the indigenous ruling class. You listen and make up your own mind. So they were experimenting with this fertilizer and trying to come up with solutions. They were learning a great deal about how much fertilizer to use. This was all beyond me. I thought all you had to do was follow the recommendations which had come from the Institute of Agricultural Research.

Ignacy-Marek Kaminski, of Polish nationality, who did fieldwork among Gypsies in Eastern Europe and later as refugee in Sweden, described his variety of methods, depending on context. This included illegal activity as refugee:

In Sweden my entire research, my entire PhD was based on participant observation, while in Poland it was a questionnaire at the beginning. In Slovakia I was always that external participant who could return to the same (privileged) status. In Sweden I was a part of the refugee community, and the difference between me and the Gypsy refugees was that they had strong bonds within the community. I was by myself. They could survive as a group, supported for political reasons by Swedish immigration. They were modern Gypsies taken from Italian refugee camps by chartered aeroplane to Sweden, given the entire welfare access with monthly payments; very high compared to what they had. Everyone had rights to a single room, plus one living room.

So I found myself suddenly not as a privileged non-Gypsy, like in Poland and in Slovakia, but in the welfare state; a refugee, under-privileged, doing illegal work and financing, from illegal work, my doctoral studies of Gypsies.

Now I can talk about it openly. When I arrived in Sweden, my Polish passport was not extended. I became a stateless refugee, but suddenly I could get a work permit as a student, *only* for three months holidays. It took three years to get residence. For three years I could only pay for my research among Gypsies, and even go to Greenland, by working for those months. It was obviously not enough. Sweden had the highest cost of living in Europe.

The only way to survive was to do an illegal job. I was working with three illegal immigrants; as the fourth person in a pyramid, with one legal immigrant, with a work permit, at the top, by delivering newspapers from 3:30 am to early morning, then studying language. I had no rights. The Gypsies realized that I was struggling. When they found that I didn't have enough food, they started helping me. There was humanity which was linking us, and ethnic differences not dividing us. I was working for an illegal immigrant who organized one person who was legal. We were four working and everybody in the pyramid was getting money. As I was a fresh immigrant, I was working most and getting the least. The Gypsies realized. During one of my visits to the community, they said: 'Marek today you are Pakistani,' I said: 'What do you mean? I am not Pakistani, I don't look Pakistani. I have green, sometimes blue eyes and blonde hair.' My best Gypsy associate thought: 'Does it matter?—The way you speak Swedish, you could be Pakistani or Turk.'

So we were going in his car. They already had complex territories divided between different Gypsy groups. We had in that Swedish town a good territory of around twenty square kilometres where he was selling carpets and I was his assistant. Then we were selling lamps and going from door to door; lamps like an aquarium with plastic fish. Usually everything was kitsch. He was playing the Pakistani role. Sometimes he was from India then Turkey. But we were losing time. He said: 'If we keep together, I will lose money. You take two blocks. I take two. You have the carpets and the lamps you have to sell.' Out of all the people I sold to, most were immigrants. I believe they already realized—how can I be a Pakistani or a Turk? They were trying to help me by buying those things.

My Gypsy friend said: 'Marek, if you want to study Gypsies, you have to learn how to pay for your bread and your rent.' The Gypsies were helping me later. He was buying from a retailer, with exotic goods. Then we are going to different Swedish towns, over which his clan had control. It was divided. Some flats were occupied by immigrants from Yugoslavia and Finland. He was telling them that we're both from Pakistan. He was moving between Romany, a number of languages, and mixing Swedish. We were selling door to door. It was illegal.

When I asked why it was good for the Polish Gypsy to say he was from Pakistan, Kaminski explained the strategy:

He doesn't look Swedish. He looks different. When we were selling carpets, and he was usually asking like 800 per cent more for what he paid, it was always the same story: 'We just came from Pakistan. The car broke and we are going to a wedding. We have to repair that car, so that gift for the wedding we have to sell.' Always there was a story related to particular goods. He was doing the talk. Finally he told me: 'You have to do the talk. You have to save us time.' They were creating added value.

I suggested that a Pakistani identity would be useful, because carpets would presumably be exotic. Kaminski confirmed the emphasis on the hand made. I found similarities with the English Gypsies who improved sales when claiming objects were handmade by themselves (Okely 2010c). Kaminski had retained contact with the same Gypsy salesman over thirty-eight years. In 2010 the salesman left the door-to-door carpet business for secondhand restaurant/pizzeria equipment transported from Sweden to Poland. Through informal networks, he exploited empty lorries returning to Poland. Thus, in contrast to past border problems, EU expansion has brought new Roma economic strategies.

Signe Howell was initially confronted by the advice of an anthropologist before fieldwork. She would not identify the person but soon ignored most of his advice:

In my first fieldwork I did it the way I thought everybody should. Before I went off, I talked to an anthropologist who had done his work in a similar region. He said that I had to get myself a tent which I then bought. Although that wasn't the way that I thought it should be. He said: 'Buy a tent.' I thought: 'But I'm going to live with them, aren't I?' But I bought a tent. Then he said: 'Don't go native. Some anthropologists think that they can really become like the people they study, but that's highly inadvisable.'

And I should always wear a halter neck: 'Don't throw away your T-shirt and your blouse and walk about with bare breasts just because the women are bare-breasted.' I thought I'll leave that. Then the last thing he said was: 'Buy a lot of provisions. Tinned food. Go out every month or so, and make a long list for a big Chinese store, and get people to carry for you, and you *can't* share it. Then there won't be enough for you. Pay people to carry stuff for you.'

This was not my interpretation of Malinowski! I bought the tent and some food. When I first came obviously I had to have something. But I was very keen to abandon all that. I never, ever bought anything just for myself again.

Whenever I went out, I bought masses of food and rice, because I knew they liked that. I didn't pay anybody to carry it. I said: 'You carry it, and we all share it.' We shared it. I never ate anything in private. I shared everything I had, and they shared everything with me.

[Okely:] So there was some nice reciprocity, in that you did bring some food in, but that was what they wanted. It wasn't you sitting like Colin Turnbull [1972] in his Landrover, eating with the curtains drawn.

[Howell:] No, not at all. I threw away my T-shirt after a while. I worked with them quite hard. They have this manioc bread which I made as well. Once a week, we would spend two days making that for the whole community. I worked as hard as anybody.

I learned a lot by it! It was through doing it that I got all those little rules about correct practice that I call cosmo-rules because they link mundane life with cosmological consideration. It's in action that those rules become expressed. It's in the way you dig up the manioc. The way you treat game. It's not the straightforward way. The way you cut the rattan strips in order to make string, to tie everything—you've got to cut it in a certain way. Nobody would think of telling you unless you are doing it. This is why my book ended up called *Society and Cosmos* [Howell 1984] because these very mundane activities are actually bringing in the spirit world in the environment.

[Okely:] If you cut the rattan the wrong way or the manioc, then they corrected you.

[Howell:] They corrected me because you are a part of it. You've got to do it right. If I do it wrong, it's not that *I* have to suffer as a consequence. It's the whole community. You activate certain forces to cause illness, or some catastrophe by doing it wrong. That is what I learned, through all this.

The minutiae of these varied examples across space and time reveal the profundity of knowledge learned through participation, not by interrogation alone. *Never* voyeurism, shared activities inspire and transform theorization.

# –6–

# Fieldwork Embodied

## Body with Mind

The Cartesian mind/body dichotomy has privileged the cerebral in fieldwork, although cross-cultural ideas of the body have been elaborated theoretically in social anthropology (Mauss 1935; Douglas 1966; Blacking 1977; Polhemus 1978; Martin 1987; Csordas 1994, 2002). The bodily experience of the fieldworker has been under-scrutinized. Granted, the discipline has moved beyond any lingering tendency to present research as if conducted by a disembodied observer, lacking specificity. Some publications have ventured eroticized encounters, with ambiguous consequences (Abramson 1987; Wade 1993; Kulick and Willson 1995). Others have courageously exposed the rape of the fieldworker (Winkler 1994; Moreno 1995). But these do not change the broader analysis.

Learning about difference beyond the familiar and the avoidance of ethnocentrism, are a living challenge for anthropologists in the field. From prior socialization, whether Western or from elsewhere, fieldworkers are likely to have internalized a taken-for-granted embodiment and experienced the body as a 'memory' (Bourdieu 1977, 1984) of cultural, class and gendered positionality (Okely 1996b: chapter 7).

As examples in the preceding chapter suggested, bodily engagement is invariably implicit in participant observation. Here, it is made explicit. The anthropologists' conscious and hitherto unarticulated bodily adaptations are disentangled. The anthropologist unlearns or at least recognizes bodily knowledge from his or her lived past that impedes alternative interpretations. Here, fieldwork is examined as a process of physical labour, bodily interaction, sensory learning and transformations which constitute emergent knowledge for the production of written texts. Anthropological fieldwork gives a very different meaning to Willis's (1977) celebrated *Learning to Labour*.

## The Body and Embodied Knowledge

Many of the practices in fieldwork, which would not pass as methods in formal proposals, involve the body and ingestion. Stoller (1989) has argued for the importance of fieldwork as taste, an anti-cerebral interconnection of all the senses with labour and vision. There is the vivid example of Lévi-Strauss and the tree grubs (chapter 5). Fieldwork is eating worms. I absorbed culture through the mouth. I had to digest it. When drinking the still warm milk from a Normandy cow, I was drinking the landscape (Okely 2001). I also noted when, for example, the Gypsies refused commensality.

Part of my exhilaration in fieldwork was the active use of the body: I had to lift scrap metal or bales of hay; I had to carry, run and toil in the potato fields. The transition from armchair means more than travel across the miles, but active movement through the culturally worked and lived space. There was the mundane and the dramatic. I was not just the heroine adventurer. It was not a simplistic escape. It was an integrated means of knowing.

Anthropologists put their bodies on the line. Myerhoff's (1974) use of peyote on the sacred journey is a compelling argument about the insider's perspective of hallucinogens, combining embodied change with prior knowledge of the cultural symbols and narratives of experience. The people argue that the taking of the cactus is very individualistic, yet her description of being in contact with the Trickster is culturally informed. She had already acquainted herself with the others' beliefs which, in turn, affected her bodily experience.

Camus suggested that the actor is like an acrobat or sportsperson. She or he uses the body on stage to convey the character, text and drama. I extend that to the anthropologist who, unlike so many other academic disciplines, takes and uses his or her body out of library, lecture hall and cloister. Action is later theorized.

Some anthropologists, in climates different from those they are accustomed to, may have to work through days or weeks of sickness. Before fieldwork, they may have to take drugs, rather than think about taking drugs as part of indigenous practice. They are fending off vulnerabilities which, tragically, the tropical forest Indians could not when first encountering invading Europeans.

Fieldwork can be manual, not just a manual. I had tended to argue it as a must, until Johnny Parry convinced me that his acceptable identity as a scholar gave Brahminical overtones in India thus precluding much physical labour. Others have found that participation entailed labour. Incompetence served to confirm the local superior skills and was a positive marker of difference from aloof strangers.

Jackson (1989) called for 'a new experiential anthropology'. 'Eschewing the supervisory perspective of traditional empiricism (which, as Foucault observes, privileges gaze as an instrument of both knowledge and control), the radical empiricist tries to avoid fixed viewpoints, by dispersing authorship, working through all five senses, and reflecting inwardly, as well as observing outwardly' (Jackson 1989: 8).

## Arrivals as Sexed and Racialized Others

The biological sex and perceived 'race' of the fieldworker were often first bodily markers of identity for the people in whose group or society the anthropologists came to live. Considerable attention has been paid to the outsider's 'arrival' scenes in anthropologists' monographs (Pratt 1986), but little or no consideration has been given to the impact of the incomer anthropologist's arrival upon the hosts. This is an important omission, however, as the body of the anthropologist can be a marker for mystery and categorization through which the outsider may be genderized and racialized as 'other'.

Signe Howell, arriving among the Chewong in tropical forest Malaysia, found that people would scream whenever she approached them. Eventually they invited her to live with them. The crucial event, she discovered months later, was being seen bathing:

> Much later I was told this, when I got to know them very well, and they became very friendly, and I'd learnt their language pretty well. One evening we were talking, and the woman who became my 'mother', was laughing. I said: 'What did you think about me when I first arrived?' She said: 'We were frightened, especially the women and the children.' I knew they were frightened, because whenever they caught sight of me at a distance they would drop whatever they had and just turn around and scream! They laughed about that. She said: 'We just didn't know really what you were, who you were, what you wanted.' They hadn't ever seen a white woman before. They had seen some white men. Then one day, then she told me (they all laughed telling me this) how I had been bathing on my own, and a man had come past and he'd seen me. I hadn't seen him, but he'd then gone to the nearby houses and he'd said, 'It! It is a woman! It has breasts!' They all felt so happy because at least then I was definable. Women are much less frightening than men—at least outsiders. They're very frightened of outside men, for good reason.

In this vivid example, the female body of the fieldworker, considerably taller than the indigenous people, was eventually genderized, indeed sexed as less threatening, and enabled the anthropologist to gain easier acceptance.

Another example in Ghana reveals how the anthropologist was perceived initially as a white 'other'. But this was soon explained away. Louise de la Gorgendière (1993), as a white Canadian woman arriving in a Ghanaian village, was believed to be a 'confused ancestor' who had been born in the wrong body:

> When I first went to the village, the old lady that I interviewed said that she had only ever seen one other white person in the village, and couldn't understand why I had come there. That other white person was a missionary who had been there in the 1940s. No other white person had ever come. This was quite a miracle. What the people decided was that I was quite a confused individual. They thought I was an ancestor who had come back in a white person's body. They insisted on coming up with this same tale over and over again. Even when we were in the shrine, people would pour libations, and they would tell the ancestor: 'One of our ancestors has returned here, in the body of a Akua Afriyie.' They said to me, several times: 'You are one of our ancestors.' I said: 'Well, how do you explain my white body, and the fact that I'm Canadian?' They said: 'Somehow your spirit got confused.

But you've come. Why else would you come to this village? How could you know our language? How could you know our customs? How can you remember all our names after only two weeks?' I said: 'I read books. I've studied the language.' They said: 'Well, why *our* village? Of all the villages in Ghana, why *our* village?' That's typical of Asante. It's like talking about witchcraft, or the supernatural. You can explain scientifically why the tree falls down—but why did the tree fall down and kill that person? We would just say: 'Well, it's fate, or it's a coincidence.' They say: 'No. There's another reason behind that' [cf. Evans-Pritchard 1937].

In England, when I was living among the Gypsies (Okely 1983), my sexuality/ gender was exploited to sanction a man criticized for his womanizing. My bodily state was seized upon and distorted by another non-Gypsy woman to divert attention away from her own well-publicized sexual misbehaviour. When I told the woman that I had a stomach upset, she passed on a complete fabrication that I was pregnant. This successfully encouraged the Travellers to focus on my alleged sexual misbehaviour rather than that of my accuser. Next, the Travellers used me as outsider to draw attention indirectly to the real past sexual misbehaviour of another Traveller. He had a reputation for womanizing and, when he ran off with another Traveller's wife some years previously this resulted in a deadly feud. For their own purposes, the camp residents claimed I was now pregnant by this same Gypsy man whom they wished to censure for his past. I, as outsider non-Gypsy, was a convenient target to settle old internal Gypsy scores. Elsewhere, I have elaborated how I managed to resolve this potentially dangerous accusation (Okely 2005).

Helena Wulff was also made aware of her gendered and racialized identity first, via her body. She had to adapt accordingly. Studying teenage girls in south London in the early 1980s, urban fieldwork was dangerous for a young woman. She and another young woman anthropologist were initially unprepared. She had to clothe her body correctly and learn how to walk, move and look in a different way from her past bodily experience:

> When we went to the cinema, we had to take precautions. People were raped and murdered all around us. It was dangerous in the tube. The area is now gentrified. We dressed casually in sneakers and jeans and tried to walk like a man so the cars wouldn't stop. I learned how to walk in the street so as to be safe—not too close to the cars. My landlady taught me that if there was a strange character approaching, you had to turn without appearing to be avoiding him. To avoid being mugged, don't have a handbag. I always put money in my shoe so I could take a taxi home. It was better that I was Swedish than being British.

Not only had Wulff to reconfigure her visible gendered identity but she was also confronted with her unchangeable white identity; something which she could not corporally change. A key incident occurred when she was queuing for a reggae concert in Brixton. She was naïvely and visibly holding up her ticket. A black boy ran past and grabbed it. Her friends said he would never have taken it from a black girl.

Although her black girl friends were angry, she realized this was what it was like for them:

> I was very upset in the tube. I was thinking: 'I'm Swedish. Sweden has never been colonialist. It's not my fault that I'm white.' It was inverted racism. I looked down at my skin. I couldn't change it. It was extremely educative to experience racism. That was what it's like—humiliation. You can't do anything about it. I couldn't change the colour of my skin.

Thus the anthropologist learned painfully how 'race', as skin colour, may permanently essentialize identity.

## The Body Moving, Sitting, Standing and Working

When anthropologists live alongside a different people, they may not be first categorized by their sex/gender and 'race'. In other instances it is not necessarily the racialized and gendered impressions which the anthropologist conveys to his or her hosts, but the total bodily language and stance. This, for Kaminski, a Polish refugee, was a vital aspect of his acceptance, not only among Irish Travellers or Roma elsewhere, but also in Lapland and Greenland. He attributed the trust he elicited to his deferential or visibly harmless, near vulnerable approach to strangers and stigmatized minorities.

In 1975, after hitchhiking to the west of Ireland, Kaminski and I pitched our tent for the night on an unauthorized Traveller camp. We were greeted with curiosity and amusement by the children and suffered no hostility. Kaminski indeed performed the naïve foreigner and years later recalled:

> Never, ever in my involvement with Gypsies has anyone stolen from me. We project onto minority groups like Tinkers. I am talking about our sleeping over inside the Tinkers' camp.

He elaborated on how bodily movement may convey inner feelings. He attributed his approach to learned experience as a child, dependent in an orphanage:

> We project patronizing, uncertain feelings with our movements. Because of my life experience, (I was living outside my home family. I had to leave when I was five years old and go to the orphanage), I had in some way gathered non-verbal communication signals which I project onto other people, because in most cases, I was entering the most dangerous situation. I should have been knifed, or killed, or raped, or whatever, and nothing happened to me. I believe in some way we project that innocence, or ignorance sometimes. It could also be interpreted as the core of humanity—we trust that other person.
>
> So my contact with Gypsies was always the same, I believe they could interpret my reaction as always friendly, as nothing hidden. Like a dog meeting the more powerful beast, they will lie on their back and show four legs. I think my entire social situation was of that dog with the four legs, so I was left un-attacked and allowed to stay.

I believe I project without knowing it, because it was the same when I was in Greenland and meeting the guys with the guns when we were shooting, or in Lapland when I was left in the forest suddenly, and alone. Then the Laplanders brought me back to their things, and allowed me to meet criminal groups—always in some way this non-verbal communication. Somebody told me that dogs attack us because, when we are scared, we have some kind of smell, which they can feel. I believe there are social situations, it could be non-verbal, but the way we look, the way we approach the person, brings hostility or welcoming. Gypsies, so many times, are trained through generations to perceive the signals, not only Gypsies, but all marginal groups.

Thus the arrival of the anthropologist is also linked to his or her prior knowledge and personality. Transformations may occur after time. The simplest and seemingly taken-for-granted bodily movements, posture and actions are subject to new, unpredictable scrutinies. The anthropologist may attempt to adjust. But sometimes such attempts reveal how skilled or culturally loaded different uses of the body can be.

For several anthropologists, the very act of walking through tropical forests was difficult, as well as hazardous. For Morris (1982), with hunter-gatherers in tropical forest India, it was especially sobering to realize that he could not keep up with an elderly woman. His relatively youthful body was exposed as incompetent:

> On one occasion this woman would've been about seventy years of age. She was only five foot and very slender. I was finding it difficult to keep up with her. It was incongruous that this thirty-four-year-old, sort of in my prime, traipsing behind this little woman and she was jumping over logs and scrambling over streams and I was trying to keep up with her.

## The Labouring Body: Skills Recognized

The anthropologists learned through embodied participation. Recognition of their own physical limitations was profoundly informative. Morris was shocked that he could not walk even at the pace of an elderly woman, neither could he slash the undergrowth as effectively as young children:

> You had to bash this creeper with an adze. Now I used to work in a foundry, so I was used to hard work. It nearly killed me this job. This particular day I was faint. I was completely exhausted. I looked around and these little kids were bashing away! There were lots of occasions like that where I thought I'm just physically not up to this.

Talib developed an entire theory from observing the stone-breakers whose labour was their value:

> Slowly I realized that these workers were earning their wage by smashing stones, producing stone chips out of huge boulders, using their chisels and their hammer. Their life energy was being expended in producing that. It had an exchange value. At the same time,

I noticed that there was body energy also spent in producing expressions. These symbols were not just idle. Life energy had gone in to it. So at the time of expression they had also undergone some experience, which, in a very fundamental way, qualified them to speak about it. If they are speaking about poverty, it is not an alien subject. It is part of their life. They've lived it.

Therefore, labour was a substratum of exchange value but it was also a substratum of symbols that the stone-breakers were using in life. It had a use value.

## Milking Cows

I asked to hand-milk cows at the first meeting with a Normandy woman farmer. She was so astonished at my seeming subversion of her French image of '*une professeur*' that she disappeared, only to return with a flash camera. She photographed me attempting to milk the cow. Thus the anthropologist's body at work was also something to be recorded and othered by the indigenous subject.

The added significance of that first encounter with hand-milking was an introduction to a bodily skill in collaboration with an animal's body and one which seemed also to respond to, if not understand, French. As a human animal, I was also relating to the named, individualized cow: 'Mère No-No'. She had been chosen for me out of the dozen others because she was more tolerant of strangers. Madame Grégoire had made me realize the specificity of cows whose personalized treatment she made an entire way of working (Okely 1996b: 227–9). My apprenticeship had eventually to be abandoned due to a repetitive strain injury (but through a very different cause from computer-bound theoreticians). Local experts explained that someone had ideally to start hand-milking from the age of five to avoid injury.

Learning to participate through labour also has its instrumental rewards. It opens avenues. When meeting aged residents in Normandy retirement homes, it was always a conversation opener when I revealed that I was learning to hand-milk cows. This evoked past and shared experiences among the women '*agriculteurs*'. They talked of their own skills and volunteered extended narratives in mutual trust (Okely 1994b). My bodily participation had redefined my identity by establishing rapport with manual labourers, beyond the bourgeoisie.

## Rolling Tent Felt or Climbing Trees

Lindisfarne, among Pashtun nomads in Afghanistan, also learned how hard domestic tasks were without practice:

> Physical learning is extremely important because of the weight, the demandingness of it. You can't really estimate how hard it is to roll wool into tent felt by just looking. They make it look easy. Because they're good at it!

Morris, in tropical forest India, spoke about tree climbing for honey:

> What really surprised me—it wasn't my lack of knowledge that made me a poor hunter-gatherer. I learned where the yams were. It was my lack of physical prowess. I could not climb these trees. I started practicing. You put your arms round the tree, as if you were going to hug it, you put your insteps on the bark. You pushed with your knees. You held on with your arms as you pushed with your feet—that created friction. Then you walked up. So the Pandaram actually walked up trees sideways. The children learnt, boys and girls, from an early stage. These trees were 100, 120 feet up. The honey is on the underside of the branches. They would do this just after dusk. I hadn't got a hope in the world of climbing up these trees like that. It wasn't common, but it was extremely dangerous if you slipped.

He subsequently realized the full extent of the risk and demands in this bodily labour when a close friend, who had acquired the skills as an indigenous member, fell to his death after years of experience.

## The Scholar Rather than Labouring Body

In some instances, the anthropologist was appreciated best as scholar, and manual labour would have no instrumental benefits. Describing his fieldwork in Greece, Herzfeld elaborated:

> We were able to go grape picking. But they wouldn't dream of letting me do any of the heavy physical labour. Now other people have managed to do this. I think it has a lot to do with where you are and how you come in. In Glendi the villagers liked the idea that they had a 'scholar', especially after I'd ceased to be a student and become, in Greek terms, a professor.

Similarly, Parry, when first conducting fieldwork in northern India, was in most contexts respected as a Brahminical scholar who did not do manual labour. Mohammad Talib explicitly recognized how the body is encultured through biography and class trajectory. An adult academic's body cannot dramatically change when contrasted with those of professional stone-breakers:

> Even to use their implements, which they would use very easily, I couldn't even lift them—something that they were using actively. Class and body are really interlinked. Being brought up in a particular class situation gives your body certain rhythms, certain levels of tolerance. The month of June in Delhi would have two sets of temperatures. If it is 47° at the quarry, it would be 45° or 44° elsewhere, because the silica stone would get heated up very easily. To be working under the sun is something that I would have difficulty tolerating—that exposure for a long time. If I used my own umbrella or any other protection, then that would set me off from them, demarcate them, contrast them, as if I'm privileged, I stand apart from them.

Some of these workers would be breaking stones under the sun. They would tolerate a certain level of exposure which I would not. The same temperature that would dehydrate me would not dehydrate them. This is the distinction which brings us to this point of biological body, physical rhythms, and class on the other hand. Maybe we get conditioned in certain ways. This is something that I explore. Then, of course, this lifting of their sledgehammer, they would use it and I won't even be able to lift it. There used [to] be that wooden cart, on which they would carry stones. They would do it effortlessly. I would have to struggle to even lift it.

## Bodily Imitation

There are more subtle ways in which the fieldworker learns about the social system in which he or she is living through unknowing, unconscious imitation or deliberate bodily mimesis. Such imitations include ways of sitting, standing and moving to music in dance. The anthropologist may find himself or herself closely scrutinized and instructed. She or he may risk causing offence by transgressing the boundaries of what was believed to be 'natural'. Conscious adjustment may be interpreted as respect.

At other times, the anthropologist may, without instruction and without knowing, empathetically pick up the mood of the other person and absorb it in similar bodily posture. A photograph (Okely 1992: 18) shows me talking with a Gypsy woman who had willingly posed for a non-Gypsy photographer whom I knew well. I had unconsciously identified with the woman's involuntary barrier posture of arms folded.

The anthropologist, if outsider, can rarely become a native in the formal sense, but through co-residence, learning the language and in dialogue and participation in the day-to-day, can modify his or her position as complete outsider. The anthropologist's posture has to reflect and fit in with those of the hosts. It may help to merge in, to become part of the crowd, if not near invisible.

Okazaki left Japan as very young man, seemingly to explore a non-literate culture. Just as Mauss (1935) argued decades earlier, Okazaki then found that the most ordinary ways of standing were culturally specific. He delighted in the embodied transformation:

When I was among the Masai, I started to learn half consciously how to rest, because their way of taking a rest is quite different from Japanese. They stand on one leg and have the spear here. It becomes comfortable. This is most fun. I can feel myself different. That is what I wanted. I become more aware of the Japanese posture and way of using the body. If I do not copy it, I can't be so much aware of that. I feel real freedom using the body in different ways. The body, I thought before, was completely fixed physically and biologically. But it was not like that. That is an amazing revelation.

So, even when I was not an anthropologist, not only in Sudan, but also when I was in a Nairobi shantytown, I tried to copy their way of sitting and their way of talking to woman and that sort of thing. It might be romantic, but it liberated my own body. Sometimes I still do, when I'm in Japan waiting for the train or something like that, (standing on one leg) with my umbrella.

McLeod reflected on posture in Ghana:

> It's not just a matter of politeness but communication and respect, as well as hierarchy. Facial expression is very important, and knowing where to look, how to look, when to show your eyes, when to look down, when to look directly at people, how to listen to them, how to sit properly. There are great subtleties there. I'm not sure how you actually learn them, except by very close and careful observation. But on the other hand, you've got to be taught how to do that. You've got to be taught that there is something worth learning there.

Also in Ghana, de la Gorgendière benefited from explicit instructions on correct bodily postures from her Ghanaian research assistant before she visited people of high rank. But for McLeod, the lessons were acquired over extended time:

> It took me *years* to notice in Asante, if a court case is being tried, or people are listening to traditions being recited, or enquiring into history, there are very high levels of detailed observation to which you are subject. There is a particular form of glance at crucial moments, when you suddenly spot someone actually putting the eye on you. It's almost like an X-ray eye, and it goes right through you. If you're not in the right position, doing the right things, when that happens, you're marked down. A lot of people never even become aware that is going on. I'm sure you pick it up unconsciously. You have to—all the very basic things. You don't cross your legs. You're not getting lefts and rights mixed up. You don't hand people things with your left hand— the distance from which you put yourself from other people, or touching them. In many circumstances, it is closer. You should touch people. You should hold them. But it's *much* more subtle! It's the facial expressions, the posture—almost the breathing. There are rhythms in the speech. There are rhythms in the dance. There are rhythms in the music. There are rhythms in the way people move, which are very subtle. You do learn them unconsciously. I have seen some very eminent experts on the Asante and their culture—European experts—doing this all wrong. They're excused, because they're outsiders. But even if you get slightly closer to them, you begin to see things like that.

Herzfeld noticed how the Greeks adjusted their bodies to linguistic subtleties and seemed to learn the same without knowing it:

> They will also stop in the middle of a sentence and savour the sound of a word, which I think is much more to do with the body, than some intellectual operation. I'm told that when I speak Greek my whole bodily appearance changes, but you'd have to ask somebody else about that.

Again, the anthropologist may pick up and absorb cultural cues through a near-unconscious empathy, not only through deliberate conscious imitation.

## Sitting

McLeod spoke of Western visitors to Ghana:

> There was a black American scholar who was waiting to make an appointment to see the King outside the King's secretary's office, and causing this slight embarrassment. He was all slumped in a chair, chewing gum, with his legs crossed, and his feet higher than his head, in the air. He could've shat on the floor. That would've made it *slightly* worse, but probably not much.

The manner of sitting in a group among settled nomads in Iran, Wright noted, was interpreted as a reflection of a person's position in the world. The wrong posture was seen as an indication of vulnerability and loss of status and control. A person had to be 'collected'; cross-legged with hands and feet all tucked in:

> I would get this *intense* care about how I behaved. That was shown in the body—an acceptable way to sit; your feet out of sight and your hands, your elbows on your knees, so that you've got a complete circle. Little children were told by their parents: 'Collect your hands and feet together.' That was the way I learnt to sit when I wanted to be in control of the situation. Because it meant that they were reading me as collected. I think the idea of balance is a crucial one. You've got cross-cutting ties all around you, if you're a tribesperson. You're trying not to offend anybody. You're trying to hold everything together, because if you can keep control, then you are not attacked. Again, particularly the way the men would sit, and would look; straight eye-contact, straight one-to-one. I didn't realize until after a while that I'd adopted this very masculine way of relating with the men. This was when I was included in men's meetings. But when walking in the alleys, I realized with a jolt that I had brought up my hand, as if holding an imaginary chador, to shield myself from the gaze of a man walking towards me.

Margaret Kenna, arriving as a young unmarried woman on a Greek island, behaved in what she thought was a modest fashion. Only years later, did she discover that sitting with crossed legs was considered to be the posture of a prostitute, because apparently this twisted the womb and prevented conception (Kenna 1992: 153). Herzfeld, in contrast, learned the subtleties of the bodily position when sitting and playing cards with the men in Crete:

> I'm not a card player, or I hadn't been. I learned some of *their* games. There's a certain kind of bodily posture, because you're trying not to give things away. You're assuming a bodily posture of comfort, but also engagement. Those things I certainly was aware of and they had to do with participating.

## The Body Culturally Clothed

In Afghanistan Lindisfarne and her partner were asked to dress like locals. She was teased for walking like a man. She had to learn to walk with yards of billowing cloth as trousers. She learned to love the chador and the invisibility it gave. As she and her husband left and travelled westwards back to the United Kingdom, she was obliged to abandon this 'comfort' cloth. It had become part of her body and identity:

> I wore the women's clothing, which included a long black veil, a *chadari,* as they called it in Pashtu, which didn't veil my face, but which was a head covering, and that went down to the ground. I wore wide dresses, which were waisted with an embroidered yoke, then trousers which were ten metres of cloth—huge, billowing harem trousers.
>
> But I was always being teased by how I wore the long black veil and by the fact that I walked like a soldier. My style of walking did not cater for the very voluminous trousers, and the veil. You had to hold your head in a certain way or the veil would fall off. When I went to the shrines I would practice trying to be invisible, so that I wasn't the foreigner. Those things were exciting to learn, and completely non-verbal. I became very fond of my veil, how I could use it to watch without being watched. I still have this sense of what you can do with a veil. Learning to go to sleep! There were always people around. But learning to do what other women did—lay down—absolutely wherever you were—pull the veil over your head and you could go to sleep. Because you weren't there!

Thus, contrary to Western ethnocentric presumptions, through bodily experience, the veil is primarily learned to be a comfort, protection and pleasure.

In other contexts, a slight shift in clothing and bodily appearance can inform the anthropologist how the subjects are perceived and treated by outsiders, as Gigengack and Alonso experienced in Mexico City. Gigengack explained:

> Body language—that's very important, also the language of what's transmitted through how people look. Once we were doing research in the bus station. We had been eating a taco which was not that good. Raquel was feeling sick so she looked pale. She had to throw up. It was cold and I had given her my sweater. We had been doing fieldwork the whole day. So the sweater was a little bit grubby and way too big for her. I had bought some water for her, which at that particular bus station, the street children use to put their solvents in.
>
> Raquel then got comments from taxi drivers—if she wanted to go home with the taxi drivers. They were whistling at her. The reactions were very different than normally. She looked like one of the girls because she was looking pale. She was looking bad, vulnerable. Her clothes were too big, grubby. She had the water which they could identify as solvent. This is an indication of how people read the street and the body language of the street children—not only anthropologists, but also bystanders.

As a visiting male, Kaminski had to retain his daytime clothing in the pristine beds which Gypsies in Sweden offered him:

> When I was going with the Gypsy to make that business and we had to stay in different Gypsy households, my Gypsy friend told me: 'Marek, you have to sleep in your trousers, because you are a man and you are visiting.' All the Gypsy households in Sweden were super-hygienic, always clean—beautiful. They took care of their houses, so they are giving

me beautiful white sheets. But then I am staying in my trousers. I felt strange, because in my own culture I would take them off.

## The Body Dancing

Changing bodily movement can be an entry into ritual and cultural representations. Laura Bohannon (Smith-Bowen 1954) and Powdermaker (1967) learned in Africa and in New Guinea the deeper knowledge gained by participating and dancing in contrast to standing as unmoving spectators. Bohannon realized through the movements required, how complex were the demands on the different parts of the body.

For Hughes-Freeland (1997, 2001; Hughes-Freeland and Crain 1998) specializing in dance in Indonesia, to dance became central. Her experience might be a condensed metaphor for other anthropologists. She had to dance differently. The movements were slow and subtle in ways unrecognized in the cultural traditions of much Western dance (Hughes-Freeland 2008b: chapter 4).

In the 1970s, the body was still seen as something to be concealed and cerebralized in public academic interchange. At an Association of Social Anthropologists conference on the Anthropology of the Body (Blacking 1977), David Brooks took the subject seriously and, as part of his presentation, performed the Bakhtiari stick dance on the platform. However, a celebrated anthropology professor at London University bizarrely declared that he 'brought the discipline into disrepute'. It was, even in the 1970s, curiously permissible for British, if not other academic anthropologists, to dance in their own ballroom style at the conference evening social, but not as cross-cultural performance on the speakers' platform (Brooks, personal communication, 1977; see also Okely 2007a: 236–8).

Yet, as the examples of Bohannon and Powdermaker have long illustrated, dance as musical movement of the body has been integral to certain contexts in fieldwork, whether or not the anthropologist chooses to focus on dance in a subsequent ethnography. Herzfeld reflects this:

> I've always been very open to new experiences and enjoyed them and looked for them. In terms of bodily carriage, some forms of Greek dancing are quite different from anything that we do in Britain as a local tradition. I think that the performance and spontaneity is one. That's when the performance and spontaneity becomes very clear. It's no coincidence that in the film *Zorba the Greek,* dance plays such an important part, especially that final scene.
>
> I knew one or two dances. I wasn't very good at picking up steps, so I tended to dance in the way that I already knew, which I partly learned when a student at Cambridge. There's a very fast Cretan men's dance called the *pendozalis* which I found exhilarating, but incredibly exhausting, if you're stuck between two burly Cretan shepherds who spend all their time prancing around in the foothills.
>
> It helped in making me feel that I was part of the scene and making *them* feel that I was more part of the scene. But I wasn't focusing all that much on dance.

Wulff used her previous ballet experience to make ethnographic sense of dance in the West. Here she used familiarity with aspects of her own culture and, unusually, years of prior balletic bodily training to interpret and produce her ethnography (Wulff 1998). Neveu, as explored earlier, found prior dance knowledge important for access and mutual respect. Likewise, Silverman drew on previous practice, explaining how dance revealed relationships and the extent of the outsider's integration:

> I'm a dancer and a musician. To me, that is body work right there. My fascination with Roma and the Balkans started, in general, through dance. In the Balkans, when you're walking down the street and you see a dance line from a wedding, you may be invited to join. People say: 'Oh you know our dances!' I've even been asked to sing: 'Offer us a song in praise of somebody'. That's important. Some Americans take this to the extreme and abuse it. They're not invited to a Bulgarian wedding, but they see one on the street and they get at the front of the line and start leading and telling people what to do. But I never get up to dance unless I'm asked or unless it's in honour of somebody. In Romany dancing there are very specific ways of using your body if you're a woman. You have to be extremely careful about what kind of sexual messages you're giving, with whom you're dancing, how far away you are, whether you're on a dance line or doing a solo in the middle. All of these embodied experiences helped me decipher social relations because the dance line is an interpretation. The dance line interprets and negotiates social relations. I've written a lot about dancing among women and men and what it says about marital status, availability, the use of the body and sexuality. I definitely feel I'm using the body.

Thus dance, as a non-cerebral, culturally flexible body, can no longer be scandalously dismissed in anthropological academic discourse as seemed once the case.

## The Body Sleeping

Overing had to learn the basics such as how to sleep in a hammock:

> The first time it took me a week to learn how to sleep on my back. But a hammock's marvellous. I was *dreaming* of a hammock in 1977, going to sleep in a hammock. My back was hurting and a hammock was right for your back. It holds you just perfect. You sleep at a diagonal—you have to know what you're doing, how it's hung—the height, and the dip, then you get the best bed you can possibly get, unless it's a cold climate, or a windy one. Because then the wind comes up underneath, and you're cold.

## The Senses

Anthropologists and social scientists in general, as well as those in the humanities, are reclaiming sensations for intellectual enquiry (Howes 2003; Okely 2001). The anthropologist in the field, whether it has been fully confronted in the past, absorbs also through the skin and learns through all the senses.

## Tasting

Through hours of participating in hand-milking and shared dialogue with Madame Grégoire, I learned her views about farming and cultivation. She refused to feed her cows concentrates and use pesticides. To prove her point, she invited me to drink her cow's pure and uncontaminated milk (Okely 1996b: chapter 10; 2001). My exploration of taste among the small farmers in Normandy, especially their knowledge of cider has countered the presumption by Bourdieu (1984: 177–200) that only the bourgeoisie have taste or 'distinction' (Okely 1994b, 2001).

## Smell

Smells are involuntarily absorbed whether they be the evocative memory of dampened vegetation and earth in Africa or the lingering odour of sheep and goats on the men with whom Herzfeld associated:

> One thing that has remained as a not very pleasant memory in my nostrils, again, given an interest in smell, was the smell of sheep. All of the men of course, their clothes smell, they reek of sheep, and goat. These people wash a great deal, they're very careful about their personal hygiene. I recognize there's a faint tinge of nostalgia now when I think about it, because I also associate it with the marvellous times I had in the village. I think smell is a tremendously important carrier of connections between periods of one's life. It's also sometimes a way of connecting those periods of one's life with larger historical periods, which is why I try to do the smellscape as a way of introducing the embodied sense of history of the people of Rehemnos [Herzfeld 1991].

Gigengack also confronted the ubiquity of odours:

> I wrote in my book on the odours, on the smells of street children, which at the time I noticed, without thinking, because people never think about what they smell unless perhaps you're trained to do so. These odours in retrospect were very important, because of how street children smell. Their smells functioned as markers of where the wastelands are. The wasteland doesn't only look like a mess but smells like a mess. That's an important part of the reality they live.
>
> They knew that they all smelt but they were very ready to indicate people who smelt worse. There were also differences amongst themselves. One guy was called Satinas . . . he smelt so bad because he never wanted to wash. So among them there were differences in smell. Also important was the drugs, because the glues and the solvents smelt. They have a very pungent odour. They tried to make up a performance, especially in front of me. I was the Dutch friend, the *compadre,* they wanted to make the impression that they didn't use

drugs. So they said: 'No, I'm not using drugs,' it's also part of drug use that very often the drug user will want to negate what's going on. But then the smell gave it away.

For others, the smell of landscape is ever evocative in a Proustian sense. Louise de la Gorgendière, described what happened on her return to the African continent:

> All of a sudden the smell of the *soil* of Africa just comes back. It has a *very* distinctive smell. If I am walking in the rain, whether in Edinburgh, Cambridge, or Canada, and I am in a forested area, or beside a garden, and that smell comes up, from damp soil, I am *instantly* transported to the village. *Instantly.* I never believed that my sense of smell was that acute. But I can just get that sense of smell, and I'm instantly transported.
>
> If I see anything in little triangle stacks, as they would have been on the tables, in Ghana, I'm instantly transported back—the colours and the music. I was far more attuned with *all* my senses than I really realized until I closed my eyes and tried to visualize it all again. Because it wasn't just visual, it was auditory *and* sensory . . . nasal.

## The Body at Risk

The anthropologist in the field cannot always hold back in caution but she or he may put her or his body, if not life, on the line. Learning through the body can be a source of pain and illness. Parry, studying death rituals in Banaras, had to ingest, against his judgement: 'One was always being given Ganges water as part of the consecrated offering, it would be poured into your hand which you would raise to drink it.'

He became very ill after drinking from a well, said to be sacred. He knew that, at that time of the year, it was likely to be risky:

> What actually gave me what was diagnosed as typhoid—I was certainly very ill—it was not Ganges water, but it was water from a particular well that was said to be sacred. It was during the beginning of the rains, so it was very hot, and that's when water tends to be most infected. Water was drawn from this well, especially for me. I had gone to see the well, and ask about it. What else would you do? But give a kind of honoured visitor, some honorific and sacred water. It wouldn't have been impossible to refuse, but it would've been extremely difficult. People in Banaras were very *assertive* about these kinds of things: 'Ganges water is pure and you come here, and you claim that you have great respect, asking us all these questions about ritual and religion.' To ostentatiously refuse would not have done my rapport much good. It was in Banaras. It was just behind the cremation ghats [burning funeral pyres].

Similarly, Okazaki found the need to accept hospitality despite the risks:

> My first trip to that area was cut short because I suffered hepatitis. I have to drink when they tried to give me some alcohol and I know that harms my liver and maybe that may be the end of my life. I couldn't refuse.

But on his return from convalescing in Japan, he found the people welcoming and sympathetic to his earlier ill health.

Overing described how she was ill, but not with malaria, in the South American tropical forest. She did not resort to Myerhoff's strategy:

> I was too ill with parasites. The irony is, I discovered later, that if I had taken them [hallucinogens], it's one of the best cures! They're a medicine! I didn't because I was just too out of it. I was not very well. I would've. But I didn't.

Some anthropologists have undergone rites of passage with the inevitable painful stages as embodied means of learning. Thus, pain and unforeseen risks may become participant experience extended from participant observation.

## Dead Bodies

The cultural fate of the dead body can be a revelation into a society's priorities. Shilling (1993) and others have confronted the dominant medicalization and privatization of death in the West, suggesting that this is consistent with the cult of the body beautiful, and secularization, which gives no recompense for death in any afterlife.

But in one centre of Western classical culture, Greece, there are different ways of dealing with the dead. The decomposition of the body is confronted. Kenna, when asked about learning through the body, volunteered a stark example: the practice of relatives digging up the grave of their dead in an exhumation a year after the burial. The near fleshless bones are lifted out of the ground and placed in containers. This focused Kenna on the continuity of genealogies and the significance of naming passed on from one generation to another in her Greek island fieldwork. The bones were stark emblems of the end of individuals, but their collection by descendants, named after them, ensured vital continuity.

## Embodied Memories for the Production of Texts

When returning from the field and writing up, as opposed to writing down field notes, the anthropologist is faced with a mass of recorded material and months of memories (Jackson 1990). Ottenberg (1990) has referred to 'headnotes'—what is not written down, remembered observations. I would prefer a less cerebral store of memory. Field notes are records for evidence, direct quotations and even quantitative data, but they may also act as mnemonic triggers of a total experience. Making sense of fieldwork is also a bodily process. The writer recognizes themes and sorts out what seemed incomprehensible puzzles because she can feel it in her bones and flesh, although she or he will be seated and relatively still, while working through the material and submerged memories (Okely 1994a).

Knowing others through the instrument of the fieldworker's own body, involves deconstructing the body as a cultural, biographical construction through lived and interactive encounters with others' cultural construction and bodily experience. This is not merely verbal, nor merely cerebral, but a kinetic and sensual process, both conscious and unconscious and which occurs in unpredictable, uncontrollable ways. The fieldworker may be newly marked as sexed, racialized and othered in different contexts. There are bodily risks, pains and pleasures. The anthropologist learns anew to sit, talk, stand, walk, dress, dance and labour at hitherto untried tasks. Fieldwork contrasts with the sedentary practices of the academic. This process is often counter-intuitive when compared to the anthropologist's original cultural socialization, yet, after extended participation, may become instinctive. Narratives reveal the anthropologists' transformations through embodiment and emerge as vital paths to the acquisition of knowledge, the analysis and the writing of cultural alternatives.

# −7−

# Specificities and Reciprocity

## Positionality

There is fear that confronting the 'observer effect' is indulgence or terrifying self-exposure. But it is not about the observer; it is about the interaction between the anthropologist and others. From that continuous encounter, the ethnographies emerge (Okely 1992). The specificity, positionality and personal history of the anthropologist are resources to be explored, not repressed. Powdermaker long ago insisted: 'A scientific discussion of field work method should include considerable detail about the observer' (1967: 9). Discrediting the lone fieldworker rests on a myth. The anthropologist was never the lone scholar, but interacting with many persons, some of whom become research associates and close friends. In contrast to many social science approaches, the anthropologist interacts, indeed *must* interact directly and daily with people as subjects.

It is even more puzzling why some multi-disciplinary ethics committees regard it as 'scientifically contaminating' if the researcher has known the people over a long time span. Anthony Simpson's research application to interview adults whom he had taught as schoolboys in Zambia (2003) was initially condemned by a non-anthropologist on his university ethics committee for that very reason (personal communication). The interviewees' answers would be 'contaminated' because they already knew the interrogator (cf. Macdonald 2010). Positivism lives. Fortunately, an eminent anthropologist on the committee explained that it is methodologically *crucial* that anthropologists get to know their subjects in depth and over time. Simpson's (2009) successful follow-up research has produced a pioneering study of HIV and masculinity.

Similarly, my doctoral student, Clive Foster (1995, 1998), was interviewed in the 1990s concerning a research grant from the chief scientist's office at the Scottish Office. Haranguing him about lack of 'control groups', they had *no* understanding of participant observation. It was deemed unscientific that the ex-borstal boys, now many HIV-positive adults through heroin needles, whom Foster had known in their teens, now asked *him* to record their perspective. They trusted him, unlike 'all these people pestering us with questionnaires', because Edinburgh was labelled 'the AIDS capital of Europe'. Foster explains:

> Since the research was to assess the nature and availability of lay care for heroin users who were HIV/AIDS, it was necessary to go before the Ethics Committee of the local health board. Their conclusion at this interrogation was that they would not sanction 'such an unstructured

research protocol'. Several weeks later, I received a letter from them to the effect that since the research was essentially anthropological they would no longer consider it their concern.

Fortunately a powerful anthropologist had enlightened the health board as to participant observation.[1]

## Insider/Outsider

The fieldworker is both researcher and analyst/author. Thus, the positionality of the researcher, with or without partner, family and assistants, has implications for access and focus (Weil 1987; Okely 2009a). Already the examples above reveal the chance advantages of long-term trust. The gender, nationality, ethnicity, age and personality will clearly affect both initial and long-term inter-relations (Whitehead and Conaway 1986; Okely and Callaway 1992; Reed-Danahay1997).

There were clear implications as to the 'foreign' or 'native' identity of the anthropologists I interviewed. Many fulfilled the image of the outsider/stranger. But some returned to the places of their childhood or where they had connections. Zulaika studied his own Basque village. Talib having, as Indian citizen, studied in Delhi, chose to research stone-breakers near the capital. Neveu, of Franco/Senegalese parentage, largely brought up in France, chose Dakar, Senegal as her field site, with early childhood memories:

> There were personal reasons. Doing the fieldwork was partly an excuse to get to know Senegal better because my father's family is from Senegal. There was a connection, but I'd never lived there. I was keen to re-establish that connection which had never really been there.

Anthropology has attracted individuals linked with more than one culture, through parentage or upbringing (Jan Mohamed 1992; Okely 2000, 2003a). Powdermaker recognized her ambivalence towards any monoculture: 'Long before I ever heard of anthropology, I was being conditioned for the role of stepping in and out of society' (1967: 19). Similarly, Hughes-Freeland stated:

> Anthropologists are often outsiders. They've had experiences in their childhood or they've lived in other countries. Something's happened or they've come from outside. Often one doesn't feel one belongs. So in the field experience, you passionately want to be accepted. Belonging is very important.

## Gender, Marital Status and Generation

The gender and status of the anthropologist, as single or accompanied, has implications. Hughes-Freeland had an idealized view of couples:

A lot of people do anthropology in couples. I envy them hugely. It's far easier if you're a husband and wife with a baby and your own house. I didn't have that high-status lifestyle. But I do have a lot of ethnography of Javanese students or Indonesian students because of where I lived—Sumatran kids and some other Javanese—all of us living in very basic rat-infested student digs.

Morris found his gendered identity problematic:

In Malawi it's difficult to talk across genders. You can't go into somebody's house even if it's a young man and an elderly woman. Two people going into a hut together, they think of only one thing. Doing things in public: you're surrounded with kids and everybody else. It was the same in India. It was difficult to speak to women on my own. *They* found it difficult. When I went with women in Malawi into the forest to collect mushrooms, they were always taking the 'micky' [teasing or making fun of] out of me.

Zulaika, initially a bachelor among his own Basque people, could be more flexible:

I was dancing at the disco. I had to show my gender a lot, no? I met a girl who had been in ETA. I came to know very personally a few of them. So they gave me the gender perspective from ETA and how much the actions were male dominated.

Silverman's specificity enhanced the comprehension of American Kalderash Roma pollution taboos:

As an unmarried woman, I had to associate with unmarried women. I was in my mid-twenties. They were in their late teens. I was in a different age-group but in the same category of persons. My unmarried status was important because everyone was watching me. They didn't want somebody around who acted inappropriately. As they taught me to clean the house, I began to understand the categories of symbolic pollution, below the waist. My analysis of pollution and gender came out of practice: being a tutor for the children, a maid, and helping with fortune telling letters. Those were the things they needed help with, that is, from a woman. There was no way that a man could have done the fortune-telling research. A male anthropologist would have done a different project. My work is not very strong in male arenas—I didn't have the access. People did trust me enough that I could talk to men, go to their car lots, and observe with other women. I had gendered access. We have to write about that instead of pretending that we are neutered. There's richness in that as well.

The traditional male anthropological perspective was to exclude children but, as this and other examples reveal, there are advantages in bringing children. Morris explained:

Heimendorf said: 'Don't take the children to the field, they'll interfere with your research.' In fact, rather than the children and being a married man being a handicap, it was the opposite. People are very suspicious of single men. There's also the fear that there might be spies. Being a married man with three children, took a lot of edge off.

My then partner, Hugh Brody (1973), was strangely advised by his sociology supervisor to do fieldwork in Catholic Ireland, only as a self-defined 'bachelor', which, like Morris, could have restricted access (Okely 2009a).

Some anthropologists in this study found recognizable contrasts, through their research trajectories, between initial identity as single, then as married fieldworker (Caplan 1992; Kenna 1992). Dubisch (1995) compared fieldwork as first married then separated. Paul Spencer (1992) bravely admitted unconsciously seeking resolution to adolescent/family problems back home. A few of the anthropologists in this study brought one child or more into the field. Heald engaged in fieldwork through months of pregnancy, gave birth and continued fieldwork for over a year with her baby daughter, alongside her teacher husband. At Heald's subsequent seminar presentation at London University in 1969, M.G. Smith lambasted her for staying in limited localities. Advocating multiple locations across a huge territory (*pace* Leach 1967), Smith insisted: 'In the interest of science, you should have left your husband and your baby!'

Heald found advantages as a married woman. But she had to be cautious with elite men:

> In Bugisu in the 1960s, I had access to both men and women. If I'd been a man, I'd have had to be circumcised, and would not have had access to the women. I was a married woman and the Bugisu peasant farmers with whom I was working, disapproved of mixed marriages in any case. Even so I was careful and avoided contacts with elites that might have made for difficulties.

Silverman moved from single to married woman and then mother. To the admiration of the Macedonian Roma, she brought her parents to help care for their grandchild. In contrast to masculinist academic perspectives, the presence of a baby daughter brought unexpected networks for Neveu (cf. Schrijvers 1993). Here was proof that the anthropologist was more than a 'grab-it-and-run' researcher:

> I chose the capital because I was going to do fieldwork with my one-year-old daughter. I didn't feel safe going into a remote area without proper access to healthcare. Almost half the Senegalese population was urban. What I had expected to be an obstacle ended up being a great advantage because I needed advice and help. People have a lot of sympathy for a mother, a family. I made friends outside the dance world, with women about my age, who had children, much faster, because I needed advice.
>
> In the dance world, people had a lot of sympathy for the fact that I was bringing my family. They saw this as a sign that it was a personal, not just a professional project. They had complete sympathy for the fact that I wanted to know my father's country better. Because I took the trouble to bring my daughter and occasionally my husband, they took as a sign I wanted to become involved with Senegal in the longer term. Not just come, take some knowledge, do my thesis then leave. The senior person in the dance world introduced me: 'This is Hélène, she's doing a thesis in anthropology, but I don't care about the thesis. What is important is that she's here with her family. She's getting to know us. Her husband is there sometimes. Her daughter recognizes me.'

Okazaki returned in his forties to live with the Gamk in Sudan with his wife and three children. But this presented unanticipated problems of finding sufficient food, because there had been famine.

For Neveu, another unexpected advantage for mutual trust in Dakar, with a practice of polygamy, was being a married woman with child:

> Having a child with me made me much less susceptible to being a competitor to other married women. There is huge competition amongst women, given that there is polygamy. There is always a threat of a second or third wife coming. When you come as a single woman you're very likely to be perceived as a potential competitor.

However, familial obligations had some restrictions:

> What I was least happy with, paradoxically, was not being able to live with a family most of the time, precisely because I had my own. Also not being able to do fieldwork for a longer time. I envy people who are able to spend two years in the field.

Fieldwork as a couple might bring problems as to divisions of research themes. Overing went with her then-husband:

> We worked together constantly. That has as much to do with his personality. He was to do the religion and I the kinship/politics. It became frustrating, because anything I wanted to write on, he wasn't publishing. I couldn't refer to it. So I didn't write [on that], for about ten years after the Piaroa. I'm still working on it. We didn't work on the analysis together. The implications of being a couple means that you have to take one another's personal quirks into account, even on the theoretical level. It's what you're able to work out between the two of you—what you're able to negotiate. It may not be what you would ideally want.

Lindisfarne joined her husband months after he had begun fieldwork in Iran:

> It was men he had access to. He was assimilated into a family of twelve sons. He became best friends with the two eldest ones. That was his identity as a young and—ostensibly—'unmarried' man. So when I came back, I was the wife. All the women were waiting. I was overwhelmed; an awful initiation into fieldwork. These zillions of women who had heard lots about me, and wanted their access to a foreigner!
>
> There are several stories I remember vividly—shaped over the years, which were so *telling*. The day I arrived in the summer pastures where Richard had been for nine months, and knew mostly men—though he knew the women's genealogies. I was immediately snaffled up by the women. There were about twenty in the camp and all of them were there. I had rudimentary Turkish that wasn't going to take me anywhere. They spent the afternoon asking me about *ijal, ijal*. I was *weak* with saying: 'Please tell me what *ijal* is!' I came crawling back to Richard: 'For Christ's sake what's *ijal*!' He started laughing: 'That's their name for me.' The women had wanted to know Richard! This was a very salutary experience about how disempowered one is in the field [Tapper and Tapper 1989].

Whereas first field research is often conducted by anthropologists in their twenties, others, such as de la Gorgendière, embarking on her first fieldwork much later, found her age and life experience positive:

> The advantage I had was being a middle-aged woman with kids and a life behind me. People identified with that. I was able to make inroads into the women's group, as well as the men's. I adopted quite an androgynous role, because I was dealing with development, committees and water provision with mainly men. Yet I was talking to women about family structure, birth control, child raising and food making—bridging the gender divide. People saw me as older. They started asking marital advice.

Relative youth may be a major restriction, as discovered by McLeod:

> I'm amused that anyone was daft enough to send an impoverished student. The analogy would be sending some northern Ghanaian refugee living on social security to study the Duke of Devonshire. I ran out of money. I took a job in a secondary school, in order to stay. After that I was offered a joint post in Cambridge and the University of Ghana. So I taught at the University of Ghana for two years.

The age of the anthropologist will also affect chosen associates. Neveu found:

> My age was very significant, as most of the best relations I've established are with people in my age range, including women with small children about the same age as mine. That we were able to look after each other's children meant a lot in building up rapport.

Sometimes age is misread across cultures and ethnicity. Heald recalled:

> It was amusing going back to Kuria and somebody saying to me: 'When you first came here, you were young. Now we see that you've got old.' I said: 'It means you've got older too.' They probably did think I was quite young when I was forty. They really had no idea. I remember, years later, when I first started working with Joseph, who was sixteen, and I was introduced at the Chief's Baraza [assembly] as this 'young married woman', and Joseph was told that he must look after me, so absolutely reversing the relationship.

The changing status of the anthropologist through the life cycle had different implications. Parry stated:

> During the village study, I had a different intimacy with the people. I was alone—before I was married. I lived with a village family, and, being very young, one was very exposed.

Later in Banaras, Parry experienced the contrasts:

> It affected the way I conducted fieldwork, also my identity. People could see that I was a respectable family man. It made it easy to be accepted. I was a visiting scholar. In friends' houses,

I would greet the young women. The men would sit with me. The women would come in and say: 'Hello, how are you?' But to sit and talk with them would not have been appropriate.

Given that the anthropologists here include those with fieldwork from the late 1960s to 2007, their varied foci reflected the theoretical, political and ethnographic priorities of the specific intellectual and political era. Moreover, individual personalities might resonate with the historical and cultural context of their early formation, as well as contemporary academic concerns. Caplan (1992) vividly outlined her changing foci, paralleling her life trajectory and political debates back home. Overing confronted the consequences of her education and culture in 1950's United States:

It depends entirely on the age you're growing up. I grew up in the 1950s. Talk about naïveté! I grew up in North Carolina. It was quite cosmopolitan, for the States. We were very active in anti-segregation battles. [Today] they go in at 25, and by the time they're writing, they're finishing up at 30, or 29. They're getting into their own, intellectually. I was impressed with how much more street-wise people became about life. It's a much more open world.

Like Caplan, Okely and others, Overing did first fieldwork when feminine gender was devalued in anthropological research (Okely 2008, 2009a). Overing stated:

The Piaroa could teach me things that the women weren't supposed to know. The women *knew* everything. They know the sacred flutes. What bothers me most is that my fieldwork was so male-oriented, although they aren't macho. I got quite a bit from the women on childbirth. But I didn't sit down systematically. The women worked *routinely.* The men would work in spurts. They had more time. The only way was for me to have worked with the women—which I wanted. I'd been taught, in the old, highly sexist way. I wasn't asking the questions I would ask afterwards. I got a lot of the information anyway.

Okely, responding to Overing, found the same masculine bias disguised as universalism:

If I did a thesis based entirely on women, it wouldn't get recognition! Those were the days when you couldn't have a doctoral title, where there were women in. I switched off from childcare—'That's women's work.' You had to prove you were an honorary male!

## Ethnic Difference

Ethnic difference and its associations were not rendered invisible. But the response varied as in the case of de la Gorgendière, a white Canadian woman, classified by her Ghanaian hosts as a 'confused ancestor' (chapter 6). McLeod, also among Asante, elaborated difference beyond 'race': You can't be invisible in Asante. Firstly, you're European. You look different, you walk different, you eat differently.'

Visible 'racial' difference can however ensure exclusion, as Hughes-Freeland discovered in desiring to perform publicly as dancer in the court in Indonesia:

> I never wanted to perform inside the court or outside. I did participate in the dance training, although other more skilled and experienced dancers did participate in the court. They were usually Asian Americans, who looked right. They would never have let a Caucasian woman perform in the court.

By contrast, Neveu's Senegalese descent was elaborated:

> People thought they could read my Senegalese connection in my body. I don't believe in that. If I tried to follow a dance, if I learnt new dance steps I learned them quickly because I'm used to dancing. I'd just watch people's bodies. I'm able to learn faster than someone who never dances. They said: 'Oh, that's because you've got Senegalese blood!'

Nevertheless the local perceptions for Neveu were culturally complex:

> In Europe people assume that because I have a Senegalese father and a French mother and because I'm black, people in Africa will relate to me in an easier way. I didn't find that. People used the same term for me as they used for white people—*Tubaab*, meaning 'white person'. It's a complicated term. It has its origins in colonial times. It's used throughout French-speaking West Africa. It doesn't only refer to race. It also refers to socio-economic status and lifestyle. Upper class urban Wolof, who speak French at home and who have a very European lifestyle, are called Wolof Tubaab. They've become associated with the category 'white people'. African Americans who come in search of their roots are also called Tubaab, although they're not white. That's the category I was associated with because I grew up in Europe and because I don't speak fluent Wolof. I have a white husband. I was an in-between category.

Gigengack, as white Dutchman, considered the implications of his ethnicity and gender in Mexico City:

> My rapport would have been very different had I been a woman, or had I been a Mexican, or a black Dutchman. There is some racism in Mexico. They make jokes about black people, but there are not many black people in Mexico. The fact that I'm white and from a Western country, influenced quite a lot in that people may like to be seen with white people. You have to be very careful because the Mexicans also deconstruct it. They may not agree with it. They always thought first that I was American. For many Latin Americans you're a white foreigner. Then you're American. Mexicans are very close to the United States, so they make a big difference between American and non-American.
>
> This was the time of the cold war. They liked me being from Europe, even the street children. They also knew the difference. Street children would say: 'You're a gringo.' When I met them a couple of weeks later they'd say: 'You're the one who's not a gringo but you're westerner.'

Personality is important because you can make jokes. The street language, you pick up easily. You can use words that are not so delicate. You can talk rough; show you're a little bit rough at times.

I was younger, so my age at that time was closer to their's. But even then they already thought I was old, because when you're over thirty, you're old.

At the time I didn't have children. I can remember some boys, rebuking me: 'What, you don't have children, why not? Next time you come here with Raquel you must have a baby.'

Wulff found it an advantage being Swedish, albeit white, in multi-ethnic South London:

It was better that I was Swedish, not British. They knew of Björn Borg and Abba. The boys would make passes. I would try to send them away in a nice way. I said: 'Fuck away'. The boy collapsed in giggles. I should have said: 'Fuck off'.

## Mixed Nationality Couple, One a Non-Foreigner

Raquel Alonso, of Mexican nationality, outlined the implications of being a co-fieldworker with Gigengack:

You are treated differently. For me it was an advantage that Roy was a foreigner. He was white. He attracted attention. I could pass unnoticed. I was able to see and hear a lot of things. My role was kind of passive. I didn't need to be very active. It was an advantage because I could write. I had the time to think about what was going on. Roy was very much part of the whole thing. I liked it that way. Some people can get upset about that. There were some activists. They wanted to have a specific role regarding organization and ways of trying to improve the situation of the children. I was there, but not there at the same time. That's why it was a great advantage to be Mexican, dark skinned—and the language, also that I was much like the children and girls around. Many interventionists mistook me for one of the street children. It was interesting to use my own nativeness and my age. Many people thought that I was younger than I was. Also the children didn't see me like a researcher. I was more like a mate, someone who was there. At the same time, I wasn't a street gang member. I was not so invasive in their space.

It also depends on how you dress, how you speak. A lot of middle-class people, who go to university, dress in a different way. Even when they were among street children, they want to have status. I was not that kind of person. I was more like shabby and informal.

## Gendered Sexuality

Alonso was confronted by a potentially vulnerable, gendered identity:

I was someone they could trust. When the police came, I had to act as advocate. I knew the situation. I was able to say to the police that they had no right to stay there. They saw me in a different light. Afterwards they were more friendly and treated me differently. But sometimes when they were angry or irritated for what was going on around them, they could threaten me. Particularly some girls were challenging me. They wanted to fight with me.

They were twenty years old. I was twenty-four. It was dangerous. I tried to be quiet, saying: 'I don't have any intention to fight you' and keep things as normal. With the boys it was more a sexual game. They wanted me like a girlfriend. They sometimes embraced me or touched me in a way which was not proper. I needed some limits. Some were really young, and just pulled their pants down. They wanted me to react. They exposed themselves. The only thing I could say was like play it back. I told him: 'Well, you called me to see that, I mean, that's a misery, it's not worthwhile.' Then I went out of the room telling everybody: 'He has so small a willy.' Afterwards he was a bit ashamed. I was alone that day. Sometimes they were playing, like saying that they will rape me, or something. It was really nasty. But it was a difficult time in the whole community.

I offered a comparable incident where Gypsy women threatened to test whether I was a virgin (Okely 2008: 59). Then I described a seduction chat up line by one unmarried Gypsy man with whom I had many engaging discussions:

He would flirt like: 'Shall I pull my caravan next to yours?' I just laughed. It was a joke. But I used it when defending him in the chief court of the land, for attempted murder and kidnapping. He mentored non-Gypsy teenagers with no history, no family. His solicitor was pleased to have me as character witness. He loved the fact that I said: 'X said he wanted to park his caravan next to mine, which meant he was heterosexual.' That was used in his defence. He was found not guilty.

Clough considered his identity as unmarried male:

I was very lucky through my male friendships getting to know their wives. I got to know a group of women who were quite conversational in their households and had a wonderful sense of humour. One of the songs which men used to love to tell among themselves, they would embroider it because in Hausa there's a great deal of local poetry. It's collective, innovative, constantly changing. There was a song of the vagina which they used to love making me write down. They'd explain it; translate it for me from advanced to elementary Hausa so that I was clear as to everything.

I was going through the fields during the farming season and I came across a field with lots of women planting. This was my second summer there. They all shouted out: 'Mr Paul, sing us the song of the vagina.' Of course they knew the song and they loved it. They were just as involved in the sexual humour as the men. I tried it out and they laughed at my mistakes. Then they added verses. I suddenly realized that this was a common humour that men and women shared.

When you're looking at West African Islam, 200 miles south of the Sahara Desert, there was not purdah. There was a system whereby women spent most of the day in these very large compounds, but from behind the semi-closed doors of their compounds they had their own fields. Women accumulated quite a bit of money. They were saving money which went in to bride wealth for their sons and dowry for their daughters. They owned most of the small livestock.

They played with words and, to the extent that I tried in Hausa, they loved it. They could conceive of me settling down. Through this it would become a marriage alliance. Since their time was spent preoccupied with thinking about who to marry, I would appear relatively powerful and rich. If they could provide me with one of their relatives as a wife then become either father-in-law or brother-in-law.

This extremely beautiful Fulani girl was brought to me and we spent several hours together. When I walked outside of my room with her, there were half the senior men of the village sitting in front of the door, they said: 'Isn't it a beautiful day Mr. Paul?' 'Is the weather nice today?' There was this dry humour. It was very freewheeling. Remember, divorce was common. Remarriage was common. Women had a great deal of authority. In Hausa society, which is ostensibly Muslim, women had immense power and freedom of movement.

Okely considered some comparisons for single women anthropologists:

> The bachelor son is a phenomenon in rural France. The bachelor son of Madame Grégoire, in his late thirties, had built his luxury house in a nearby village but still lived with his parents. Someone said: 'He has this beautiful cage which he's built but doesn't have *une oiseau* [a bird] to go in it.' I overheard people say I was his fiancée. They couldn't understand anything else.

## Individual Personality

The anthropologists were asked to consider the possible consequences of their specific personalities in fieldwork relations. Overing explained:

> I'm very diffident with new people. I have to get to know people slowly. I formed very close friends. But it took time. With the Indians, if you didn't go slowly, you'd have trouble. They are diffident, slowly disclosing more and more. It depends on who you're with. You're fortunate if you get people that you enjoy psychologically at a very deep level.

Morris revealed a similar modest self-description:

> I'm quite a shy person. I find it difficult to contact people and push myself. So my research is very limited. The only times I can do that [be pushy] if there's a real issue or a problem, to sort out.

Zulaika, also with the self-description of shyness, had to overcome this to inter-relate:

> I tend to be shy. They gave me this role of being the leader of the group for this thing [organizing a disco] and then to promote it. We had to organize concerts around the Basque country to pay our debts. Suddenly I'm presenting these concerts to large audiences. They forced me on stage. When Lennon was murdered, the next day we had 3,000 people for a concert in one of the Basque capitals and we devoted it to John Lennon. I was put on the stage for this. But I felt always shy. It wasn't my thing. So I was put up by my own fieldwork.

Anthropologists may thus have to go against what they previously considered a fixed persona. Zulaika continued:

> I would say that, if not for being a fieldworker and a writer, I wouldn't have talked to so many people. I have said many times, that the one good thing about being an anthropologist is that is forces me into interaction, interviewing people, and into being sociable, which otherwise I would not be.

In response, Okely suggested:

> But often people who are the most shy are best performing on a platform. Because you're not relating, you're a persona—distant. You've got the audience out there. You can be per-fectly shy afterwards. Getting up on a platform, like giving a public lecture, you can do it, however shy, because the people are distant and remote.

## The Stranger's Biography Is Ignored

Whereas some anthropologists were interrogated in considerable detail by their hosts, in other contexts, personal biographical detail beyond the first classification was irrelevant. Heald found this in her first fieldwork in Uganda:

> In Bugisu in the 1960s, I was simply an alien being, in whom they were really not inter-ested . . . This is hard to explain now, because globalization has made a difference . . . I was totally depersonalized. That was the most difficult thing for me, that 99 per cent of what I thought I was, or my experiences, were totally irrelevant.
>
> They were living this one particular life. It wasn't a closed system, of the classic sense, in that they were well aware of the historical changes in their lives. But they hadn't imag-ined beyond, even though they had travelled beyond. Many had travelled to Kampala or Nairobi in Kenya. Some men had fought in the Second World War. But if I asked them about their experiences in the war, they could tell me very little. They had been in Burma, in Egypt, all over, but it was irrelevant. They came back to the Bugisu hills, to Masaba and that environment totally absorbed everyone. So someone coming from outside had to be absorbed into that, and seemingly, brought nothing into it.

## Transgressive Identity and Personality

Stepping in and outside society (Powdermaker 1967), the anthropologist may have to engage in behaviour which is transgressive in terms of his or her own society or in a wider context of the fieldwork. This may be consistent with humanitarian justice but against the hegemonic racism of the majority population, if the anthropologist is engaged with a persecuted minority. Kaminski, for example, remonstrated against non-Gypsy Slovaks who were beating up Gypsies at a bus stop. He suggested that his rejection of neutrality related to his own positionality:

> In Slovakia we were waiting for the bus and suddenly Slovak hooligans came and attacked the Gypsies. I was with them and waiting. It was an automatic response: 'Why the hell are they beating these guys who are waiting for the bus?' That event brought me into their community. I took their side in this struggle. The area I was studying was not far from the Slovak/Polish border. There were districts where the majority were Gypsy inhabitants. You are waiting for the bus from this district town, as it was the only access to these Gypsy settlements. Then there came some drunkards, non-Gypsy Slovaks, who are, just for the sport, attacking waiting Gypsies. Sometimes the Gypsies would defend themselves, but usually, they were extremely passive. They were beaten, but no reaction. I was from Poland, an outsider, and a privileged position, because in Eastern Europe a foreigner, even from a neighbouring socialist country, was a privileged person, because the community couldn't travel easily. We didn't have passports, so being an outsider and taking their side and shouting at Slovaks in Polish, I was suddenly projecting that fight into some international affair at the local level. I was told that this was frequent. They were beaten at that time, all the time. We talk about Jewish pogroms in East Europe in the twentieth century. But I am talking about Slovakia in 1968/69/70—regular pogroms against the Gypsies by non-Gypsies.
>
> The community was divided by internal domestic regulations. You had to have a residence permit to stay in one area. You had to have a work permit to move to another. Within Eastern Europe you had domestic divisions. The Gypsies had no chance if they had criminal records, by fighting back. The entire police force had no Gypsy who admitted to being a Gypsy. Whenever they were attacked and beaten up, they had no chance of defence. That I recognized.

Kaminski revisited Slovakia between 2000 and 2008 and noted that such 'pogroms' continued, even after Slovakia joined the European Union. Meanwhile a new generation of anthropologists is emerging with important studies of Gypsies in the Czech and Slovak Republic (Jakoubek and Budilova 2006; Budilova and Jakoubek 2009).

The individual may draw on his or her individual transgressive biography which becomes a means of empathy through fearless protest, enhanced or even exploited in fieldwork. The anthropologist may be both rebel and compliant—a 'critic at home and a conformist abroad' (Lévi-Strauss 1955/1973: 386). 'Home' may be one's own designated culture. Abroad may be other but in the same territory. Kaminski's potential empathy as incoming stranger is revealed in chapter 5, but he is a critic in the previous example. Similarly, my barbaric boarding school as 'home', with its British 'stiff upper lip', became a reason to reject that culture. Forbidden to cry, hours after learning of my father's death, I found resolution through the contrasting Gypsy death rituals. Here children were permitted to express grief at parental loss (Okely 2008).

## Full Participation Withheld

Political engagement can take a challenging turn and the anthropologist, while resisting the chimera of detached scientist, will nevertheless feel obliged to stand back from participation as violence. David Brooks, who did fieldwork among the Bakhtiari in Iran, described how he was challenged to shoot one of the group's neighbouring enemy. Brooks refused. From then on he was ridiculed as 'not a real man'. He joked that my challenge was specifically female when I was used as outsider to censor a womanizing Gypsy man. I turned the joke around (Okely 2005: 707–8). Brooks observed that he, the man, was expected to kill, while I, the woman, was represented as giving life.

Zulaika was directly confronted with the extremity of dilemmas over specific types of political engagement. The participant observer had to make decisions unsolved by scientific 'objectivity'. Rejecting any suggestion of joining ETA, he felt compelled to witness their detailed commitment. Direct exchanges, based on mutual trust, gave unique coherent perspectives:

> Suddenly I'm going to be writing about these guys and I cannot look at them as Rosaldo writing about headhunters in the Philippines [Rosaldo 1993]. We could write about how headhunting is part of their cultural initiation. Their set of values and my values are totally different. I could not distinguish myself. These guys were what we all had pretty much desired. We had fought against Francoism. It was a defence of the local culture. Suddenly I see myself having to be a witness to what these guys are doing. I see myself unable to murder for political reasons.
>
> But I see them the way they see themselves, as quasi-soldiers' identities, defending their own view of a certain country. I could have my disagreements, but they were not for me vulgar murderers. I see myself being a witness to their lives was a legitimate intellectual task. Writing about them, even if I don't agree, I had to be a witness. This was quite uncomfortable I thought I was just crazy. This was a terrorist group—illegal. It's not that by then the Spanish state was illegal. It was a normal European state, as legitimate as any other. Yet, this other tradition of political resistance, with violence and murder, had its own different legitimacy. I, as anthropologist, didn't want to privilege one over another. I wouldn't say that the political legitimacy of these guys was superior. They were both there and I had to witness these guys' lives. I got too close. I was relieved when they told me they didn't want me around. I look back now. It was totally crazy. But I had no control.
>
> I knew I was overstepping. I couldn't tell my professors. This was academically crazy. Yet, I felt if I was unwilling to be a witness to their own lives, as if I was not up to my job as a writer of their lives. I had fallen into a mirage in the distinction I make between metaphor and sacrament. I was identifying too much with their political cause, not because I had wanted to be in ETA.

## Dissonance or Resonance

Qualities of personality may be more fully appreciated if they resonate with those valued by the research subjects. Inter-relations of difference or commonality affect rapport. Howell provided insight:

> I was quite different in my second fieldwork. In my first fieldwork, I always felt on the defensive. I was anxious about not doing anything wrong. I could have been more forthcoming. I was waiting for them to take initiatives. They are shy, timid people, and I didn't push them. It may be that they gave me so much—it's difficult to say.
>
> In Indonesia, the people were completely different. They were very belligerent. Far from running away when I first arrived, they nearly mobbed me! And bullied me! It was a very different relationship. It's probably relational. I was cautious with the cautious people. I was more demanding with the demanding people!'

Invariably, values may not be predicted in advance. They are specific to the people encountered.

After her possessions were stolen, Neveu was admired for her self-control:

> I was so shell shocked that I reacted in the way when I'm under great levels of stress, which is by shutting down and withdrawing, not saying very much, looking very calm, and locking all emotions inside. That's something which is a personality trait but which people took as a sign of strength. There is great value placed on restraining your emotions and not showing anything, even under great stress. Several friends and my best friend's mother, who saw me immediately after, often commented: 'When *it* happened, I could see that she was a good person because she kept calm. She was so cool. She didn't shout. She didn't say anything.' The fact that I was so quiet gave me status. It was a sign of moral strength, not something I intended.

Neveu recalled another very different incident where indeed emotions broke out:

> There was one occasion during which I cried, which made me very embarrassed, but it ended up being a good thing. I had gone to see a Senegalese scholar, a brilliant scholar who's since become a friend, whom I didn't know very well but whom I'd visit occasionally to exchange ideas with. The third or fourth time we met, he asked me a personal question on a day when I was extremely tired. I was emotionally vulnerable. He asked about my father's family. I started crying without being able to control it. But it created a bond. He reacted extremely well and started telling me some of his personal stories. It changed our relationship for the better immediately. With a different person it would have been the other way around, but with him it was a turning point.

Okely shared a fieldwork incident:

> Shared empathy or shared emotions completely challenges the positivistic ghost that we have about being the detached researcher, which is still lingering with most of what some

other disciplines teach. I remember one point where I exploded with anger. It enhanced my reputation. The Gypsy kids had smashed up something in my trailer. I absolutely exploded. They really liked that I could show anger. There can be no blue prints for personal interaction. Detachment as objectivity is relational, not a universalized research mode.

## Shared Illegalities

Kaminski found commonality with Roma crossing borders in communist Eastern Europe and was trusted to smuggle consumer goods, for example, a simple matter of shoes for a child and taking messages across countries. All this is now legal, but, in the past, such actions were criminal offences. His vulnerability to police surveillance helped create a common bond:

> We were both helped, the Gypsies and myself, to come closer to each other, and we were helped by the police dealing with minority groups, which were residing around the borders. I was living with thousands of Roma, living near the Czech border, on both sides of the borders, and during the Communist time. When I started my research in 1967, it was an extremely and carefully guarded area. I was always asked: 'What are you doing and why are you meeting with Gypsies?' and the Gypsies were asked: 'Why are they doing this or that?' It took me a time to realize they were smuggling goods across the border and were, for different reasons, suspected by the police. So being subjected to Communist institutions, in different ways we were in communion, we were both suspicious and both suspected, myself and the Gypsies. If in a more open community, I would probably have not had such access, but being in a Communist country it was such a reason.
>
> At the beginning, I didn't establish good contacts with the Polish Roma, but if I was moving and studying the Slovak Roma, they needed me to pass the information, or boxes, or goods to the Roma families living on the other side of the border, so I became useful as an anthropologist who was delivering goods; I could smuggle a couple of shoes for children needed in Poland, or take some vodka on the other side.

## Historical and Political Contexts

Beyond gender, age, marital status and ethnicity, the anthropologist is defined and othered by nationality, class and colonial legacies. Parry confronted the variable colonial legacy and class category of his British identity:

> In *my* experience, in different parts of India, people have very different stereotypes. It means something very different to be an Englishman. Kangra was a hill district, from which the British had recruited army regiments. A lot of the men, particularly the older men, had been in the army, and served under British officers. They had very firm ideas. There were two types of Brits: 'Officers and gentlemen' and 'barbaric foot soldiers'. There would be questions to establish which I should be slotted into.

The people I was working with tended to have a very low opinion of the British—Westerners don't have family. They don't have philosophy. They don't have kinship. What they've got is science. You'd say: 'I want to know about ritual in religion.' They'd say: 'That's what you people *need* to know about!' The whole attitude towards being British and a Westerner was one of a certain disdain, if not hostility. There were interesting ways in which British or foreigners, Americans, would be referred to as the descendants of terrible demons in Hindu mythology. In Bhilai, the notion of the foreigner was of Russians. People who don't know tend to assume that I'm a Russian.

Heald, in Africa, witnessed negative 'othering' of Europeans, especially women:

They despised white women. It was: 'We are Bagisu, we marry our own.' There had been marriages of Bagisu and white people, and even an anthropological couple. These marriages, they reckoned, didn't work.

There was a colonial legacy also for McLeod:

In Ghana was there was no obvious division between Africans and Europeans. It's down to the Asante. They're so self-confident in their own innate superiority. It was one of the refreshing things about being in Ghana, particularly in the 1960s: Europeans and Africans mixed extremely easily, and on pretty equal terms. However, you are still associated with an ex-ruling group, the remnants of empire. Being British had a special significance. It imposed obligations, because Britons were expected to behave in a proper, decent way. I remember my forty-year-old research assistant complaining bitterly that Myer [Fortes] had sent out a researcher from Cambridge who ate peanuts in the street. This was not the way a Briton should behave!

Far from the caricature of anthropologists importing ethnocentricity, they are transformed through interaction in the field. McLeod explained:

All the slight social graces I may have, the ability to deal with things, and the way I behave: anything that's of any use, I've learned from them. I went out as a naïve, brash, immature person and, over the years, the Asante have educated me into something passable. By their standard, it's a pretty rudimentary model. I feel much more at home there than I do here.

The ability of Heald to adapt to local contexts was appreciated in Uganda and Kenya:

They see me as a chameleon, in both places. I've heard it said they really like and admire me, because I can move in all worlds. In Kuria I talk to everyone, they say, and in Bugisu the same.

As Hendry (1992), studying in Japan, has recounted, anthropologists do not necessarily study relatively underprivileged groups. They also 'study up' (Nader 1974; Okely 1996b: chapters 7, 8) McLeod stated that:

> Ghana was probably the wrong place to try and work, at least among the Asante. I had a very small grant. I couldn't afford a car until late. That made getting around difficult. The Asante are a highly hierarchical group. They expect Europeans to be rich. They don't pay much attention to young boys. I'd have been much better working in one of the poorer groups in northern Ghana, which were far less status-conscious, and didn't have the money that many Asante had. It's only thirty years later, when I've grown old in Asante, and done a lot of things with them, that I have much easier access to all sorts of information.

## Key Associates

The specificity of the fieldworker will also have implications for the most welcoming and encouraging research associates. Anthropology has, in contrast to stereotypes, recognized that indigenous intellectuals are in all cultures. For many anthropologists these became significant intermediaries and interlocutors facilitating future collaboration (Sanjek 1993; Lassiter 2005). Specific individuals and clusters had crucial significance for unfurling discovery and in-depth knowledge. Encountering key individuals can be compared again to chaos theory. Embarking on research into an iron and steel works, Parry had a chance meeting with an individual who was impressed by a European male, competent in Hindi:

> I was in this steel plant in the reception area. I needed a pass. There were thousands of company representatives milling around. It's absolute chaos, queues. I was talking to a Bengali businessman. We were speaking Hindi, having a fairly inconsequential conversation. A young man came up, obviously curious and listening. Then the businessman's number came up. He went away. This young man said: 'It's very interesting. Where are you living? I'll come and see you.' A few days later, this guy showed up and told me all sorts of interesting things: 'You'd better come and see me. You're interested in these labour colonies. I live in one the other side of town.' He became my research assistant. It was through him that I picked the second of these ex-villages cum labour colonies.

The anthropologist seized this chance and changed focus, thanks to the intellectual curiosity of one individual.

Cultural or biographical hybridity is often found in key associates (cf. Jan Mohamed 1992). Okely found her closest links were with Gypsies who either had one non-Gypsy parent and had lived for a while in a house and attended school or one who had experienced national army service. They had a bifocal perspective and were sensitive to articulating the differences across the ethnic divide. Howell moved from one field site in Malaysia:

> This was too much on the edge of the forest. They'd always talked about this place that was paradise, far away. There were waterfalls, lots of meat, and wild fruit. Eventually, somebody was going—two days quite heavy walk. As I came, this old woman came out of one of the houses. She smiled! She could speak a little Malay. She said: 'Come inside.' She pointed: 'This is where you're going to sleep.' That was very unusual. Even when people accepted me, they were completely non-demonstrative. They were always passively waiting. It was really hard to make contact. To see this woman who came out and made contact—it was terrific! She then became my mother. That is where I lived.
>
> She had heard that I was there. She was a very unusual person. She was the only woman alive (her younger sister had been like this) who had been outside of the forest territory. The British game warden, Ogleby, in 1947 was stationed deeper in the forest, but near a town near the railway. In 1952 he sent for two young men of the Chewong, and said: 'Why don't you come, and be my guides and live with me?' These two young men came. That was her husband, and her husband's brother.
>
> Her husband's brother I had met when I first arrived in the other place, and they took their wives with them. They had lived for about six months with Ogleby in this other reserve area and had been bearers for him.
>
> She had lived there, she and her sister. Two sisters had married two brothers.
>
> That's why she spoke Malay, why she knew the way of the world! That was in 1950/1953. As we got to know each other, she taught me so much. She was so intelligent. She understood fairly fast what I was after, what I was doing. This woman was a focus. People always liked visiting her. She was very hospitable. I just tagged along.

Overing insisted:

> You have to find people you can work with, and people you're comfortable with. I did spend time with the women, but not talking. Maybe I got just as much by not talking, knowing them as people. They are very important in my book. When I talk about equality in the genders, I know, because I watched! I watched them yell at their men. I know what they felt like! But I would've liked to have had a more verbal, relationship. Later it was again, these young men—I really enjoyed them! The Piaroa really make good conversationalists, they *love* talking. They're very verbal. They're the kind of people you stay up till two talking.

Key associates may come to be a vital means of ensuring reciprocity between the anthropologist and the people. Parry experienced the dramatic imprisonment of the same man whom he first encountered when seeking his permit and who became his research assistant. In a twisted political drama, the man was imprisoned as a 'terrorist'. Parry assisted in the eventual campaign, using his professorial status to seek his release as innocent (Parry 2010). His wife, Margaret Dickinson, made a DVD for relevant publicity (2008).

As with the examples of the anthropologist revealing emotions, Clough narrated a major breakthrough via reciprocity. Answering a request to help was misunderstood as self-interest:

> From the first day, a man in his mid-thirties took to me—the uncle of my young friend in Zaria township. We became close friends. He was reflective by nature, not economically successful. He liked to sit back and look at things, but was wonderfully responsive to my needs. Whereas other villagers would not understand my research and would be worried that I was a spy, he accepted that I needed to find out a great deal of information. In a quiet way he helped me. He did not have a motorcycle and when, at harvest the very competitive cotton-buying season began, the four other cotton traders all had motorcycles and were speeding around the inter-lying villages buying cotton. So I became his carrier. I took him around the villages on my motorcycle.
>
> I was trying to be a detached sociologist, to keep my emotions under control, to keep smiling even when my leg was being furiously pulled. I was not developing friendships with older men, apart from two. I was not in a family situation where I could get to know the wives.
>
> Then something happened. I began mapping the farms of the village, measuring acreages. One man came to me and said would I please come to measure his fields. I was very busy. I had some research plans. I said: 'OK when and where do we meet? What field do we measure?'
>
> I went to the field to measure with my tape. There he was farming with his mother and she began grumbling in a way I'd heard before. She said to me in Hausa: 'You are here to exploit us. You are here to eat our villages.' It's a well-known expression in other African languages, which has become the centre of a book by Bayart—*The Politics of the Belly*. This 'eat' idea is popular in West Africa, a word for exploitation. She said: 'You are eating us. You are going to go back to England with your notebooks to make money out of your notebooks.' I'd heard this before. I was fatigued. Since I knew her son had called me to do this for his benefit, I blew my top. I lost control. I started shouting: 'Damn you, I don't want to be out in this bloody field, (all in Hausa). I only came because your son invited me. I'm happy to leave this bloody field this moment.' Their mouths dropped. For the first time, after a year, they had seen this white man show emotion. He was a human being. From that moment she became my firm friend.

## Intellectual Exchange between Equals

Heald spoke of the individuals who worked closely with her:

> They become close friends. I'm very against all this anonymization we're being forced into. They are equals, for heaven's sake. They are co-participants, co-researchers, because the ones you work with are the ones who get turned on by the same kind of problems, and often discover a real interest in their own culture, and beliefs, and work with you on them.

I've worked closest with men for an obvious reason; they are the ones with time. The women have the children, and the children are a twenty-four-hour task. Men, on the other hand, can take time off when they feel like it. Thus, I could pay a man to be my assistant, but I couldn't select a woman, because they wouldn't have that kind of freedom. At first in Kuria, as a much older woman, I was surprised that the first two men I became friendly with who 'picked me up', so to speak, were young. Then I realized that it was because the young men who had less responsibility than anybody else. They had the time to be interested in this 'stranger'.

The anthropologist, as guest and participant observer, necessarily becomes engaged with the fate of specific individuals and that of the peoples as a whole. They may have often found themselves allied to those who have been relatively powerless. This counters the myth that anthropologists collude solely with the powerful, merely extracting information for their personal career. They are intellectually fired up and drawn towards defending difference whenever attempts are made to draw subordinated or alternative others into an overbearing hegemony.

Fieldwork is more than research for instrumental ends. There are ways in which the anthropologist learns how to reciprocate in appropriate ways for what has been given and shared through time. None of the anthropologists in this study were embedded spies for some superpower, nor any other institution intent on exploitation or conquest. As throughout these multiple examples of fieldwork from around the world, through decades, and by individuals of some sixteen varied nationalities, the contexts for reciprocity and exchange varied according to context and the specificity of the individual fieldworker.

Gigengack, as anthropologist ally of street children in Mexico City, found himself recruited as honorary kin, more especially when faced with the death and subsequent mortuary rituals of a child. In some cases he was asked by them to make the arrangements with a priest:

> I remember at least four, five or six [children's deaths]. I didn't go to all the funerals. But these were ones that I remember well. It was very important with one little boy. Omarito died at the age of fourteen of sudden sniffing. Some die of violence. As far as I know most of the deaths are because they don't wake up. It was very important for me to have been at the funeral. It was also important for the group, because they knew Omarito. That's one of the moments when they did not sniff. It was also a landmark in the memory because quite often, even years afterwards: 'Do you remember that we talked about it at the funeral of Omarito?' That was a memory mark. Being there, in terms of acceptance, the funeral was important. I've been to a number of others. Especially when I came back. For example, my *comadre* died in 1998. She was not a child anymore but a young adult.
>
> They usually are buried, as far as I could find out, in the grave for the paupers and there is no marking, no names. I came back when another boy had died, less than a year later. But the grave disappeared. There were a number of other graves that were opened. I think they exhumed the bodies, to destroy them. They need the space.
>
> There were a number of coffins lying open there. There were dogs walking around so they could have eaten the remnants. I even found a small skull. So there was this very

obvious non-remembering from the side of the State. For the children themselves also to have, for example, Day of the Dead is very important. There were institutions who organized a Day of the Dead to remember the dead street children, because they did not always do it in a ritualized sense. The grave of Omarito, when I told them that I went back to the grave but it was gone, the family members of the bombe Bande, said: 'That's bad', his cousins: 'it shouldn't be like that', but they themselves hadn't been there.

In other cases the anthropologist enters into political dialogue across national and cultural divides.

## Politics Become Intellectual Exchange

Questions within participant observation are potentially powerful in an explicitly political dialogue. Rejecting the notions of academic and scientific neutrality, the researcher might explore the political implications of his or her research by presenting her observations and tentative findings to the people as subjects for their own response and assessment (Huizer and Mannheim 1979). The researcher's queries and suggestions can elicit counter-arguments and correctives, a possible synthesis and the impetus for informed action and change.

Relevant to the past links with colonialism and Western imperialism, individual anthropologists were confronted with their branded national identity and history, whether or not they wished it. Wright could not escape her label as British. At first she was ignored by an older generation who had fought the British:

> In the main village, for the first three months, some of the older generation of men wouldn't even say hello to me, when I'd pass them in an alleyway. They wouldn't acknowledge my existence as a human being. Because I was British, and because they had been involved in a movement against the British and Americans in the Second World War.

At the same time, the extensive dialogues she had with the former nomads about British history were illuminating for what she could learn of their perceptions and memory at grass-root level and also for competing representations found in official British accounts:

> There was a very great deal of aggression to begin with, all done through Persian etiquette. So nobody actually wanted to hit me or attack me, but the questions were very strong. There was an attempt to land on my shoulders, the whole blame of British history, and British current policy. I spent hours and hours discussing this. Their telling me what they thought had happened in Iran, and my saying what I'd learnt from school and university in England.
>
> They could see how my mind was closed to certain things through the education system. We discussed how I'd grown up, and how they'd grown up, and how we had these different perspectives. I accepted their version of history, but explained that I'd never been

given insight into it before. Then regarding England's involvement in Iran, I emphasized: 'I don't agree with everything that's going on in England at the moment.' Gradually, we got to a situation where I was positioned within England; the history of Britain's use of Iranian oil and other resources from around the world, converted into the welfare state, had given me privileges—it was those privileges that had got me to my doctoral research in their village. Therefore, to some extent, I was reproducing privilege in the UK. But on the other hand, I couldn't be landed with total responsibility for everything that ever happened in England historically or in the present.

We got to a really nuanced understanding of difference, and how, as individuals, we are responsible for reproducing systems and structures of privilege, but on the other hand, aren't.

The questions they were asking were: 'How many colonies does Britain still have? Why did they try and colonize Iran? Why did they send their army in 1940-whenever? Why were they trying to kill us? Why did they give the Shah the planes to strafe us?'

It transpires that Britain sold military helicopters to the Shah. When the Shah was trying to settle the tribes, they used a road that had been built years before with British engineers, that transversed the migration route of the tribes. They cut the growth back on either side, so they were very visible. Then they went with the aeroplanes down this road, and strafed the tribes and killed them. This is just after the Second World War. There was one of the Qashqai groups which specialized in horses. In one crossing of that road, they lost 200 horses. I'd done a history degree. I'd specialized in Middle Eastern history and British diplomatic history in the Middle East. I'd done a primary document-based course on British diplomatic history in the Middle East. I hadn't known any of this angle of British involvement. Of course it was the thing they knew about Britain. So I was educated very, very quickly!

In Iran Lindisfarne, American with a British husband, found that the different nationalities were less relevant than the generic Anglophobia they met. The pastoralists they worked with in Azerbaijan believed that whatever major conflict was occurring across the globe, the British would be behind it, even claiming 'the British had managed to get the Americans to fight in Vietnam for them.' In Afghanistan, by contrast, the two anthropologists were not seen as extracting information, just entertaining. Lindisfarne stated:

What they said, which is just about as honest as anything, is: 'we are an occasion for *saat tireh*'—which means passing the time.

They thought we were amusing, because we asked them all kinds of silly questions. We'd gotten to the stage where we were authorities on genealogical matters. We were interested in stories, in music. They said we were a way of passing the time. We were not seen by most of the people as more intrusive than that. We were a diversion they enjoyed. There were other kinds of fears, on the part of the local governor, on the part of the tribal leaders, but it had very little to do with us learning things. Because what we were learning, they all knew anyway.

It was unimaginable that it would be turned into any kind of nefarious use by the government. Ironically, these are people that now, all of them, have been forced to flee during, following the Russian invasion of Afghanistan. So, what materials we collected have now become a memorial to a way of life. I strangely have no conscience, but a good one about these things.

On the other hand, Lindisfarne and her partner were assailed with extensive dislike and stereotyping of the Russians:

> It was quite a remote place. We were not Russian. That was very important, because the Russians held the huge empire just over the northern border. The Russians were characterized as all that was opposite of decent humanity.

Tragically, the people would soon suffer from the Russian invasion. Lindisfarne noted that many of the people with whom she had worked were scattered as internal refugees in refugee camps in Pakistan and further afield. She wrote about their lives in Saripul (Lindisfarne 1991), but regretted that a new job required her switching to another region of the world (Lindisfarne 2000, 2001) and made it hard to search for the Pashtun in disconnected places.

## Expertise as Reciprocity

The anthropologists in this study were often in a position to use their expertise as some exchange and reciprocity for the hospitality, shelter and knowledge they had been given. Their intellectual endeavour and participant observation brought political enlightenment and engagement. Silverman was at first a witness, recorder and analyst of Bulgarian Roma music when musicians were subject to extreme persecution. They were banned from making music and, if they were caught, they had their hair shaved and were imprisoned. Subsequently, Silverman was able to assist in asylum cases to the United States. She was also asked by the musicians to act as introducer and impresario for touring musicians. She wrote liner notes for CDs. This was not recognized in curriculum vitae applications for promotion:

> I have worked collaboratively with Roma, not only in scholarship, but in semi-activist agendas, organizing music tours. I work with the only Romany NGO in the US, Voice of Roma; it's run by a Rom from Kosovo. He understands all of the Balkan groups that I have contact with. His agenda is aligned with mine—using music as an educational medium. I have worked collaboratively in applied settings with Romany musicians, to produce their music on respectable labels in the US, or to lobby for West European contracts. This is something I can offer. I have contacts that they don't have. So during post-socialism, a Western researcher very often becomes a conduit for ideas, for commercial enterprises. Advocacy has a very important place. These musicians are talented and the field is being dominated by some non-Romany people in the West who have appropriated Romany music. I see my music activism and scholarship as intertwined. My name is circulated widely, which is not a good thing because I have to say no to a lot to people. I have also helped with asylum applications. I take those very seriously. I look at each one on its own merits, deciding whether I will serve as an expert witness. Again, my name is being circulated. But in legitimate cases I will help out.

The anthropologists can reciprocate in both the short and long term. As with the example of Silverman, anthropologists, despite their employers' regulations, may insist on reciprocity or the giving of their acquired skills and knowledge. The obligation to return lives on (Mauss 1954). Okely was ordered by her research centre to take time out of her four weeks annual leave for any time spent visiting a Gypsy in Wandsworth Gaol and for appearing as character witness in court. In contrast to managerial speak, Okely saw such actions as a minimum return, especially because the specific individual had spent many hours in shared discussion about Traveller life. Fortunately, the Gypsy was found not guilty on all serious counts and the testimony of an Oxford graduate, dressed for the occasion, with 'appropriate' accent, impressed even the gaolers.

Recently, the managerial and capitalist/consortium ideology of universities has brought an increased priority of income generation and so-called outreach (Okely 2006a). But this is very specific. Chapter 1 signalled how, in collaboration with a former MA pupil, Okely assisted (unpaid) in a social anthropology course in Hull prison. One inmate was a Gypsy. The next year, at least one new undergraduate revealed that the course had inspired him to come to university after his release. In Okely's annual appraisal this was rubbished by the departmental head because it was not 'income generating'. Thus intellectual exchange and transformation go unrecognized even among fellow academics. Talib spoke of the context and limitations of reciprocity:

To be a Brahmin among the stone quarry workers was very difficult because there were no Brahmins around. They were all lower-caste people. They had their own autonomy. I saw the like of one Brahmin in the quarry. This was the priest who conducted the prayers at the temple. He would be a butt of jokes when he was outside the temple. People would say: 'Who says that you are superior to us?' They would touch him and he would say: 'Don't touch me.' He would only find protection in the precincts of the temple, but outside it, he would be chased from here to there. He would not share food with them. In caste idiom, they make a distinction between cooked food and the uncooked food. This was his plight. He would only take uncooked food, which was the cereals, the grains, whatever, the pulses. He had minimal commensality with them.

I established that I should befriend them and in a way which need not be part of my research. One informant, my friend had asthma. Today we know it is silicosis. In the mid-1980s we called it asthma. They used to say it's a cough problem, but it was stone dust pollution, which had damaged their lungs. I wanted to take this person to a hospital. I knew the doctor in the hospital. I would do these kinds of reciprocities, not strictly part of my research but I thought I should do. I made a mistake one day of actually calling Raja Ram to my home. He needed a book and says: 'I need it immediately.' I said: 'This is at my home, why don't you just come with me?' That was when my research was almost complete.

When he came to my house he was rendered speechless. He had not seen resources organized to that level. He sat in the drawing room. He was just quiet. I gave him that book, wanting to share the same jokes and he was not responsive. While he was leaving, he says: 'It never appeared that you lived so comfortably.' So it's not a very easy thing to befriend because you are doing it with an agenda. You are doing research, collecting material, and befriending is really an instrumentality. But the other person has given his heart to you, with an understanding that you are also sharing common conditions of life. Which was not true. That perhaps would have shocked him. He didn't tell me in so many words but I think that is probably what has happened. Unfortunately, I never met him after that because he got a job and he left.

Talib outlined a very local intervention:

I spoke to one educational school entrusted with the situation of marginalized workers. I told him after this experience of school where these children of the stone quarry workers' families would go, that the curriculum was very alienating. I did a content analysis of some of the textbooks that the children were reading. For example, they would describe an animal zoo. The children had never seen an animal, other than the dogs and the cats. A lion's or tiger's cage was so clean. The caretaker would give them vitamins and clean them every week. This had no meaning because the 'cage' *they* were in had mosquitoes. The caretaker is never going to come. They were clearly malnourished. There were no vitamins there.

Here was a textbook that was telling them stories about animals who were living a cleaner life than they. This was an alienation to which this textbook material actually subjected them. On the one hand they had very intimate folk tales which were never codified into texts. This was the mismatch between the life they lived, which was meaningless, and some of the ideas or the codes which their school would produce and which made little sense to them.

Reciprocity can feature sometimes through other significant means. Neveu found this in offering her photographic skills and camera for the dance group's publicity. Hughes-Freeland as often as possible shared her research money, employing her associates as assistants. Then, most dramatically, when the people she had known for decades were the victims of an earthquake, she changed her research agenda. She set up a fund to which many contacts via mass email, including academics throughout the West, contributed. This helped in providing basic emergency accommodation. She oversaw the operation, ensuring the contributions were not inappropriately diverted.

Heald has for years, with Malcolm Ruel, organized a special fund for girls' education in schools in Kenya. Again, the hands-on knowledge and involvement of the anthropologist ensures the funding goes direct by using trustworthy local contacts. The anthropologists' day-to-day and often time-consuming involvement saves costly overheads.

Another form of reciprocity is the anthropologist as public figure. Overing found that signing a petition in the name of the indigenous people's land rights banned her from returning to the tropical forests in Venezuela. She defied a long-nurtured caution of signing petitions from memories of McCarthysm in the United States, but felt compelled to break family traditions.

This had unexpected twists for her return fieldwork. The Piaroa had become more acquainted with urban trips out of the woods. Confined to the urban, Overing had unique and extended visits from former trusted associates who came to her hotel. There she found new stimulus in protracted dialogues with a people whom she described as the most intellectual of all the tropical forest groups in the region:

> It was just at the time when they were planning the development of the Amazon. They didn't want anthropologists overlooking that. They were planning hydroelectric power plants, all kinds of things. I didn't know it then. The year before, I had signed a petition at the Americanist meetings in Paris—300 hundred of us—Lévi-Strauss was among them. Unfortunately, I organized them. So, my name was at the top. Venezuela didn't want any bother with foreign anthropologists. This was the frontier town.

She spent six months in the hotel, where she achieved an:

> amazing amount of work. All the young men came in, and the various shamans coming in to town. They'd like coming to visit. It was a grapevine—constant stream of people coming in.
> They wanted to tell the world about the Piaroa, not listen. They really enjoyed [it] at that period. They came later to hate anthropologists, I don't know what went on in Venezuela—it was upheaval at that time. It was about 1977, the young men would say: 'We haven't had an anthropologist in our village! We want our anthropologist!' A lot of the development agency people, came in under the guise of being anthropologists. That was not good.
> I grew up in the McCarthy years. Never sign petitions because you'll go to gaol. You won't get your passport. We're being asked to sign petitions all over the place. We had Communist friends followed by the FBI. We grew up with such a cloud from the 1950s, that I wouldn't trust any government. I would still have signed the petition for Brazil on that, and immediately get another one, for Venezuela. You'd have to be shrewd. If you knew enough of what's going on, you could also use the papers to keep Venezuela in mind. But you'd have to know enough, at the time.
> If I were there, I'd be drawn in, in various ways—certainly from Venezuela. It's been frustrating being so far away. Also not being a very good politician, or not being a very good networker. Also Colombia was very dangerous. There are machineguns everywhere. Venezuela is a very legalistic country. That's what saved us. Else we would've been thrown in gaol.

Anthropologists have acted as witnesses in land claims, for example for the indigenous Australians. Here the people have specifically asked for their assistance. They may know the requirements and practices across the cultural and historical divides, especially when land rights and ownership have been previously established by alien sedentarist and hegemonic criteria (Morphy 1993; Layton 1995).

As outlined in the Eric Wolf lecture, Okely (2006b) explored how the state may make use of the anthropologist's ethnographic evidence when it suits, but reject it when the political context changes. Thus, the early research (Adams et al. 1975) helped influence the 1978 Labour government to recognize the Gypsies' right to travel and receive assistance in site provision. But this was revoked in 1994 by the Conservative government. The negative consequences continue.

Research is not merely top-down, but can be collaborative. In another arena, from the mid-1990s, Okely acted as expert witness in cases of racial discrimination, especially on behalf of the Scottish Travellers hitherto unrecognized as an ethnic group. Her evidence, along with that of her former doctoral student, Colin Clark, of Scottish Traveller descent, was used in a successful 2008 court case which recognized the Travellers as an ethnic group.

Global changes bringing greater migration have consequences for anthropologists. Clough, as professor of anthropology in Malta, responded to the mass influx of asylum seekers who could make claims after Malta's accession to the European Union. The majority had intended to land in Italy from North Africa but had been shipwrecked. Many were of Nigerian or Somali origin and of Muslim faith provoking extreme Islamophobia in a deeply Catholic island. Clough organized festivals in the camps, brought his students as allies and assisted regularly in asylum claims.

As a non-Roma, Silverman and her musical expertise showed potential for unpredicted reciprocity:

> As a result of my vocal background and my helping Roma with their tours, helping the Roma, I have been invited to perform with them and record with some of the top stars from Bulgaria and Macedonia. That is a tremendous honour. I don't deserve it. I don't have the skills they have, but I feel like I'm helping them in an educational and in a commercial way, and we're in a reciprocal relationship. I'm glad that it happened.
>
> Another methodology I've used is playing videos of various events back for the participants and then having them comment on them. I record those sessions. So we'll look at a wedding together and will say: 'So and so is trying to match up so and so.' I'll say: 'How did you know that?' He'll say: 'He got in the dance line right next to her and he's the cousin of someone who's trying to find a bride for him.' So you can understand the workings of the community through watching a video of a dance.

Finally, de la Gorgendière used her bureaucratic, development expertise for raising funds for installing a well in the Ghanaian village where she had conducted fieldwork. She discovered that the people were victims of bilharzia, an illness derived from snails in stagnant water. Her creative response brought clean drinking water. Without the unexpected discovery of the people's vulnerability to this illness, she would not have been challenged to explore new forms of mastering the relevant bureaucracy. Through intervention and specific expertise, she achieved a transformation in the villages' long-term health. In a marvellous return, the people appointed her as Queen Mother in a traditional ceremony. Here is a supreme example of the anthropologist/fieldworker able to and choosing to give a life-enhancing return.

## To Conclude

There are multifaceted ways in which anthropologists can return their expertise, something already enhanced by the people as subjects. The micro context of fieldwork can resonate to transform lives and minds for decades. The search for simplistic generalizability or universals of banality can be misleading distractions. Anthropological practice, through sharing others' 'imponderabilia' of every day life, alongside the strange and familiar, enlarges our knowledge of difference as well as similarity. Texts emerging from lived participation and experiences have unpredictable creative consequences. Some texts may be misused for destructive ends, but optimists prefer to recognize the greater good. The anthropologists in this text migrated from armchair, desk and even laptop for embodied fieldwork across the globe, in unknown, tiny or well-trampled places. They were open to what confronted them rather than following some formulaic agenda. The people whom they encountered helped show the way. The anthropologists learned and were transformed. In turn, the emergent knowledge in so many contexts, across time and place around the world, has contributed to ever-subtle awareness of the full range of humanity, alongside its commonalities. The recorded words in extended, informal dialogues, later selected in this text, reveal crucial insights of discovery and practice. The anthropologists' narratives of fieldwork continue to resonate.

# Appendix: Questions for the Anthropologist
### *By Judith Okely*

1. What were, if any, your initial ideas? In what way, if any, were they changed in the field?
2. How did you establish connections?
3. Were there any key events/encounters?
4. Did serendipity play a part?
5. How did you go about your research?
6. What were the most successful approaches?
7. What were the least successful approaches?
8. Did you learn by mistakes?
9. In what ways did you use (a) participant observation and (b) interviewing; either structured or semistructured?
10. Did you learn with your body and all your senses?
11. What, if at all, was the importance of memory?
12. Who were your main informants or associates?
13. What, if any, were the effects on rapport and your approach of your gender/age/'race'/ethnicity/nationality/and personality?
14. How did you record and make use of field notes?
15. Did photography or other images feature in your research?
16. What was the role of memory in analysis?

# Notes on Anthropologists and Interviewees

PAUL CLOUGH (BA. DPhil, Oxford University) is associate professor of anthropology, the University of Malta. His doctoral thesis was runner-up for the Audrey Richards Prize by the African Studies Association, United Kingdom. For twenty years, he has done fieldwork in West Africa on the cultural dimensions of rural economy. Recent publications are 'Polygyny and the Rural Accumulation of Capital' (2003), ' "Knowledge in Passing": Reflexive Anthropology and Religious Awareness' (2006) and 'The Impact of Changing Political Economy on Gender Relations in Islamizing Rural Hausaland, Nigeria' (2009). He is currently the chief editor of the *Journal of Mediterranean Studies*, and he co-edited *Powers of Good and Evil* (2001). Apart from rural political economy and economic anthropology, his main research interest is the dimension of morality in culture (2007).

LOUISE DE LA GORGENDIÈRE is associate professor of anthropology at Carleton University, Ottawa, Canada. She taught at Edinburgh University and worked as a social development adviser for the Department for International Development (UK; DFID), the French government and the United Nations (International Labour Office [United Nations]/United Nations Development Program [ILO/UNDP]). Her Ghanaian research began with an examination of Asante marriages (MA, University of Calgary), then shifted to development and education (PhD, Cambridge University). She conducted a study on HIV/AIDS in Congo (formerly Zaire). She is conducting research with the Ghanaian diaspora in Canada—investigating people's ongoing ties to Ghana, life histories and associational ties through Ghanaians' lived experiences within multicultural Canada.

ROY GIGENGACK, assistant professor of development anthropology, Wageningen University, Netherlands, graduated from the Amsterdam School for Social Science Research. Author of *Young, Damned and Banda: The World of Young Street People in Mexico City* (in press), he has held positions at Amsterdam University, the Free University, Amsterdam, Oxford University, and the Public Health Foundation of India. His research interests include street youth in Mexico City, Delhi and elsewhere; drug use and harm reduction strategies; child and adult prostitution; police work in developing countries; urban violence and qualitative methods. Gigengack worked alongside his partner Raquel Alonso Lopèz.

SUZETTE HEALD has extensive field experience in Africa. Her early research concentrated on issues of violence, masculinity and ritual among the Gisu of Uganda, and she is the author of *Controlling Anger: The Anthropology of Gisu Violence* (1998 [1989]);

*Manhood and Morality: Sex, Violence and Ritual in Gisu Society* (1999). Her interests
have moved into HIV/AIDS and vigilantism in East Africa. This latter research builds
upon twenty-five years' intermittent fieldwork among Kuria in Kenya, resulting in
articles and an ethnographic film titled *Law and War in Rural Kenya*. In 2010–11, she
was awarded a fellowship at the Institut d'Études Avancées in Nantes.

MICHAEL HERZFELD (DPhil, Oxford University, 1976) is professor of anthropology at Harvard University, where has taught since 1991. He is an ethnographic filmmaker, the author of ten books and a recipient of the J. I. Staley Prize and the Rivers
Memorial Medal (both in 1994) as well as honorary doctorates from the Université
Libre de Bruxelles (2005) and the University of Macedonia (Thessaloniki) (2011)
and a DLitt from the University of Birmingham (1989), He was editor of *American
Ethnologist* (1995–98) and is currently editor-at-large (responsible for "Polyglot Perspectives") at *Anthropological Quarterly*. His research in Greece, Italy and Thailand
has addressed the social and political impact of historic conservation and gentrifica-
tion, the dynamics of nationalism and bureaucracy and the ethnography of knowledge among artisans and intellectuals.

SIGNE HOWELL (DPhil. Oxford University, 1981) is professor of social anthropology at the University of Oslo. She previously lectured at Edinburgh University. Her
engagement with the Chewong hunter-gatherer-shifting cultivators in the rainforest
of peninsular Malaysia continues until today since her original fieldwork in the late
1970s. She has also done fieldwork in Indonesia and undertook a major research
project on transnational adoption as a national and global practice. She has published
widely as a result of her three main research projects.

FELICIA HUGHES-FREELAND (BA, English, Cambridge University; PhD, social
anthropology, School of Oriental and African Studies, London) has researched dance
in Indonesia for thirty years. Her publications cover performance, ritual, media, gender,
Indonesian society and culture and anthropological theory. She has edited and co-edited
several books and authored *Embodied Communities: Dance Traditions and Change in
Java* (2008). Trained in documentary filmmaking at the National Film and Television
School, her films *The Dancer and the Dance* (1988) and *Tayuban: Dancing the Spirit
in Java* (1996) are distributed by the Royal Anthropological Institute (RAI). Current research includes ritual performance, intangible heritage and ownership in Southeast Asia
and women filmmakers in post-Suharto Indonesia.

I-M. KAMINSKI (PhD, social anthropology, Gothenburg University, 1980) is associate at Linacre College, Oxford University and Tokyo Mejiro University. A Polish-
born, Swedish anthropologist and filmmaker, he was elected to the Swedish Writers'
Union. His work has been translated into eleven languages. After eighteen years in
exile (1972–90), he frequently revisits Poland, where he teaches cultural anthropology at Warsaw University. He has done fieldwork among the Inuit, Ainu, Okinawans
and Roma. His 2007 documentary *The Ainu* (Anthropos Pictures) was screened at

the Fourth International Symposium, Linguapax Asia, Tokyo University. Father of two Eurasian children, he lives in Tokyo, Bruges, and Oxford.

MARGARET KENNA, emeritus professor of social anthropology at Swansea University, studied anthropology at University College London and was a doctoral student at the London School of Economics, then the University of Kent, Canterbury. Her fieldwork (covering a forty-five-year span) focuses on the small Greek island of Anafi and Anafiot migrants in Athens, dealing with kinship, inheritance, ritual, migration and tourism. She is an honorary member of the Anafiot Migrants Association and an honorary citizen of the island. Publications include *Greek Island Life: Fieldwork on Anafi* (2001), *The Social Organization of Exile* (2001) and numerous articles.

NANCY LINDISFARNE taught social anthropology at the School of Oriental and African Studies, London until 2001. She has done fieldwork in Iran, Afghanistan, Turkey and Syria and published articles on gender, marriage and Islam in the Middle East. As Tapper, she published *Bartered Brides: Politics, Gender and Marriage in an Afghan Tribal Society* (1991). As Lindisfarne, she was co-editor with Cornwall of the pioneering *Dislocating Masculinity* (1994), and her short stories about elite families in Syria appeared in Arabic in 1998 and in English in 2000. Her 2001 publication about nationalism, secularism and practised Islam anticipated her 2002 Audrey Richards Lecture, Oxford, which later appeared in *Taking Sides: Ethics, Politics and Fieldwork in Anthropology* (2008). She retired from teaching to study at St. Martins School of Art and Design London. Her exhibition of photographs of Iran appeared in London and Manchester. Another exhibition of prints, paintings and photographs, 'Reconsidering Iran', was held at Wolfson College, Oxford. She has been studying a former Welsh mining community.

RAQUEL ALONSO LÓPEZ qualified in psychology postgraduate studies at the University of Mexico. She has an MA in social science at the University of Amsterdam. She is a PhD student at the New School graduates sociology programme. Her main research interest is in corruption and violence, police and policing in Mexico City. She has ethnographic field research experience among street youth populations and police officers in Mexico City.

MALCOLM DONALD MCLEOD retired in 2006 from his post as vice-principal, University of Glasgow, where he was director of the Hunterian Museum and Art Gallery and professor of African Studies. He read history then social anthropology at Oxford University. He carried out research in Ghana before returning to Cambridge University to teach anthropology. In 1974 he was appointed keeper of ethnography at the British Museum and ran the Museum of Mankind until 1990, when he moved to Glasgow. A trustee of National Museums Scotland from 2005, he continues to work on several projects in Ghana, where he set up a museum for the Asante in 1995.

BRIAN MORRIS (BEd, PhD, London School of Economics) is emeritus professor of anthropology, Goldsmiths College, London University. Leaving school at fifteen, he was a foundry worker, seaman and tea planter in Malawi before becoming a teacher. He carried out fieldwork among the hunter-gatherer people in South India. He has published books on a variety of subjects, including the anthropology of religion, conceptions of the individual, the Self and herbalism in Malawi. He has also published numerous articles on ethnobotany, ethnozoology, classification, ritual and symbolism. He has carried out fieldwork regularly in Malawi, most recently researching human-insect interactions.

HÉLÈNE NEVEU KRINGELBACH (DPhil, social anthropology, Oxford University, 2005) is departmental lecturer in anthropology and African studies at Oxford University. She conducted research on dance troupes in Dakar, Senegal, and is currently completing a monograph from her doctoral thesis. The research is set in historical perspective and examines the ways in which urban identities in Senegal are formed through dance, both in everyday life and as a professional occupation and through varied genres. Whilst still following the trajectories of Senegalese performers, she is beginning a new research project on Euro-Senegalese families in locations across Europe and Senegal.

AKIRA OKAZAKI (PhD, social anthropology, School of Oriental and African Studies, London University) is professor at the Graduate School of Social Sciences in the Faculty of Social Sciences, Hitotsubashi University, Japan. With specialisms in social anthropology and African studies, he has done fieldwork among the Masai in Kenya and the Gamk in the Sudan, about whom he has published numerous articles. He was visiting fellow at the Max Planck Institute for Social Anthropology, Halle, Germany.

JOANNA OVERING (BA, Duke University, MA, history, University of Connecticut, PhD, anthropology, Brandeis University) is professor emeritus in social anthropology, St Andrews University. Her research interests include egalitarianism, gender, linguistics, philosophical anthropology, indigenous cosmologies, aesthetics and the ethnography of Amazonia. Formerly lecturer at the London School of Economics, with a joint appointment at the Institute of Latin American Studies, her many publications include *The Piaroa; A People of the Orinoco Basin: A Study in Kinship and Marriage* (1975), *Reason and Morality* (ed., 1985), *Anthropology of Love and Anger: The Aesthetics of Conviviality in Native South America* (co-editor with A. Passes, 1998) and *Key Concepts in Social Anthropology* (with N. Rapport, 2000).

JONATHAN PARRY (BA, PhD, social anthropology, Cambridge University) is emeritus professor of anthropology at the London School of Economics. He has done field research in north and central India on different topics. His publications include *Caste and Kinship in Kangra* (1979) and *Death in Banaras* (1994). He co-edited *Death and the Regeneration of Life* (1982), *Money and the Morality of Exchange* (1989) and others.

CAROL SILVERMAN, professor of anthropology and folklore, the University of Oregon, has examined the intersection of politics, social position, gender and performance arts among Roma, exploring their nuanced identity in the Balkans and transnational spaces, including New York. Musician and human rights educator, Silverman investigates Romani music as embedded in political economy and interethnic relationships. Her current project, supported by a Guggenheim fellowship, explores the globalization of Balkan Gypsy music in Western Europe and the United States, analysing its performance, consumption and production. Considering how collaborations and hybridity may be liberating and/or exploitative, she documents strategies through which non-Roma, including celebrity patrons, appropriate and transform Gypsy music.

MOHAMMAD TALIB held a faculty position in sociology at Jamia Millia Islamia University, Delhi (1980–2000). He is Sultan Bin Abdul Aziz fellow in the anthropology of Muslim societies at the Oxford Centre for Islamic Studies. He is also Islamic Centre lecturer at the Institute of Social and Cultural Anthropology, Oxford. His ethnography of urban migrant workers in stone quarrying led to *Writing Labour: Stone Quarry Workers in Delhi* (2010). His interest in anthropology of Muslim societies and Islam focuses on the institutions of religious education and Sufi groups in India as well as the United Kingdom. Current research—*Madrassahs in the Recent History: An Alternative View between Anthropology and International Relations*—surveys studies on the madrassahs within the broad reference of geo-political dynamics around Afghanistan before 9/11.

SUE WRIGHT (BA, history, Dunelm University; DPhil, social anthropology, Oxford University) is professor of educational anthropology, Aarhus University, Denmark. Formerly director of the Centre for Learning and Teaching—(C-SAP) and senior lecturer in cultural studies, Birmingham University, and lecturer in social anthropology, Sussex University, she has done fieldwork in Iran, England and Denmark. From 1974 she studied political organization in Doshman Ziari, Iran during the Shah's modernization, with a return study after the Islamic revolution. Her work on anthropology of policy arose from political transformations under the Thatcher, Major and Blair governments, including central government's promotion of the 'enterprising individual', local government's mobilizing of 'community' to resist the rollback of the state and how people subject to both policies responded. Later studies include participant observation on culture and world governance in the United Nations Educational, Scientific and Cultural Organization (UNESCO) and university reform from the perspectives of students, academics, managers and national and international policymakers in England and Denmark.

HELENA WULFF is professor of social anthropology at Stockholm University, Sweden. Her current research engages with expressive cultural forms in transnational perspective. The transnational world and social memory through dance have generated questions in relation to place, mobility, the emotions and visual culture. She has recently focused on writing and Irish contemporary literature as process and form. Wulff's monographs include *Ballet across Borders* (1998) and *Dancing at the Crossroads* (2007). She has edited and co-edited numerous volumes (1995, 2003, 2007, 2010). She was co-editor of *Social Anthropology,* journal of the European Association of Social Anthropologists, and was its vice president.

JOSEBA ZULAIKA (PhD, Princeton University, 1982) is professor of anthropology and Basque studies at the University of Nevada, Reno (UNR), since 1990. He is the co-director of the Center for Basque Studies at UNR. He is the author of fourteen books, including *Basque Violence: Metaphor and Sacrament* (1982), *Terror and Taboo* (with W. A. Douglass, 1996), and *Terrorism: The Self-Fulfilling Prophecy* (2009). He is working on an ethnography of the city of Bilbao, addressing the role of architecture in reviving urban centres with particular attention to the apocalyptic aspects of contemporary culture.

Okely also recorded dialogues with Alan Campbell, Edinburgh University, tropical forest Brazil; Susan Drucker-Brown, Cambridge University, Ghana; Narmala Halstead, University of East London, Guyana and diaspora; Roy Willis, Edinburgh University, East Africa. If not directly quoted, their insights have informed the text.

# Notes

## Chapter 1

1. I was awarded a one-year Senior Fellowship (1996–7). In my application, I had naïvely and over-optimistically aimed to complete two books, one on field methods and the other on my six month's 1980s fieldwork in Normandy. I eventually concluded that the latter was insufficient for a monograph so concentrated on further articles.

   By 1997 I had completed detailed draft chapters of the methods book when I submitted my Economic and Social Research Council (ESRC) Final Report. But already transcripts of dialogues with several anthropologists had made me recognize that these, and others planned, needed an *entire* transformation of that text. The interviewees offered unique and original insights. Hence my extended intellectual quest and refusal to submit the draft in the Report.

   The ESRC telephoned me to say that my explanation and satisfactory proof of alternative publications; a book containing new articles and complex re-editing of others (Okely 1996b), a field trip to Normandy, filming and other material eventually used for my 1998 Inaugural (Okely 2001), along with additional articles, had initially encouraged a favourable assessment. I had been given one below the top rating. But subsequently, the committee's positive assessment was overturned and I was awarded the *lowest but one* rating. It was wrongly asserted that my publications had been completed *before* the Fellowship. No appeal was permitted to prove otherwise. Apparently the unknown 'correct procedures' had not been followed within the time limit.

   Thus intellectual integrity and openness to new knowledge and discovery, emerging through years of re-thinking, listening, learning and editing are punished. The judgement would severely block any future grant applications. As chapter 2 fulsomely demonstrates, anthropologists are best if open to changing their initial focus. It was, paradoxically, my freedom to think far from administrative and departmental pettiness, that I re-envisaged the core of this book. Thus I should, notwithstanding, thank the ESRC for those rare months, despite its brutal penalty for having responded creatively to the unpredictable.

   Meanwhile, driven by intellectual dedication, I have personally carried the massive costs of over ninety hours of tape transcriptions of interviews, each often lasting four hours. A few transcriptions were generously subsidized by a Hull University research award.

2. Given the informal conversational exchange, I have edited out repetitions, interjections and link phrases such as 'You know', 'I believe', 'And so'. Some anthropologists corrected each phrase of the transcripts, believing the entire text would be published. When I explained that I sought the spontaneity of the spoken word, most agreed to only minor adjustments and necessary corrections.

3. *Reflexive Ethnography* (Aull Davies 1999) is a key text. My reservation is the tendency towards injunctions, for example pp. 86–7. Ellen's classic (1984) has less discussion of participant observation.

4. In a sociology department, I witnessed empiricist colleagues interrogating bewildered undergraduates exploring innovative, qualitative dissertation topics. At the outset, they were expected to produce hypotheses to 'operationalize'.

5. When I was appointed to a lectureship in the Essex sociology department, a leading communist feminist organized an (unsuccessful) petition, protesting my selection. She presumed that anthropology was anti-leftist 'symbolic-interactionism', denying political economy and asserting biological racial 'types'. She was incredulous that my social anthropology course was so popular (Okely 2007a: 240–2).

## Chapter 2

1. Addressing such issues in the 2004 Association of Social Anthropologists-conference, my paper, marginally mentioning Gypsies, was not integrated in sessions on movement. Thus lessons from nomads are archived, then 'discovered' by those engaged with the sedentarized.

2. Literary UK celebrities, if not elsewhere, plagiarize published autobiographies and analytic ethnography because they are deemed mere 'reportage'. McEwan's novel (2001) reproduced, without quotation marks, a passage from an autobiography (Andrews 1977). Headlined in *The Guardian* (27 November 2006), McEwan denied plagiarism defining the material merely as 'superb reportage'. Seemingly, novelists can plagiarize non-fiction because, like anthropology, it is downgraded as reportage. Okely's analysis of Gypsy animal classification (1983: 89–104; 1994a) was plagiarized then hailed years later as Martin Amis's wife's original discovery (Armitstead 2008).

3. My doctorate included a study of Gypsy conflict resolution, so withheld from circulation. Publication, decades later, coincided with anti-Traveller publicity by the Conservative Leader before the 2005 election (*The Independent,* 20 March 2005). Ethnographic details were withheld (Okely 2005).

4. This publication was the only ethnography of private all-girls' institutions. Earlier research had focused on all-boys institutions, thus privileging taken-for-granted masculine power. In 2010 it was selected for a Harvard psychology course.

# Chapter 3

1. 'Experts' on terrorism in the 1980s emphasized the pathological psychology of individuals as isolates. The wider political/ethnographic context, as meaningful system, was not considered.

# Chapter 7

1. Recently labelled 'evidence-based research', which privileges 'statistical meta-analysis', may be appropriate in medicine. Granted 'anecdotal evidence and intuition' (Dunifon et al. 2004: 3) may indeed be insufficient. But this hegemonic model risks inappropriate extension to ethnographic research.

# References and Further Reading

Abramson, A. (1987), 'Beyond the Samoan Controversy in Anthropology: A History of Sexuality in the Eastern Interior of Fiji', in P. Caplan (ed.), *The Cultural Construction of Sexuality*, London: Tavistock, pp. 193–216.

'Academic Fury over Government Order for the AHRC to Study the Big Society', *The Observer* (27 March 2011).

Adams, B., Okely, J., Morgan, D., and Smith, D. (1975), *Gypsies and Government Policy in England*, London: Heinemann Educational Press.

Agar, M. (1980), *The Professional Stranger: An Informal Introduction to Ethnography*, London: Academic Press.

Amit, V. (ed.) (2000), *Constructing the Field: Ethnographic Fieldwork in the Contemporary World*, London: Routledge.

Anderson, P. (1969), 'Components of the National Culture', in A. Cockburn and R. Blackburn (eds.), *Student Power: Problems, Diagnosis, Action*, Harmondsworth: Penguin, pp. 214–84.

Andrews, L. (1977), *No Time for Romance*, London: Corgi Books.

Ardener, E. (1987), '"Remote Areas": Some Theoretical Considerations', in A. Jackson (ed.), *Anthropology at Home*, London: Routledge, pp. 38–54.

Arens, W. (1979), *The Man Eating Myth: Anthropology and Anthropophagy*, Oxford: Oxford University Press.

Armitstead, C. (2008), 'Plagiarism Is Nothing New in Academia: Few Professors Will Have Been Shocked by the Raj Persaud Story'. *Guardian Books Blog* (18 June), www.Guardian.co.uk.

Asad, T. (ed.) (1973), *Anthropology and the Colonial Encounter*, Ithaca, NY: Humanities Press.

Asad, T. (ed.) (1986), 'The Concept of Cultural Translation in British Social Anthropology', in J. Clifford and G. Marcus (eds.), *Writing Culture*, Berkeley: University of California Press, pp. 141–64.

Attwood, R. (2007) 'Study of Terrorism Steps up to New Level', *Times Higher Education* (22 June).

Augé, M. (1995), *Non-places: An Anthropology of Supermodernity* (trans. J. Howe), London: Verso.

Aull Davies, C. (1999), *Reflexive Ethnography: A Guide to Researching Selves and Others*, London: Routledge.

Battersby, C. (1989), *Gender and Genius: Towards a Feminist Aesthetics*, London: Women's Press.

Beeman, W. (2001), 'Writing for the Crisis', Guest editorial, *Anthropology Today*, 17/6: 1–2.

Beeman, W. (2007), 'Anthropology for the Authorities—Then and Now', Paper presented for panel 'Against the Weaponisation of Anthropology: Critical Perspective on the Military, War and US Foreign Policy', American Anthropological Association, Washington DC, November 28–December 2.

Beatty, A. (2009), *A Shadow Falls: In the Heart of Java*, London: Faber and Faber.

Beck, U. (1998), *World Risk Society*, Cambridge: Polity Press.

Becker, H. S. (1963), *Outsiders: Studies in the Sociology of Deviance*, New York: Free Press.

Bell, C. (1984), 'The SSRC Restructured and Defended', in C. Bell and H. Roberts (eds.), *Social Researching: Politics, Problems, Practice*, London: Routledge and Kegan Paul, pp. 14–31.

Bell, D., Caplan, P., and Karim, W. (eds.) (1993), *Gendered Fields: Women, Men and Ethnography*, London: Routledge.

Benjamin, W. (1992), *Illuminations* (trans. H. Zohn), London: Fontana.

Berg, M. (2009), 'Between Cosmopolitanism and the National Slot: Cuba's Diasporic Children of the Revolution', *Identities: Global Studies in Culture and Power* 16/2: 129–56.

Berg, M. (2011), *Diasporic Generations: Memory, Politics, and Nation among Cubans in Spain*, Oxford: Berghahn.

Besteman, C. (2008), 'Beware of Those Bearing Gifts': An Anthropologist's View of AFRICOM, *Anthropology Today*, 24/5 (October): 20–1.

Blacking, J. (ed.) (1977), *The Anthropology of the Body*, London: Academic Press.

Bloch, M., and Bloch, J. (1980), 'Women and the Dialectics of Nature in Eighteenth-century French Thought', in C. McCormack and M. Strathern (eds.), *Nature, Culture and Gender*, Cambridge: Cambridge University Press, pp. 25–41.

Boffey, D. (2011), 'Row over Research Funding and David Cameron's Big Society: Academics Claim Research Council Behaviour Is "Craven" ', *The Observer* (April 3).

Borneman, J. (2009), 'The Fieldwork Encounter, Experience, and the Making of Truth: An Introduction', in J. Borneman and A. Hammoudi (eds.), *Being There: The Fieldwork Encounter and the Making of Truth*, Berkeley: University of California Press, pp. 1–24.

Borneman, J. and A. Hammoudi (eds.) (2009), *Being There: The Fieldwork Encounter and the Making of Truth*, Berkeley: University of California Press.

Bourdieu, P. (1977), *Outline of a Theory of Practice*, Cambridge: Cambridge University Press.

Bourdieu, P. (1984), *Distinction: A Social Critique of the Judgement of Taste* (trans. R. Nice), London: Routledge & Kegan Paul.

Bradburd, D. (1998), *Being There: The Necessity of Fieldwork*, Washington DC: Smithsonian Institution Press.

Breton, A. (1937), *L'Amour fou*, Paris: Gallimard.

Brody, H. (1973), *Inishkillane: Change and Decline in the West of Ireland*, London: Allen Lane, Penguin.

Brooks, D. (1993), 'Living with Ventilation: Confessions of an Addict', *Care of the Critically Ill*, 8/5 (Sept./Oct.): 205–7.

Browne, J. (2010), *Securing a Sustainable Future for Higher Education in England*, Independent report commissioned by the Labour government and presented to the coalition.

Bryceson, D., and Vuorela, U. (eds.) (2002), *The Transnational Family: New European Frontiers and Global Networks*, Oxford: Berg.

Budilova, L., and Jakoubek, M. (2009), 'Anthropological Fieldwork Site and Roma Communities: Roma/Gypsies in the Czech and Slovak Republic', *Anthropological Notebooks*, 15/2: 5–14.

Burgess, R. (1984), *In the Field: An Introduction to Field Research*, London: Allen & Unwin.

Byatt, A. (1996), *Book Mark*, BBC2 TV, March 30.

Campbell, A. (1995), *Getting to Know WaiWai: Amazonian Ethnography*, London: Routledge.

Caplan, P. (1992), 'Spirits and Sex: A Swahili Informant and His Diary' in J. Okely and H. Callaway (eds), *Anthropology and Autobiography,* London: Routledge, pp. 64–81.

Caplan, P. (1997), *African Voices, African Lives: Personal Narratives from a Swahili Village*, London: Routledge.

Caplan, P. (ed.) (2003a), *The Ethics of Anthropology: Debates and Dilemmas*, London: Routledge.

Caplan, P. (2003b), 'Introduction: Anthropology and Ethics' in P. Caplan (ed.), *The Ethics of Anthropology: Debates and Dilemmas*, London: Routledge, pp. 1–33.

*Chambers 20th Century Dictionary* (1983), New Edition, Edinburgh: Chambers.

Clark, C. (2001), '"Invisible Lives": The Gypsies and Travellers of Britain', PhD dissertation, Edinburgh University.

Clifford, J. (1988), 'On Ethnographic Authority', in J. Clifford (ed.), *The Predicament of Culture*, Cambridge, MA: Harvard University Press, pp. 21–54.

Clifford, J. (1997), 'Spatial Practices: Fieldwork, Travel, and the Disciplining of Anthropology', in J. Clifford (ed.), *Routes: Travel and Translation in the Late Twentieth Century*, Cambridge, MA: Harvard University Press, pp. 52–91.

Clifford, J., and Marcus, G. (eds.) (1986), *Writing Culture*, Berkeley: University of California Press.

Clough, P. (1981), 'Farmers and Traders in Hausaland', *Development and Change*, 12: 273–92.

Clough, P. (2003), 'Polygyny and the Rural Accumulation of Capital: Testing a Model Based on Continuing Research in Northern Nigeria', *Etnofoor* 16/1: 5–29.

Clough, P. (2006), '"Knowledge in Passing": Reflexive Anthropology and Religious Awareness', *Anthropological Quarterly*, 79/2 (Spring): 261–83.

Clough, P. (2007), 'Between Anthropology and Philosophy: The Relevance of Kinship to Moral Reasoning in Culture and in Moral Theory'. *Social Analysis*, 51/1: 135–55.

Clough, P. (2009), 'The Impact of Rural Political Economy on Gender Relations in Islamizing Hausaland, Nigeria', *Africa*, 79/4: 595–613.

Clough, P., and Mitchell, J. (eds.) (2001), *Powers of Good and Evil*. Oxford: Berghahn.

Clyde Mitchell, J. (1969), *Social Networks in Urban Situations: Analysis of Personal Relationships in Central African Towns*, Manchester: Manchester University Press.

Coffey, A. (1999), *The Ethnographic Self: Fieldwork and the Representation of Identity*, London: Sage.

Condominas, G. (1965), *L'exotique est quotidien: Sar Luk, Vietnam Central*, Paris: Plon.

Cornwall, A., and Lindisfarne, N. (eds.) (1994), *Dislocating Masculinity: Comparative Ethnographies*, London: Routledge.

Crapanzano, V. (1980), *Tuhami: Portrait of a Moroccan*, Chicago: University of Chicago Press.

Csordas, T. (ed.) (1994), *Embodiment and Experience: The Existential Ground of Culture and Self*, Cambridge: Cambridge University Press.

Csordas, T. (ed.) (2002), *Body/Meaning/Healing*, New York: Palgrave Macmillan.

Davis, J. (1987), *Libyan Politics: Tribe and Revolution*, London: Tauris.

Dawson, A. (1990), 'Ageing and Community in a Post-mining Town, N. E. England', PhD dissertation, Essex University.

de Beauvoir, S. (1949), *Le Deuxième Sexe*, Paris: Gallimard.

de Beauvoir, S. (1958), *Mémoires d'une jeune fille bien rangée*, Paris: Gallimard.

de la Gorgendière, L. (1992), 'Asante Residence: Searching for Norms', in J. Sterner and N. David (eds.), *An African Commitment: Papers in Honour of P. L. Shinnie*, Calgary: University of Calgary Press, pp. 87–103.

de la Gorgendière, L. (1993), Education and Development in Ghana: An Asante Village Study, PhD dissertation, Cambridge University.

de la Gorgendière, L. (1995), 'When You Educate a Woman, Do You Really Educate a Nation? Females and Education in Ghana', *Proceedings from the International Conference at the University of Cambridge on the Case for Girls' Education in Sub-Saharan Africa*, July, Cambridge University, pp. 1–16.

de la Gorgendière, L. (1999), 'Women's Life Stories and the Next Generation in Ghana: Educate a Woman', *Social Analysis*, 43/1: 53–72.

de la Gorgendière, L. (2005), 'Rights and Wrongs: HIV/AIDS Research in Africa', *Human Organization, the Journal of the Society for Applied Anthropology*, 64/2: 166–78.

Dendrinos, P. (2008), Contemporary Greek Male Homosexualities: Greek Gay Men's Experiences of the Family, the Military and the LGBT Movement, PhD dissertation, Glasgow University, formerly Hull.

Deutscher, I. (1970), 'Words and Deeds', in W. Filstead (ed.), *Qualitative Methodology: Firsthand Involvement with the Social World*, Chicago: Markham, pp. 27–51.

De Soto, H., and Dudwick, N. (eds.) (2000), *Fieldwork Dilemmas: Anthropologists in Post Socialist States*, Madison: University of Wisconsin Press.

Dickinson, M. (2008), *New State; Old Problems: Anjam,* DVD.

Ditton, J., and Williams, R. (1981), *The Fundable versus the Doable*, Glasgow: Glasgow University Press.

Douglas, M. (1966), *Purity and Danger*, London: Routledge & Kegan Paul.

Doyle, J. (2000), 'Nationalism and Belonging: The Politics of Home for English Speakers of Montreal, Quebec', PhD dissertation, Hull University.

Dresch, P., James, W. and Parkin, D. (eds.) (2000), *Anthropologists in a Wider World: Essays on Field Research*, Oxford: Berghahn.

Dubisch, J. (1995), 'Lovers in the Field: Sex, Dominance, and the Female Anthropologist' in D. Kulick and M. Wilson (eds.), *Taboo, Sex, Identity and Erotic Subjectivity in Anthropological Fieldwork*, London: Routledge, pp. 29–50.

Dunifon, R. et al. (2004), Evidence-based Extension, *Journal of Extension*, 42/2: 1–9, www.joe.org.

Durakbasa, A. (1991), 'A Cross Cultural Study of Female Identity: Kemalist Feminists in Turkey and British Suffragettes', PhD dissertation, Essex University.

Durkheim, E. (1897/1952), *Suicide, a Study in Sociology* (trans. J. Spaulding and G. Simpson), London: Routledge & Kegan Paul.

Dwyer, K. (1982), *Moroccan Dialogues: Anthropology in Question*, Long Grove, IL: Waveland Press.

Dyson-Hudson, N. (1972), 'Introduction', in W. Irons and N. Dyson-Hudson (eds.), *Perspectives on Nomadism*, Leiden: Brill, pp. 1–15.

Eco, U. (1998), *Serendipities: Language and Lunacy* (trans. W. Weaver), London: Orion.

Edgar, I. (1995), *Dreamwork, Anthropology and the Caring Professions*, Aldershot: Avebury.

Ellen, R. (ed.) (1984), *Ethnographic Research: A Guide to General Conduct*, London: Academic Press.

Elyas, N. A. (2011), 'Care of Elderly Women in Saudi Arabia: A Comparison of Institutional and Family Settings', PhD dissertation, Hull University.

Evans-Pritchard, E. (1937), *Witchcraft, Oracles and Magic among the Azande*, Oxford: Oxford University Press.

Evans-Pritchard, E. (1940), *The Nuer*, Oxford: Clarendon Press.

Evans-Pritchard, E. (1962), *Essays in Social Anthropology*, London: Faber and Faber.

Fabian, J. (1983), *Time and the Other: How Anthropology Made Its Object*, New York: Columbia University Press.

Falk Moore, S. (2009), 'Encounter and Suspicion in Tanzania', in J. Borneman and A. Hammoudi (eds.), *Being There: The Fieldwork Encounter and the Making of Truth*, Berkeley: University of California Press, pp. 151–82.

Fog Olwig, K., and Hastrup, K. (eds.) (1997), 'Introduction', in *Siting Culture: The Shifting Anthropological Object*, London: Routledge.

Foster, C. H. (1995), 'Drug Users in a Therapeutic Cul-de-sac', PhD dissertation, Edinburgh University.

Foster, C. H. (1998), 'Of Tales, Myth, Metaphor and Metonym', in R. S. Barbour and G. Huby (eds.), *Meddling with Mythology: AIDS and the Social Construction of Knowledge*, London: Routledge, pp. 144–59.

Foucault, M. (1977), *Discipline and Punish* (trans. A. Sheridan), London: Allen Lane.

Frankenberg, R. (1957), *Village on the Border. A Social Study of Religion, Politics, and Football in a North Wales Community*, London: Cohen and West.

Frazer, J. (1890), *The Golden Bough: A Study in Magic and Religion*, vols. 1 and 2.

Frean, A., and Evans, M. (2006), 'Universities "Asked to Act as Spies for Intelligence Services" ', *The Times* (Oct. 19).

Freud, S. (1900/1954), *The Interpretation of Dreams* (trans. J. Strachey), London: George Allen Unwin.

Ghassem-Fachandi, P. (ed.) (2009), *Violence: Ethnographic Encounters*, Oxford: Berg.

Geertz, C. (1975), *The Interpretation of Cultures*, London: Hutchinson.

Geertz, C. (1988), *Works and Lives*, Cambridge: Polity.

Gibb, R. (1999), 'A Republic under Threat? Multiculturalism, Anti-racism and Social Movements in Contemporary France', PhD dissertation, Edinburgh University.

Gibb, R. (2003), 'Constructions et mutations de l'antiracisme en France', *Journal des anthropologues*, 94–95, 165–79.

Gigengack, R. (in press), *Young, Damned and Banda: The World of Young Street People in Mexico City, 1990–1997*, Oxford: Berghahn.

Glaser, B., and Strauss, A. (1967), *The Discovery of Grounded Theory: Strategies for Qualitative Research*, New York: Aldine.

Gledhill, J. (2006), in P. Baty, 'Life-risking 'Spy Plan Pulled'', *Times Higher Education*, 20 October.

Gomoll, L. (2010), 'Anthropology and US Militarization', *Anthropology News* (February): 9.

Gonzalez, R. (2007), 'Phoenix Reborn? The Rise of the "Human Terrain System" ', *Anthropology Today*, 23/6 (December): 21–2.

Goodman, R. (1990/1993), *Japan's 'International Youth': The Emergence of a New Class of Schoolchildren*, Oxford: Clarendon Paperbacks.

Goody, E. (1975), 'Towards a Theory of Questions', in E. Goody (ed.), *Questions and Politeness*, Cambridge: Cambridge University Press, pp. 17–43.

Gough, K. (1968), 'New Proposals for Anthropologists', *Current Anthropology*, 9/5: 403–35.

Gullestad, M. (1984), *Kitchen-Table Society*, Oslo: Universitetsforlaget.

Gupta, A., and Ferguson, J. (1997a), 'Culture, Power and Place: Ethnography at the End of an Era', in A. Gupta and J. Ferguson (eds.), *Culture, Power and Place: Explorations in Critical Anthropology*, Durham, NC: Duke University Press, pp. 1–29.

Gupta, A., and Ferguson, J. (1997b), 'Discipline and Practice: "The Field" as Site, Method, and Location in Anthropology', in A. Gupta and J. Ferguson (eds.), *Anthropological Locations: Boundaries, and Grounds of a Field Science*, Berkeley: University of California Press.

Halstead, N. (2004), 'Being There: "Non-places," Home and the Rituals of Leave-taking', paper delivered to the European Association of Social Anthropologists (EASA) conference, Vienna.

Halstead, N. (2008), 'Introduction: Experiencing the Ethnographic Present: Knowing through "Crisis"', in N. Halstead, E. Hirsch and J. Okely (eds.), *Knowing How to Know: Fieldwork and the Ethnographic Present*, Oxford: Berghahn, pp. 1–20.

Halstead, N. (in press), 'Gift Practices in Guyanese East Indian Diaspora: Belonging, Loss and Status', *Journal of Latin American and Caribbean Anthropology.*

Hammersley, M., and Atkinson, P. (1983), *Ethnography: Principles in Practice*, London: Tavistock.

Hammoudi, A. (2009), 'Textualism and Anthropology: On the Ethnographic Encounter, or an Experience of the Haji', in J. Borneman and A. Hammoudi (eds.), *Being There: The Fieldwork Encounter and the Making of Truth*, Berkeley: University of California Press, pp. 25–54.

Hannerz, U. (1969), *Soulside: Inquiries into Ghetto Culture and Community*, New York: Columbia University Press.

Harding, S. (1986), *The Science Question in Feminism*, Milton Keynes: Open University Press.

Hardman, C. (1973), 'Can There Be an Anthropology of Children?', *Journal of the Anthropology Society Oxford*, 4/1: 85–99.

Hastrup, K. (1992), 'Writing Ethnography: State of the Art', in J. Okely and H. Callaway (eds.), *Anthropology and Autobiography*, London: Routledge, pp. 116–33.

Hastrup, K., and Fog Olwig, K. (eds.) (1997), *Siting Culture: The Shifting Anthropological Object*, London: Routledge.

Hastrup, K., and Hervik, P. (eds.) (1994), *Social Experience and Anthropological Knowledge*, London: Routledge.

Heald, S. (1998 [1989]), *Controlling Anger: The Anthropology of Gisu Violence*, Oxford: James Currey.

Heald, S. (1999), *Manhood and Morality: Sex, Violence and Ritual in Gisu Society.* London and New York: Routledge.

Heald, S. (2000), 'Tolerating the Intolerable: Cattle Raiding among the Kuria', in G. Aijmer and J. Abbink (eds.), *Meanings of Violence*, Oxford: Berg, pp. 101–21.

Heald, S. (2006), 'State, Law and Vigilantism in Northern Tanzania', *African Affairs*, 105: 265–83.

Heald, S. (2007), 'Controlling Crime and Corruption from Below: Sungusungu in Kenya', *International Relations*, 21/2: 183–99.

Heald, S. (2010), *Law and War in Rural Kenya.* Film presented at the Royal Anthropological Institute Film Festival, University College, London.

Hendry, J. (1992), 'The Paradox of Friendship in the Field: Analysis of a Long-term Anglo-Japanese Relationship', in J. Okely and H. Callaway (eds.), *Anthropology and Autobiography*, London: Routledge, pp 163–73.

Herzfeld, M. (1985), *The Poetics of Manhood: Contest and Identity in a Cretan Mountain Village*, Princeton, NJ: Princeton University Press.

Herzfeld, M. (1991), *A Place in History: Social and Monumental Time in a Cretan Town*, Princeton, NJ: Princeton University Press.

Hindes, B. (1973), *The Use of Official Statistics in Sociology: A Critique of Positivism and Ethnomethodology*, London: Macmillan.

Hirsch, P., James, W. and Parkin, D. (eds.) (2000), *Anthropologists in a Wider World*, Oxford: Berghahn.

Hockey, J. (1990), *Experiences of Death: An Anthropological Account*, Edinburgh: Edinburgh University Press.

Horowitz, I. L. (ed.) (1967), *The Rise and Fall of Project Camelot*, Cambridge, MA: MIT Press.

Houtman, G. (1988), 'Interview with Maurice Bloch', *Anthropology Today*, 4/1: 18–21.

Howell, S. (1984), *Society and Cosmos: Chewong of Peninsular Malaysia*, Oxford: Oxford University Press.

Howell, S. (2006), *The Kinning of Foreigners*: *Transnational Adoption in a Global Perspective*, Oxford: Berghahn.

Howell, S., and Talle, A. (eds.) (2011), *Returns to the Field: Multi-temporal Research and Contemporary Anthropology*, Bloomington: Indiana University Press.

Howes, D. (2003), *Sensual Relations: Engaging the Senses in Culture and Social Theory*, Ann Arbor: University of Michigan Press.

Huby, G. (1998), 'On Networks and Narratives: Research and the Construction of Chaotic Drug User Life Styles', in R. Barbour and G. Huby (eds.), *Meddling with Mythology*: *AIDS and the Social Construction of Knowledge*, London Routledge, pp 160–79.

Hugh-Jones, C. (1979), *From the Milk River: Spatial and Temporal Processes in Northwest Amazonia*, Cambridge: Cambridge University Press.

Hugh-Jones, S. (1977), *The Palm and the Pleiades: Initiation and Cosmology in Northwest Amazonia*, Cambridge: Cambridge University Press.

Hugh-Jones, S. (1989), 'Waribi and the White Men: History and Myth in Northwest Amazonia', in E. Tonkin, M. McDonald and M. Chapman (eds.), *Ethnicity and History*, London: Taylor & Francis, pp. 53–70.

Hughes-Freeland, F. (1997), 'Consciousness in Performance: a Javanese Theory', *Social Anthropology*, 5/21: 55–68.

Hughes-Freeland, F. (2001), 'Dance, Dissimulation, and Identity in Indonesia', in J. Hendry and C. W. Watson (eds.), *An Anthropology of Indirect Communication*, ASA Monographs 37, London, Routledge, pp. 145–62.

Hughes-Freeland, F. (2008a). 'Cross-dressing across Cultures: Genre and Gender in the Dances of Didik Nini Thowok', Working Paper Series 108, Asia Research Institute, National University of Singapore, 37 pp.

Hughes-Freeland, F. (2008b), *Embodied Communities: Dance Traditions and Change in Java*, Oxford: Berghahn.

Hughes-Freeland, F., and Crain, M. (eds.) (1998), *Recasting Ritual*, London: Routledge.

Huizer, G. (1979), 'Research through Action: Some Practical Experiences with Peasant Organisations', in G. Huizer and B. Mannheim (eds.), *The Politics of Anthropology*, The Hague: Mouton, pp. 395–420.

Huizer, G. and B. Mannheim (eds.) (1979), *The Politics of Anthropology: From Colonialism and Sexism toward a View from Below*, The Hague: Mouton.

Hume, L., and Mulcock, J. (eds.) (2004), *Anthropologists in the Field: Cases in Participant Observation*, New York: Columbia University Press.

Irvine, J., Miles, I. and Evans, J. (eds.) (1979), *Demystifying Social Statistics*, London: Pluto Press.

Issa, H. (2005), 'New Insights into Bedouin Culture: A study of Three Bedouin Descent Groups in Northeast Egypt'. PhD dissertation, Hull University.

Jackson, A. (ed.) (1987), *Anthropology at Home*, London: Routledge.

Jackson, J. (1990), '"I Am a Fieldnote": Fieldnotes as a Symbol of Professional Identity', in R. Sanjek (ed.), *Fieldnotes: The Makings of Anthropology*, London: Cornell University Press, pp. 3–33.

Jackson, J. (1995), '"Deja Entendu": The Liminal Qualities of Anthropological Fieldnotes', in J. Van Maanen (ed.), *Representation in Ethnography*, London: Sage, pp. 36–78.

Jackson, M. (1989), *Paths toward a Clearing: Radical Empiricism and Ethnographic Inquiry*, Bloomington: Indiana University Press.

Jakoubek, M., and Budilova, L. (2006), 'Kinship, Social Organization and Genealogical Manipulation in Gypsy Osadas in Eastern Slovakia', *Romani Studies*, 16/1 (June): 63–82.

James, W. (1973), 'The Anthropologist as Reluctant Imperialist', in T. Asad (ed.), *Anthropology and the Colonial Encounter*, London: Ithaca Press, pp. 41–69.

James, W., and Mills, D. (eds.) (2005), *The Qualities of Time: Anthropological Approaches*, Oxford: Berg.

Jan Mohamed, A, (1992), 'Worldliness-without World, Homelessness-as-Home: Toward a Definition of the Specular Border Intellectual', in M. Sprinkler (ed.), *Edward Said: A Critical Reader*, Oxford: Blackwell, pp. 96–120.

Jansen, S. (1998), 'Homeless at Home: Narrations of Post-Yugoslav Identities', in N. Rapport and A. Dawson (eds.), *Migrants of Identity: Perceptions of 'Home' in a World of Movement*, Oxford: Berg, pp. 85–109.

Jansen, S. (2000), 'Anti-nationalist Resistance in the Former Yugoslavia', PhD dissertation, Hull University.

Jarman, N. (1993), 'Intersecting Belfast', in B. Bender (ed.), *Landscape: Politics and Perspectives*, Oxford: Berg, pp. 107–38.

Johnson, M. (1984), 'Women in Iceland', PhD dissertation, Durham University.

Jorgensen, J. G., and Wolf, E. (1970), 'A Special Supplement: Anthropology on the Warpath in Thailand', *New York Review of Books* (Nov. 19): 1–4.

Kaminski, I-M. (1980), *The State of Ambiguity: Studies of Gypsy Refugees*, Gothenburg: Anthropological Research.

Kaminski, I-M. (2004), 'Applied Anthropology and Diplomacy: Renegotiating Conflicts in the Eurasian Diplomatic Gray Zone by Using Cultural Symbols', in H. J. Langholtz and C. Stout (eds.), *The Psychology of Diplomacy*, London: Greenwood Press, pp. 175–206.

Kaminski, I-M. (2007), 'Involve the Ainu in Japan-Russia Border Talks', Point of view column, *Asahi Shimbun and International Herald Tribune* (August 18–19), Tokyo.

Kaminski, I-M. (forthcoming), 'Identity without Birthright: Negotiating Children's Citizenship and Identity in Cross-Cultural Bureaucracy', in J. Waldren and I-M. Kaminski (eds.), *Learning from the Children: Childhood, Culture and Identity in a Changing World*, Oxford: Berghahn.

Keenan, J. (2008a), 'Ethical Questions for the Embedded', Review of D. Price, *Anthropological Intelligence*, *Times Higher Education*, 2 (October): 48–49.

Keenan, J. (2008b), 'US Militarization in Africa: What Anthropologists Should Know about Africom', *Anthropology Today*, 24/5 (October): 16–20.

Kenna, M. (1992), 'Changing Places and Altered Perspective: Research on a Greek Island in the 1960s and in the 1980s', in J. Okely and H. Callaway (eds.), *Anthropology and Autobiography*, London: Routledge, pp. 147–62.

Kenna, M. (2001a), *The Social Organisation of Exile: Greek Political Detainees in the 1930s*, Amsterdam: Harwood Academic.

Kenna, M. (2001b), *Greek Island Life: Fieldwork on Anafia*, Amsterdam: Harwood Academic.

Kenna, M. (2005), 'Why Does Incense Smell Religious? Greek Orthodoxy and the Anthropology of Smell', *Journal of Mediterranean Studies*, 15/1: 51–70.

Knowles, J. (1993), 'Masai Women and Gender Roles in Kenya', PhD dissertation, Durham University.

Kuczynski, M. (2006), Michael Posner, Obituary, *The Independent* (9 March).

Kuhn, T. (1962), *The Structure of Scientific Revolutions*, Chicago: University of Chicago Press.

Kuklick, H. (1991), *The Savage Within: The Social History of British Anthropology, 1885–1945*, Cambridge: Cambridge University Press.

Kuklick, H. (2011), 'Personal Equations: Reflections on the History of Fieldwork, With Special Reference to Sociocultural Anthropology', *Isis*, 102: 1–33.

Kulick, D., and Willson, M. (eds.) (1995), *Taboo: Sex, Identity and Erotic Subjectivity in Anthropological Fieldwork*, London: Routledge.

Lassiter, L. (2005), *The Chicago Guide to Collaborative Ethnography*, Chicago: University of Chicago Press.

Law, J. (2004), *After Method: Mess in Social Science Research*, London: Routledge.

Layton, R. (1995), 'Relating to the Country in the Western Desert', in E. Hirsch and M. O'Hanlon (eds.), *The Anthropology of Landscape: Perspectives on Place and Space*, Oxford: Oxford University Press, pp. 210–31.

Leach, E. (1964), *Political Systems of Highland Burma: A Study of Kachin Social Structure*, London: London School of Economics, Bell and Sons.

Leach, E. (1967), 'An Anthropologist's Reflections on a Social Survey', in D. Jongmans and P. Gutkind (eds.), *Anthropologists in the Field*, Assen: Van Gorcum, pp. 75–88.

Leach, E. (1968), *Pul Eliya: A Village in Ceylon: A Study of Land Tenure and Kinship*, Cambridge: Cambridge University Press.

Lienhardt, G. (1961), *Divinity and Experience: The Religion of the Dinka*, Oxford: Oxford University Press.

Lévi-Strauss, C. (1949/1969), *Les Structures élémentaires de la parenté* (trans. J. H. Bell, J. R. von Sturmer and R. Needham), Paris: Mouton.

Lévi-Strauss, C. (1955/1973), *Tristes Tropiques* (trans. J. Weightman and D. Weightman), London: Jonathan Cape.

Lévi-Strauss, C. (1966), *The Savage Mind* (trans. anon), London: Weidenfeld and Nicholson.

Lévi-Strauss, C. (1973/1977), *Structural Anthropology*, vol. 2, (trans. M. Layton), London: Allen Lane.

Lewis, H. (2007), 'Interrogating Community: Dispersed Refugees in Leeds' PhD dissertation, Hull University.

Lindisfarne, N. (Tapper) (1991), *Bartered Brides: Politics, Gender and Marriage in an Afghan Tribal Society*, Cambridge: Cambridge University Press.

Lindisfarne, N. (Tapper) (2000), *Dancing in Damascus: Stories*, Albany: State University of New York Press.

Lindisfarne, N. (Tapper) (2001), *Thank God, We're Secular: Gender, Islam and Turkish Republicanism*, Ankara, Turkey: Iletism.

Lindisfarne, N. (Tapper) (2008), 'Starting from Below', 2002 Audrey Richards Lecture, IGS Oxford, in H. Armbruster and A. Lareke (eds.), *Taking Sides: Ethics, Politics and Fieldwork in Anthropology*, Oxford: Berghahn.

Lutz, C. (2008), 'Selling Ourselves? The Perils of Pentagon Funding for Anthropology', Guest editorial, *Anthropology Today*, 24/5 (October): 1–3.

Macdonald, S. (2010), 'Making Ethics', in M. Melhuus, J. Mitchell and H. Wulff (eds.), *Ethnographic Practice in the Present*, Oxford: Berghahn, pp. 80–94.

MacClancy, J., and McDonaugh, C. (eds.) (1996), *Popularising Anthropology*, London: Routledge.

McDonald, M. (1989), *'We Are Not French!' Language, Culture and Identity in Brittany*, London: Routledge.

McEwan, I. (2001), *Atonement*, New York: Anchor Books.

McEwan, I. (2006), *The Guardian* (27 November): 1–2.

Malenou, J. (2001), 'Place and Identity in a Greek Mountain Village'. PhD, University of Hull.

Malinowski, B. (1922), *The Argonauts of the Western Pacific*, London: Routledge & Kegan Paul.

Malinowski, B. (1926), *Crime and Custom in Savage Society*, London: Routledge & Kegan Paul.

Malinowski, B. (1967), *A Diary in the Strict Sense of the Term*, London: Routledge & Kegan Paul.

Malkki, L. (1995), *Purity and Exile: Violence, Memory, and National Cosmology among Hutu Refugees in Tanzania*, Chicago: University of Chicago Press.

Mahnken, T. G. (2008), 'Partnership for Mutual Benefit: The Pentagon's Perspective, *Anthropology Today*, 24/5 (October): 3.

Maquet, J. (1964), 'Objectivity in Anthropology', *Current Anthropology*, 5: 47–55.

Marcus, G. (1998), 'Ethnography in/of the World System: The Emergence of Multisited Fieldwork', in G. Marcus, *Ethnography through Thick and Thin*, Princeton, NJ: Princeton University Press, pp. 79–104.

Marcus, G., and Okely, J. (2007), 'How Short Can Fieldwork Be?' Debate section, *Social Anthropology*, 15/3 (October): 353–67.

Marshall, G. (ed.) (1994), *The Concise Oxford Dictionary of Sociology*, Oxford: Oxford University Press.

Martin, E. (1987), *The Woman in the Body: A Cultural Analysis of Reproduction*, Milton Keynes: Open University Press.

Marx, K. (1887/1961), *Das Kapital/Capital: A Critical Analysis of Capitalist Production*, vol 1 (trans. S. Moore and E. Aveling), Moscow: Foreign Languages Publishing House.

Mascarenhas-Keyes, S. (1987), 'The Native Anthropologist: Constraints and Strategies in Research', in A. Jackson (ed.), *Anthropology at Home*, London: Routledge, pp. 180–95.

Mauss, M. (1935), 'Les Techniques du corps', in *Journal de Psychologie Normale et Pathologique*, 35: 271–93.

Mauss, M. (1954), *The Gift* (trans. I. Cunnison), London: Cohen & West.

Mayer, P. (1961), *Townsmen or Tribesmen*, Oxford: Oxford University Press.

Melhuus, M., Mitchell, J. P. and Wulff, H. (eds.) (2010), *Ethnographic Practice in the Present*, Oxford: Berghahn.

Meskell, L., and Pels, P. (eds.) (2005), *Embedding Ethics*, Oxford: Berg.

Mills, D. (2003), 'Like a Horse in Blinkers'? A Political History of Anthropology's Research Ethics', in P. Caplan (ed.), *The Ethics of Anthropology: Debates and Dilemmas*, London: Routledge. pp. 37–54.

Ministry of Housing and Local Government (1967), *Gypsies and Other Travellers*, London: Her Majesty's Stationery Office.

Mitchell, J. P. (1996), 'Gender, Politics and Ritual in the Construction of Social Identities: The Case of San Pawl. Valetta, Malta'. PhD, University of Edinburgh.

Mitra, B. (1999), 'The Impact of Television Advertising on Rural India', PhD dissertation, Hull University.

Moreno, E. (1995), 'Rape in the Field: Reflections from a Survivor', in D. Kulick and M. Wilson (eds.), *Taboo: Sex, Identity and Erotic Subjectivity in Anthropological Fieldwork*, London: Routledge, pp. 219–50.

Morphy, H. (1993), 'Colonialism, History and the Construction of Place: The Politics of Landscape in Northern Australia', in B. Bender (ed.), *Landscape: Politics and Perspectives*, Oxford: Berg.

Morris, B. (1982), *Forest Traders*: *A Socio-Economic Life of the Hill Pandaram*, LSE Monographs, London: Athlone Press.

Morris, B. (1987), *Anthropological Studies of Religion*, Cambridge: Cambridge University Press.

Morris, B. (1991), *Western Conceptions of the Individual*, Oxford: Berg.

Morris, B. (1994), *Anthropology of the Self: The Individual in Cultural Perspective*, London: Pluto Press.

Morris, B. (1998), *The Power of Animals: An Ethnography*, Oxford: Berg.

Myerhoff, B. (1974), *Peyote Hunt: The Sacred Journey of the Huichol Indians*, Ithaca, NY: Cornell University Press.

Nader, L. (1974), 'Up the Anthropologists: Perspectives from Studying Up', in D. Hymes (ed.), *Reinventing Anthropology*, New York: Vintage, pp. 284–311.

Nakhleh, K. (1979), 'On Being a Native Anthropologist', in G. Huizer and B. Mannheim (eds.), *The Politics of Anthropology*, The Hague: Mouton, pp. 343–52.

Nash, J. (1979a), 'Anthropology of the Multinational Corporation', in G. Huizer and B. Mannheim (eds.), *The Politics of Anthropology*, The Hague: Mouton, pp. 421–46.

Nash, J. (1979b), 'Ethnology in a Revolutionary Setting', in G. Huizer and B. Mannheim (eds.), *The Politics of Anthropology*, The Hague: Mouton, pp. 353–70.

Needham, R. (1967), 'Blood, Thunder, and Mockery of Animals', in J. Middleton (ed.), *Myth and Cosmos: Readings in Mythology and Symbolism*, New York: American Museum Sourcebooks in Anthropology, pp. 271–85.

Neveu Kringelbach, N. (2007a), 'Le poids du succès: construction du corps, danse et carrière à Dakar', *Politique Africaine*, pp. 81–101.

Neveu Kringelbach, N. (2007b), 'Cool Play: Emotionality in Dance as a Resource in Senegalese Urban Women's Associations', in H. Wulff, (ed.), *The Emotions: A Cultural Reader*, Oxford: Berg.

Newby, H. (1977a), *The Deferential Worker: A Study of Farm Workers in East Anglia*. London: Allen Lane.

Newby, H. (1977b), 'In the Field: Reflections on the Study of Suffolk Farm Workers', in C. Bell and H. Newby (eds.), *Doing Sociological Research*, London: George, Allen and Unwin, pp. 108–29.

Nordstrom, C., and Robben, A. (eds.) (1995), *Fieldwork under Fire: Contemporary Studies of Violence and Survival*, Berkeley: University of California Press.

*Notes and Queries on Anthropology: RAI Committee* (1874/1951), London: Routledge & Kegan Paul.

Oakley, A. (1981), 'Interviewing Women: A Contradiction in Terms', in H. Roberts (ed.), *Doing Feminist Research*, London: Routledge & Kegan Paul, pp. 30–61.

Okazaki, A. (1997), 'Dreams, Histories and Selves in a Borderland Village in Sudan', PhD dissertation, School of Oriental and African Studies, University of London.

Okazaki, A. (2002), 'The Making and Unmaking of Consciousness: Two Strategies for Survival in a Sudanese Borderland' in R. Werbner (ed.), *Postcolonial Subjectivities*, London: Zed Books, pp. 63–83.

Okazaki, A. (2003) 'Translating Gamk Notions of Dream, Self and Body: "Making Sense of the Foreign"', in T. Maranhão and B. Streck (eds.), *Translation and Ethnography: The Anthropological Challenges of Intercultural Understanding*, Tucson: University of Arizona Press, pp. 152–71.

Okely, J. (1975), 'The Self and Scientism', *Journal of the Anthropology Society of Oxford*, republished in Okely (1996), *Own or Other Culture*, London: Routledge, pp. 27–44.

Okely, J. (1983), *The Traveller-Gypsies*, Cambridge: Cambridge University Press.

Okely, J. (1986), *Simone de Beauvoir: A Re-reading*, London: Virago.

Okely, J. (1987), 'Fieldwork up the M1: Policy and Political Aspects', in A. Jackson (ed.), *Anthropology at Home*, London: Tavistock, pp. 55–73.

Okely, J. (1992), 'Anthropology and Autobiography: Participatory Experience and Embodied Knowledge', in J. Okely and H. Callaway (eds.), *Anthropology and Autobiography*, London: Routledge, pp. 1–28.

Okely, J. (1994a), 'Thinking through Fieldwork', in R. Burgess and A. Bryman (eds.), *Analysing Qualitative Data*, London: Routledge, pp. 18–34. Part reprinted in S. Yates (1998), *Doing Sociological Research*, London: Sage/Open University, pp. 211–15.

Okely, J. (1994b), 'Vicarious and Sensory Knowledge of Chronology and Change: Ageing in Rural France', in K. Hastrup and P. Hervik, (eds.), *Social Experience and Anthropological Knowledge*, London: Routledge, pp. 45–64.

Okely, J. (1996a), 'Against the Motion: Social Anthropology Is a Generalizing Science or It Is Nothing', in T. Ingold (ed.), *Key Debates in Anthropology*, London: Routledge, pp. 36–54.

Okely, J. (1996b), *Own or Other Culture*, London: Routledge.

Okely, J. (1997), 'Some Political Consequences of Theories of Gypsy Ethnicity: The Place of the Intellectual', in A. James, J. Hockey and A. Dawson (eds.), *After Writing Culture*, London: Routledge, pp. 224–43.

Okely, J. (1998), 'Anthropology's Practice Brings Subject and Theory', Distinguished Lecture, Society for the Anthropology of Europe, American Anthropological Association, Washington DC.

Okely, J. (1999a) 'Writing Anthropology in Europe: An Example from Gypsy Research', *Folk*, 41: 55–75.

Okely, J. (1999b), 'Love, Care and Diagnosis', in T. Kohn and R. McKechnie (eds.), *Extending the Boundaries of Care: Medical Ethics and Caring Practices*, Oxford: Berg, pp. 19–48.

Okely, J. (2000), 'Rootlessness against Spatial Fixing: Gypsies, Border-intellectuals and "Others"', in R. Bendix and H. Roodenberg (eds.), *Managing Ethnicity: Perspectives from Folklore Studies, History and Anthropology*, Amsterdam: Het Spinhuis, pp. 13–39.

Okely, J. (2001), 'Visualism and Landscape: Looking and Seeing in Normandy', *Ethnos*, 66/1: 99–120.

Okely, J. (2003a), 'Hybridity, Birthplace and Naming', *Journal of Mediterranean Studies*, 13/1: 1–19.

Okely, J. (2003b), 'The Filmed Return of the Natives to a Colonizing Territory of Terror', *Journal of Media Practice*, 3/2: 65–74.

Okely, J. (2003c), 'Hidden Commonalities at the Heart of the Ethnographic Project', Conference of the American Ethnological Society, Providence, RI.

Okely, J. (2005), 'Gypsy Justice and Gorgio Law: Interrelations of Difference', *Sociological Review*, 53/4 (November): 691–709.

Okely, J. (2006a), 'The Bureaucratization of Knowledge: Or What Are Universities For?' in D. Carter and M. Lord (eds.), *Engagements with Learning and Teaching in Higher Education*, C-SAP, Birmingham University, pp. 127–37.

Okely, J. (2006b), 'Ethnographic Knowledge Has the Power to Transform: It May Also Be Ignored, Blocked or Misappropriated', Third Eric Wolf Lecture, Vienna University.

Okely, J. (2006c), 'Changing senses across cultures' review of "The Senses" *Etnofoor* 18(1) 2005. Guest editors Regina Bendix and Donal Brenneis', in *Senses and Society*, 1/2: 277–80.

Okely, J. (2007a), 'Gendered Lessons in Ivory Towers', in D. Fahy Bryceson, J. Okely and J. Webber (eds.), *Identity and Networks: Fashioning Gender and Ethnicity across Cultures*, Oxford: Berghahn, pp. 228–46.

Okely, J. (2007b), 'Fieldwork Embodied', in C. Shilling (ed.), *Embodying Sociology: Retrospect, Progress and Prospects*, Oxford: Blackwell, pp. 65–79.

Okely, J. (2007c), 'How Short Can Fieldwork Be?', Debate with G. Marcus, *Social Anthropology*, 15/3 (October): 353–67.

Okely, J. (2008), 'Knowing without Notes', in N. Halstead, E. Hirsch and J. Okely (eds.), *Knowing How to Know: Fieldwork and the Ethnographic Present*, Oxford: Berghahn, pp. 55–74.

Okely, J. (2009a), 'Written out and Written in: Inishkillane Remembered', *Irish Journal of Anthropology*, 12/2: 50–5.

Okely, J. (2009b), Reply to Amy Pollard's 'Field of screams: Difficulty and ethnographic fieldwork', in www.Anthropologymatters.com 11 (2). (The official postgraduate network of the Association of Social Anthropology of the UK and Commonwealth.)

Okely, J. (2010a), 'Crossing Borders', Obi Igwara Memorial Lecture, The Association for the Study of Ethnicity and Nationalism (ASEN), London School of Economics (LSE).

Okely, J. (2010b), 'Fieldwork as Free Association and Free Passage', in M. Melhuus, J. Mitchell and H. Wulff (eds.), *Ethnographic Practice in the Present*, Oxford: Berghahn, pp. 28–41.

Okely, J. (2010c), 'Constructing Culture through Shared Location, Bricolage and Exchange: The Case of Gypsies and Roma', in M. Stewart and M. Rovid (eds.), *Multi-disciplinary Approaches to Romany Studies*, Central European University Ebook.

Okely, J. (2011), 'Retrospective Reading of Fieldnotes: Living on Gypsy Camps', *Behemoth*, 4/1.

Okely, J. (2012), 'The Isle of Wight as a Site for English-British Identity', in J. Matthews and D. Travers (eds), *Islands and Britishness: A Global Perspective*, Cambridge: Cambridge Scholars Publishing, pp. 40–52.

Okely, J., and Callaway, H. (eds.) (1992), *Anthropology and Autobiography*, London: Routledge.

Oliver, C. (2008), *Retirement Migration: Paradoxes of Ageing*, Abingdon: Routledge.

Omvedt, G. (1979), 'On the Participant Study of Women's Movements: Methodological Definitional and Action Considerations', in G. Huizer and B. Mannheim (eds.), *The Politics of Anthropology*, The Hague: Mouton, pp. 373–93.

O'Reilly, K. (2009), *Key Concepts in Ethnography*, London: Sage.

Ottenberg, S. (1990), 'Thirty Years of Fieldnotes: Changing Relationships to the Text' in R. Sanjek (ed.), *Fieldnotes: The Makings of Anthropology*, London: Cornell University Press, pp. 139–60.

Overing, J. (1975), *The Piaroa; A People of the Orinoco Basin: A Study in Kinship and Marriage*, Oxford: Clarendon Press.

Overing, J. (ed.) (1985), *Reason and Morality*, Association of Social Anthropologists Monograph 24, London: Tavistock.

Overing, J., and Passes, A. (eds.) (1998), *Anthropology of Love and Anger: The Aesthetics of Conviviality in Native South America*, London: Routledge.

Overing, J., and Rapport, N. (2000), *Key Concepts in Social Anthropology*, London: Routledge.

Owuso, M. (1979), 'Colonial and Postcolonial Anthropology of Africa: Scholarship or Sentiment?' in G. Huizer and B. Mannheim (eds.), *The Politics of Anthropology*, The Hague: Mouton, pp. 145–60.

Parry, J. (1979), *Caste and Kinship in Kangra*, London: Routledge.

Parry, J. (1994), *Death in Banaras*, Cambridge: Cambridge University Press.

Parry, J. (2010), 'The Anthropologist's Assistant: A Story from India', Paper presented at the International Centre for Gender Studies Seminar Series, 'Political and Reciprocal Aspects of Cross-cultural Research', convened by J. Okely and S. Sanders, Queen Elizabeth House, University of Oxford.

Parry, J., Astuti, R. and Stafford, C. (eds.) (2007), *Questions of Anthropology*, Oxford: Berg.

Parry, J., and Bloch, M. (eds.) (1982), *Death and the Regeneration of Life*, Cambridge: Cambridge University Press.

Parry, J., and Bloch, M. (eds.) (1989), *Money and the Morality of Exchange*, Cambridge: Cambridge University Press,

Parry, J., Breman, J. and Kapadia, K. (eds.) (1999), *The Worlds of Indian Industrial Labour*, London: Sage.

Pero, D. (2008), *Exclusionary Rhetoric/Exclusionary Practices: Left-wing Politics and Migrants in Italy*, Oxford: Berghahn.

Polhemus, T. (ed.) (1978), *Social Aspects of the Human Body*, Harmondsworth: Penguin Books.

Popper, K. (1961), *The Poverty of Historicism* (2nd ed.), London: Routledge.

Powdermaker, H. (1967), *Stranger and Friend: The Way of an Anthropologist*, London: Secker & Warburg.

Pratt, M. L. (1986), 'Fieldwork in Common Places', in J. Clifford and G. Marcus (eds.), *Writing Culture*, Berkeley: University of California Press, pp. 27–50.

Price, D. (2004), *Threatening Anthropology: McCarthyism and the FBI's Surveillance of Activist Anthropologists*, Durham, NC: Duke University Press.

Price, D. (2006), 'Anthropology and Spying. Response to Sebag Montefiore', *Anthropology Today*, 22/1 (February): 21.

Price, D. (2007), 'Anthropology as Lampost? A Comment on the Counterinsurgency Field Manual', *Anthropology Today*, 23/6 (December): 20–21.

Price, D. (2008), *Anthropological Intelligence: The Deployment and Neglect of American Anthropology in the Second World War*, Durham, NC: Duke University Press.

Punch, M. (1986), *The Politics and Ethics of Fieldwork*, London: Sage.

Reed-Danahay, D. (ed.) (1997), *Auto/Ethnography: Rewriting the Self and the Social*, Oxford: Berg.

Rohde, D. (2007), 'Army Enlists Anthropologists as Advisers', *New York Times*, in association with *The Observer* (14 October): 1, 4.

Rosaldo, R. (1993), 'Grief and a Headhunter's Rage', in R. Rosaldo (ed.), *Culture and Truth*. London: Routledge, pp. 1–21.

Rose, H. (1983), 'Hand, Brain and Heart: A Feminist Epistemology for the Natural Sciences', in *Signs: Journal of Women in Culture and Society*, 9/1: 73–90.

Rose, H. (1984), 'Is a Feminist Science Possible?' Paper presented to MIT Women's Studies Program, Cambridge, MA, April.

Rose, S. (1997), *Lifelines: Biology, Freedom and Determinism*, London: Allen Lane, Penguin Press.

Sanjek, R. (ed.) (1990), *Fieldnotes: The Makings of Anthropology*, Ithaca, NY: Cornell University Press.

Sanjek, R. (1991), 'Ethnographic Present', *Man*, New Series, 26/4 (December): 609–28.

Sanjek, R. (1993), 'Anthropology's Hidden Colonialism: Assistants and Their Ethnographers', *Anthropology Today*, 9/2: 13–18.

Sarkar, N. K., and Tambiah, S. (1957), *The Disintegrating Village*, Colombo: Ceylon University Press.

Schrijvers, J. (1993), 'Motherhood Experienced and Conceptualised', in D. Bell, P. Caplan and W. Karim (eds.), *Gendered Fields: Women, Men and Ethnography*, London: Routledge.

Segalen, M. (1980), *Mari et femme dans la société paysanne*, Paris: Flammarion.

Shields, R. (1994), 'Fancy Footwork: Walter Benjamin's Notes on flânerie', in K. Tester (ed.), *The Flâneur*, London: Routledge, pp. 61–80.

Shilling, C. (1993), *The Body and Social Theory*, London: Sage.

Shilling, C. (ed.) (2007), *Embodying Sociology: Retrospect, Progress and Prospects*, Oxford: Blackwell.

Shostak, M. (1981), *Nisa: The Life and Words of a !Kung Woman*, Cambridge, MA: Harvard University Press.

Silverman, C. (2000), 'Researcher, Advocate, Friend: An American Fieldworker among Balkan Roma, 1980–1996', in H. De Soto and N. Dudwick (eds), *Fieldwork Dilemmas: Anthropologists in Post socialist States,* London: University of Wisconsin Press, pp. 195–217.

Silverman, C. (2007), 'Trafficking in the Exotic with "Gypsy" Music: Balkan Roma, Cosmopolitanism, and "World Music" Festivals', in D. Buchanan (ed.), *Balkan Popular Culture and the Ottoman Ecumene: Music, Image, and Regional Political Discourse,* Lanham, MD: Scarecrow Press, pp. 335–61.

Silverman, C. (2008), 'Transnational Chochek: Gender and the Politics of Balkan Romani Dance', in A. Shay (ed.), *Balkan Dance: Essays on Characteristics, Performing, and Teaching,* Jefferson, NC: McFarland Press, pp. 37–68.

Silverman, C. (2011), *Romani Routes: Cultural Politics and Balkan Music in Diaspora,* Oxford: Oxford University Press.

Silverman, D. (1985), *Qualitative Methodology and Sociology,* Aldershot: Gower.

Silverman, D. (2000), *Doing Qualitative Research,* London: Sage.

Simpson, A. (2003), *'Half-London' in Zambia: Contested Identities in a Catholic Mission School*, Edinburgh: International African Library.

Simpson, A. (2009), *Boys to Men in the Shadow of AIDS: Masculinities and HIV Risk in Zambia*, London: Palgrave Macmillan.

Simpson, B. (2011), 'Ethical Moments: Future Directions for Ethical Review and Ethnography', *Journal of the Royal Anthropological Institute*, 17/2 (June): 377–93.

Smith-Bowen, E. (L. Bohannon) (1954), *Return to Laughter*, New York: Doubleday Anchor.

Southall, A. (ed.) (1973), *Urban Anthropology: Cross-Cultural Studies of Urbanization*, New York: Oxford University Press.

Sondheim, S. (1970), 'The Anthropologist as Hero', in E. N. Hayes and T. Hayes (eds.), *Claude Lévi-Strauss: The Anthropologist as Hero*, Cambridge, MA: MIT Press, pp. 184–96.

Spencer, J. (2010), 'The Perils of Engagement: A Space for Anthropology in the Age of Security?' *Current Anthropology*, 51/Supplement 2 (October): S289–99.

Spencer, P. (1992), 'Automythologies and the Reconstruction of Ageing', in J. Okely and H. Callaway (eds.), *Anthropology and Autobiography*, London: Routledge, pp. 50–63.

Spradley, J. (1980), *Participant Observation*, New York: Holt, Rinehart and Winston.

Stewart, M. (1997), *The Time of the Gypsies*, Boulder, CO: Westview Press.

Stewart, M., and Rovid, M. (eds.) (2011), *Multi-disciplinary Approaches to Romany Studies*, CEU Central European University Ebook.

Stanley, L., and Wise, S. (1990), 'Method, Methodology an Epistemology in Feminist Research Processes', in L. Stanley (ed), *Feminist Praxis: Research, Theory and Epistemology in Feminist Sociology*, London: Routledge, pp. 20–60.

Stocking, G. (1983), 'The Ethnographer's Magic: Fieldwork in British Anthropology from Tylor to Malinowski', in G. Stocking (ed.), *Observors Observed: Essays on Ethnographic Fieldwork*, Madison: University of Wisconsin Press, pp. 70–120.

Stolcke, V. (1995), 'Talking Culture: New Boundaries, New Rhetorics of Exclusion in Europe', *Current Anthropology*, 36: 1–24.

Stoller, P. (1989), *The Taste of Ethnographic Things: The Senses in Anthropology*, Philadelphia: University of Pennsylvania Press.

Strathern, M. (1981), *Kinship at the Core: An Anthropology of Elmdon, A Village in North-West Essex in the Nineteen Sixties*, Cambridge: Cambridge University Press.

Sutherland, A. (1975), *Gypsies: The Hidden Americans*, London: Tavistock.

Taleb, A. (1987), 'The Algerian Emigration to France: A Sociological Study of the Background, Origins and Present Difficulties', PhD dissertation, Essex University.

Talib, M. (2002), 'Soul of the Soulless: An Analysis of Pir-Murid Relationship in Sufi Discourse', in C. W. Troll (ed.), *Muslim Shrines in India*, Oxford: Oxford University Press.

Talib, M. (2008), 'Sufis and Politics' (updated Johansein's version), in John Esposito (ed.), *The Oxford Encyclopaedia of the Modern Islamic World*, Oxford: Oxford University Press, pp. 233–43.

Talib, M. (2010), *Writing Labour: Stone Quarry Workers in Delhi*, Delhi and Oxford: Oxford University Press.

Tambiah, S. (1970), *Buddhism and the Spirit Cults in North-East Thailand*, Cambridge: Cambridge University Press.

Tapper, R., and Tapper, N. (1989), Anthropological Couples, *Focaal*, 10: 54–60.

Tester, K. (ed.) (1994), *The Flâneur*, London: Routledge.

Tett, G. (2009), *Fools Gold: How Unrestrained Greed Corrupted a Dream, Shattered Global Markets and Unleashed a Catastrophe*, London: Little, Brown.

Thompson, T. W. (1922), 'The Uncleanness of Women among English Gypsies', *Journal of the Gypsy Lore Society*, third series, 2/3: 113–39.

Tonkin, E. (1995), *Narrating Our Past: The Social Construction of Oral History*, Cambridge: Cambridge University Press.

Toynbee, P. (2009), *The Guardian* (28 November): 37.

Turnbull, C. (1972), *The Mountain People*, New York: Simon & Schuster.

Turner, V. (1969), *The Ritual Process*, London: Penguin.

Turner, V., and Bruner, E. (eds.) (1986), *The Anthropology of Experience*, Chicago: University of Illinois Press.

Van Maanen, J. (1988), *Tales of the Field: On Writing Ethnography*, Chicago: University of Chicago Press.

Van Maanen, J. (ed.) (1995), *Representation in Ethnography*, London: Sage.

Vines, G. (1994), 'Gail Vines Profiles Henrietta Moore Who Refuses to Produce Anthropological "Soft Porn" or Even Soap Opera', *Times Higher Education Supplement* (23 September): 20–1.

Wade, P. (1993), 'Sexuality and Masculinity among Colombian Blacks', in D. Bell, P. Caplan and W. Karim (eds.), *Gendered Fields: Women, Men and Ethnography*, London: Routledge, pp. 199–214.

Wallace, T. (2009), 'Developmental Issues', Paper delivered to the IGS International Gender Studies Center seminar, Oxford.

Wallerstein, I. (1974), *The Modern World-System: Capitalist Agriculture and the Origins of the European World-Economy in the Sixteenth Century*, London: Academic Press.

Wax, R. (1971), *Doing Fieldwork: Warnings and Advice*, Chicago: University of Chicago Press.

Weil, S. (1987), 'Anthropology Becomes Home; Home Becomes Anthropology', in A. Jackson (ed.), *Anthropology at Home*, London: Tavistock, pp. 196–212.

Whitehead, T. L., and Conaway, M. E. (eds.) (1986), *Self, Sex and Gender in Cross-Cultural Fieldwork*, Chicago: University of Illinois Press.

Whyte, W. F. (1943/1955), *Street Corner Society: The Social Structure of an Italian Slum*, Chicago: University of Chicago Press.

Willis, P. (1977), *Learning to Labour: How Working Class Kids Get Working Class Jobs*, Aldershot: Gower.

Winkler, C., with K. Wininger, (1994), 'Rape Trauma: Contexts of Meaning', in T. Csordas (ed.), *Embodiment and Experience: The Existential Ground of Culture and Self*, Cambridge: Cambridge University Press, pp. 248–68.

Wolff, J. (1990), *Feminine Sentences: Essays on Women and Culture*, Cambridge: Polity.

Wolff, K. H. (1994), 'Surrender and the Other', *Anthropological Journal on European Cultures*, 3/2: 155–68.

Wright, S. (1978), 'Prattle and Politics: The Position of Women in Doshman Ziari, Iran', *Journal of the Anthropology Society of Oxford*, 9/2: 98–112.

Wright, S. (1981), 'Place and Face: Of Women in Doshman Ziara, Iran', in S. Ardener (ed.), *Women and Space: Ground Rules and Social Maps*, London: Croom Helm, pp. 136–57.

Wright, S. (1996), 'Patterns and Representations', in E. Hallam and N. Levell (eds.), *Communicating Otherness: Cultural Encounters*, Sussex University, Graduate Research Centre in Culture and Communication, pp. 45–62.

Wright, S., and Shore, C. (eds.) (1997), *Anthropology of Policy: Perspectives on Governance and Power*, London: Routledge.

Wulff, H. (1988), *Twenty Girls: Growing Up, Ethnicity and Excitement in a South London Micro Culture*, Stockholm: Almqvist & Wiksell International.

Wulff, H. (1998), *Ballet across Borders, Career and Culture in the World of Dancers*, Oxford: Berg.

Wulff, H. (2002), 'Yo-yo Fieldwork: Mobility and Time in a Multi-local Study of Dance in Ireland', *Anthropological Journal on European Culture*, 11: 117–36.

Wulff, H. (2007a), *Dancing at the Crossroads: Memory and Mobility in Ireland*, Oxford: Berghahn.

Wulff, H. (ed.) (2007b), *The Emotions*, Oxford: Berg.

Wulff, H. (ed.) (forthcoming), *The Anthropologist as Writer*, Chicago: University of Chicago Press.

Wulff, H., and Amit-Talai, V. (eds.) (1995), *Youth Cultures*, London: Routledge.

Wulff, H., and Garsten, C. (eds.) (2003), *New Technologies at Work*, Oxford: Berg.

Xiang Biao (1970), *Global 'Body Shopping': An Indian Labor System in the Information Technology Industry*, Princeton, NJ: Princeton University Press.

Young, D. E., and Goulet, J. G. (eds.) (1994), *Being Changed by Cross-Cultural Encounters: The Anthropology of Extraordinary Experience*, Ontario: Broadview Press.

Young, M. (1991), *An Inside Job*, Oxford: Oxford University Press.

Zonabend, F. (1984), *The Enduring Memory: Time and History in a French Village* (trans. A. Forster), Manchester: Manchester University Press.

Zontini, E. (2008), *Transnational Families, Migration and Gender: Moroccan and Filipino Women in Bologna and Barcelona*, Oxford: Berghahn.

Zulaika, J. (1982), *Basque Violence: Metaphor and Sacrament*, Reno: University of Nevada Press.

Zulaika, J. (1995), 'The Anthropologist as Terrorist,' in C. Nordstrom and A. Robben (eds.), *Fieldwork under Fire: Contemporary Studies of Violence and Survival*, Berkeley: University of California Press, pp. 205–22.

Zulaika, J. (2009), *Terrorism: The Self-Fulfilling Prophesy*, Chicago: University of Chicago Press.

Zulaika, J., with Douglass, W. A. (1996), *Terror and Taboo: The Follies, Fables and Faces of Terrorism*, New York: Routledge.

# Index

holism, 17, 19–20, 53, 78; holistic,
17–18, 20–1, 48, 53, 75
Howell, Signe, 29, 37, 50, 57, 105–6,
109, 139, 143, 158
Huby, G., 73
Hughes-Freeland, Felicia, 10, 50, 63,
79, 93, 96, 119, 126, 132, 150, 158
Hugh-Jones, Christine, 1, 92
Hugh-Jones, Stephen, 1, 29, 92, 99
Hull prison, 149; University, 9, 164
Hunterian Museum, 159
hybridity, 142
hypergamy, 50, 58, 59

Iceland, 1, 73
identity, 36–8, 41, 63, 68, 73, 79, 91,
105, 108, 110–11, 113, 118, 126–30,
133–4, 140, 146, 160
immigrants, 104–5
imperialism, 33, 146
India, 1, 3, 22, 28, 38–9, 42, 49–50, 59,
71, 73, 93–4, 105, 108, 112, 114,
127, 140, 157, 160–1; Indian, 4, 58,
80–1, 93, 126
indigenous, 53, 160; peoples, 15,
18, 32–4, 66, 76, 79, 81, 85, 104,
108–9, 113–14, 142, 150–1
Indonesia, 3, 119, 132, 139, 158
informal networks, 105
informants, 1, 40, 45, 47, 58, 85, 94, 155
Ingessana, *see* Gamk
inheritance, 13, 159
insider(s), 41, 55, 80, 97, 99, 108, 126
Institute of Agricultural Research, 104
interdependence, 99
International Labour Office (ILO), 157
interviewing, 2, 18, 44, 136, 155
Inuit, 33–4, 158
Iran, 3, 34, 36, 40–2, 44, 50, 57, 87,
117, 129, 138, 146–7, 159, 161;
Iranian, 40, 44, 147
Iran, Shah of, 42, 44, 50, 147, 161

Iraq, 35, 36, 37
Ireland, 3, 4, 43, 75, 111, 128
Ishaqzai, 90
Islam, 36–7, 66, 134, 159, 161; Islamo-
phobia, 152; *see also* Muslim
Issa, Hesham, 50, 73
Italy, 152, 158

Jackson, M., 108
James, W., 33
Jamia Millia Islamia University, 69
Jansen, S., 73
Japan, 38, 99, 115, 123, 142, 160;
Japanese, 4, 28, 115
Johnson, M., 73
Joseph, Keith, 8

Kaminski, Ignacy-Marek, 27, 30, 63,
104–5, 111, 118, 137, 140, 158
Kampala, 136
Kangra, 58, 60, 93, 140, 160
Kenna, Margaret, 1, 30–1, 40, 42,
66–7, 95, 117, 123, 159
Kenya, 3, 32–3, 62–3, 73, 77, 136, 141,
150, 158, 160
Keynesian economics, 8
kinship, 19–20, 28, 48, 50, 53, 56–9,
62, 87, 129, 141, 159; kinship
system, 28, 53, 57
Knowles, J., 73
Kosovo, 148
Kroeber, Alfred L., 33
Kula expeditions, 19
Kurdistan, 42, 44
Kuria, Kenya, 63, 130, 141, 145, 158

labour, 24, 88, 92, 97, 103, 107, 113,
124; agricultural, 93; bonded, 71;
colonies, 142; craft, 78; division of,
84; indentured, 50; manual, 67, 88,
114; participant, 88; physical, 107–8,
112, 114; shared, 88; wage, 65